INVESTING
IN PEACE

INVESTING IN PEACE

How Development Aid Can Prevent Or Promote Conflict

Robert J. Muscat

M.E. Sharpe
Armonk, New York
London, England

Copyright © 2002 by M. E. Sharpe, Inc.

All rights reserved. No part of this book may be reproduced in any form
without written permission from the publisher, M. E. Sharpe, Inc.,
80 Business Park Drive, Armonk, New York 10504.

Library of Congress Cataloging-in-Publication Data

Muscat, Robert J.
    Investing in peace : how development aid can prevent or promote conflict / by
Robert J. Muscat.
    p. cm.
Includes bibliographical references and index.
ISBN 0-7656-0978-9 (alk. paper) — ISBN 0-7656-0979-7 (pbk. : alk. paper)
    1. Economic assistance. 2. Economic development. 3. Ethnic conflict. 4. Conflict
management. I. Title.

HC60.M833 2002
338.91--dc21   2001057822

Printed in the United States of America

The paper used in this publication meets the minimum requirements of
American National Standard for Information Sciences
Permanence of Paper for Printed Library Materials,
ANSI Z 39.48-1984.

| MV (c) | 10 | 9 | 8 | 7 | 6 | 5 | 4 | 3 | 2 | 1 |
| MV (p) | 10 | 9 | 8 | 7 | 6 | 5 | 4 | 3 | 2 | 1 |

For my children

David, Joshua, and Elysabeth

Contents

Preface

As I headed for the front door of the hotel on Zagreb's main square—it was in 1996, four years after the end of the Croatian phase of the Yugoslav breakup conflict—straight from the airport and dragging my luggage, I was approached by a shabbily dressed old woman. She thrust a piece of paper in my face, which I could not read. No one in the passing crowd stopped to help an obviously puzzled foreigner. Bewildered, I entered the hotel lobby. The man behind the registration desk had seen my little encounter. "Just a Gypsy!" he sneered.

A little later I was back in the lobby to meet three of the people with whom I had come to work. One was a woman who told a chilling story about her family. She came from Vukovar, a city in northeastern Croatia that the Yugoslav army had reduced to rubble during a three-month siege. While the siege was under way she had managed to escape, taking her four-year-old daughter but leaving her husband behind. Soon after, another Vukovar refugee who had escaped a bit later told her that her husband was dead. Their next-door neighbor had bludgeoned the husband with a hammer. They had known the killer and his family for years. The two families often had eaten together and their children were playmates.

Why had the neighbor turned into a killer of a fellow besieged? My brush with contempt for Gypsies had been a foretaste. The families of the husband and the killer were all Catholic and considered themselves Croatian, ethnically and historically (setting aside the decades of the shared Yugoslav identity, which proved to be only a veneer). The husband, however, had had a Serb grandfather and bore his grandfather's Serb family name. As with the "racial" laws of Nazi Germany, this was enough Serb ancestry to brand the husband an enemy outsider in the neighbor's eyes, despite the husband's own complete identity with, and loyalty to, his Croatian Catholic ethnicity. The woman's concluding account of life in Zagreb seemed to show that the dominance of ethnic identity for determining behavior and rules in Croatian society at the time was not limited to the places like Vukovar experiencing extremes of fear and combat. In Zagreb, because the woman's family name was Serb, her four-year old, when she fell ill, was refused the free health care routinely provided to refugees from Vukovar and other areas the Serbs had occupied. After the mother learned she was a widow, she reverted to her Croatian maiden name. The government then acknowledged the child's reestablished Croatian identity and thereby her eligibility for medical attention.

That same year I visited Lombok Island in Indonesia as a member of a team evaluating some U.S. Agency for International Development (USAID) food aid projects. Lombok had seen some of the worst slaughter during the anticommunist rampage in Indonesia in 1965. One of my local interlocutors talked about the killings. He said a friend of his was among several youths who were rounded up by an army unit and pressed into a few hours' service to slay "communists" the military had taken into custody. Neither his friend nor anyone else, as far as he could remember, had the slightest idea then what a communist was. The soldiers told them communists were people who wanted to banish Islam and the worship of Allah from Indonesia, and that this was sufficient reason for them to be killed. The youths were handed machetes and proceeded to dispatch the prisoners. The friend killed two, then begged to be excused. According to my informant, his friend (I began to suspect he was actually speaking about himself), now a middle-aged and better-informed adult like the rest of us, has labored under feelings of guilt ever since.

The apparent motivations for the egregious behavior described to me in these two conversations, continents and cultures apart, illustrate the opposite ends of the range of explanations one finds in the literature on conflict. In Vukovar a man kills spontaneously, going so far as to attack one-on-one; he acts individually, motivated by internalized conviction that "Serb-ness"— and its ineluctably associated threat to Croats—is inherent in any Serb derivation, even unto the third generation from one grandparent, not offset by the Croat three-quarters. This is an example of "primordialism"—the deep infusion of an ethnic identity-based worldview, a view that ethnicity (a term that can encompass, in different degrees for different groups, language, religion, culture, homeland, and a group's shared belief in common origin) is the fundamental determinant of vital interests and the fundamental source of conflict behavior. In Lombok the aggression was invoked by manipulative authorities. Having conjured up primordial fear and hostility, the local military authorities induced violence by activating religious apprehension that had otherwise remained dormant or, more likely, had never been known before by the drafted killers. Even if one grants (the facts remain in dispute) that the national coup leaders, and perhaps the local coup implementers, were (at least partly) driven by concerns for the nation's well-being, much of the local violence was individual score-settling in the guise of anticommunism.

Speaking of this episode and of all the domestic violence since independence, Indonesia's most prominent writer, Pramoedya Ananta Toer, observed, "Everything came from the government, everything was a provocation." In his view, the army attacked the communists in 1948 to impress the West. The Left then responded by killing many Muslims. Then perhaps a million communists and suspected sympathizers, a large number of whom were ethnic Chinese, were killed in 1965 in response to an alleged communist coup.[1] Thus, precipitating this violence there were many strands, many motivations, among actors at different levels of the society—a mix of religion, ethnic prejudice, opportunism, political ambition, and national interest.

The primordial interpretation suggests that these hostilities are inevitable and recurrent. Such conflicts would be difficult if not impossible to prevent. It has been a commonplace to attribute Balkan wars to primordial hostility. After all, whatever the particular circumstances may have been that sparked each conflict, Balkan history seems marked by a propensity of the region's peoples to leap at each other's throats. The Muslim Moros rebelling in the southern Philippines since the country's independence in 1946 also fought against the American takeover of the islands from Spain in the nineteenth century after resisting Spanish rule back to the sixteenth century. The facile characterization of such histories of recurrent conflict as primordial is intellectually seductive; it enables one to avoid the difficult task of mastering complex realities and to sustain a flattering conviction that one has plumbed the depths of the problem. A primordial explanation can also lead one to conclude that interventions to prevent or resolve such conflicts are futile. Why risk loss of life or incur pointless expenditures?

In fact, despite the overwhelming evidence that aggression is a strong propensity of our species, the primordialism explanation for violent behavior, especially organized warfare between particular large *groups* of people, is virtually always simplistic and, consequently, a naive basis for public policy. Apparently primordial fears and hatreds often obscure and mix with hardnosed issues of economics and power. By the same token, it would be a mistake to underestimate or dismiss the power of nonmaterial, non-Realpolitik issues—such as remembered histories, recent or even remote violence against a group's collective forebears, perceptions of religious or cultural hostility, ancient schisms that appear to outsiders as doctrinal minutiae, rival claims to places of symbolic or cultic importance only—to motivate groups to take up arms. The realities of violent conflict are often dense in the complexity of their origins and their accumulated motivations. Conflicts that have roots in economic and political competition often become inflamed and turn "primordial" through the arousal of identity differences.

For most people, ethnicity is a given at birth and inculcated in childhood as the core of the individual's identity, a core that is shared with all others who claim (or even reluctantly partake of) a common ancestry. Under this definition,[2] ethnicity is the widest and most elastic concept of kinship. For convenience I use "ethnicity" (rather loosely) to refer to any group that may be described, or describes itself, in terms of caste, tribe, nationality (in the anthropological, not legal, sense), culture, or race, all categories that may or may not coincide with religion and language. Typically, even in the absence of defining physical characteristics, a group's ethnicity is evident to itself and to nonmembers through "markers" such as language or dialect, customs, traditional costume, and rituals.

Many writers have expatiated on the complexity of group identity and the multiplicity of ascriptive patterns found among human societies. In some cases several critical markers coincide to define multifaceted differentiation between one or more "ethnic" or "national" groups within a state. In Sri Lanka, for example, the Sinhalese majority and Tamil minority are differentiated by regional concentration, language, and religion. Some of the ethnic Chinese minorities in Southeast Asia are differentiated from the population groups of longer residence by physical appearance, religion, (second) language, cuisine, and economic occupations. In other cases, many markers may be shared by groups that differ only with respect to one significant marker, a single difference that may be sufficiently delineating to be the basis for enmity. One example is the Protestant–Catholic differentiation in Northern Ireland.

Ethnic communities commonly claim a primordial within-group attachment and a history that is uniquely theirs, separating "us" from all other "them." Writers on ethnicity often observe that the historical and primordial character of many communities is "imagined," resting on beliefs that are partially fictional if not deliberately (and often recently) invented; this is done to create a sense of nationhood, and political common interests, within an ethnic group that previously had only loose common identity and weak cohesion for pursuing political objectives as a bloc. It is of more than academic interest that the history of many ethnic groups has been misconstrued, often deliberately, to overstate the continuity, homogeneity, and differentiating characteristics that are claimed to define their uniqueness and to support the justice of their present-day claims. The view that contemporary ethnic groups are historically and socially primordial would appear to support the idea that (at least many) ethnic conflicts are recurrently unavoidable. Under this view, the conflicts also are primordial, based on divisions and relations too deeply antipathetic to be overcome or transformed. The adoption by one group of an "imagined" communal myth implying hegemony over another group may provoke the latter to develop a countervailing myth of its own.

The historical facts often belie all these assertions. The modern Sinhalese racial reinterpretation of its ancient history and relationship with the Tamils is an example of retrospective myth-making.[3]

Daniel Patrick Moynihan and others have described how ethnicity has reemerged in the modern state, especially since World War I and despite the powerful ideology of the liberal state, based on individual citizenship and shared founding principles, and despite the long and now waning hold of Marxism, based on class consciousness and class interests that would purportedly override the primitivism of ethnicity and ascriptive association. Whether along the lines of the American "melting pot" or the European nation-state in which historic cultural–linguistic differentiation would be attenuated through assimilation into the dominant national community, ethnicity had seemed for a time to be diminishing in salience. Among most developing countries, however, there are few signs of ethnicity being submerged under concepts of citizenship or due to the effects of technological globalization and the spread of mass cultures. Ethnic politics, low rates of intermarriage, and widespread ethnic conflict give vivid indication of the continuing, perhaps rising salience of ethnicity.

In the short run, especially in societies that are in the midst of, or just emerging from, violent conflict, it may seem as if ethnic differences and their associated animosities are immutable social facts, divisions that are unbridgeable. In fact, numerous examples exist of ethnicities that have merged with other groups, or assimilated. Many languages have disappeared or have become cultural relics spoken by small, aging populations. The intermarriage rate among sharply differentiated ethnicities is seldom above 10 percent, and even where the rate is significantly higher, as it was in Yugoslavia, especially in Bosnia, intermarriage is no guarantee that old animosities cannot be revived by extremist politicians.

Conversely, there are also examples where intermarriage has been extensive for several generations, easing interethnic tension and producing a new ethnic amalgam, as with the Sino–Thai and the Sino–Filipino. These ethnic and cultural changes are long-run phenomena, but they do attest to the mutability of ethnic identity.

In the years ahead, as in the past few decades, it is the developing countries—not the wealthy democratic countries—that are at risk of falling into internal armed conflict. The "international development community"—that is, the bilateral and multilateral development assistance banks, aid agencies, and nongovernmental organizations—may be able to contribute to peaceful resolution of material differences, inequalities, and grievances before the parties find themselves on a downslide toward violent conflict. These organizations are often deeply involved in the financing and shaping of the economic development process, years before such downslides occur. International intervention, especially problematic when the only remedy appears to be military, is usually contemplated at the eleventh hour or when violent conflict is already under way and producing humanitarian disaster. This book is an effort to explore conflict prevention—how the international development agencies, working on fundamental, long-run economic and institutional problems, can alleviate some of the problems that have often been at the roots of contemporary civil wars in developing countries.

The concept of fundamental, nonviolent resolution is deeply embedded in the institutions, political processes, acceptance of rule of law, and shared value systems of the established democratic states. Resolution of differences takes place constantly at all levels of governance and jurisprudence, and in the institutions of civil society. Though all cultures have traditional systems of conflict management, the developing countries, especially the recently independent states with little history of self-government as entities within the inherited colonial boundaries, generally have conflict management institutions and norms that are weak for resolving differences at the state level, or between rival subpopulations. For better or for worse, the only instruments the (official) international community has for influencing the underlying tensions and structures (even in the exceptional cases where, as occupiers, the international powers forcing the resolution impose political structures, as in Bosnia, Cambodia, and Kosovo) are the development agencies (and to a more limited degree, the International Monetary Fund [IMF]). There remain grounds for doubt that the transplants will not be rejected. The ability of the development agencies to contribute to conflict-mitigating economic change is much greater before violent conflict embitters the antagonists than after. That these agencies can be significantly relevant to conflict will be demonstrated throughout this book. The problem is how to make such relevance mitigating rather than exacerbating, that is, how to identify mitigating and prevention possibilities, and how to capitalize on them.

The development agencies whose activities are the main focus of this text comprise both the international, or multilateral, institutions (i.e., the World Bank and the Asian, African, and Inter-American regional development banks, and the various development assistance funds and agencies of the United Nations [U.N.] system), and the bilateral, or individual country, agencies that administer the separate foreign aid programs of donor countries. The leading bilateral aid providers, in terms of influence and funds, are among the twenty-one member countries of the Development Assistance Committee (DAC) of the Organization for Economic Cooperation and Development (OECD). Taking together their bilateral programs and their contributions to the international agencies, the largest bilateral aid providers are Japan, the

United States, Germany, France, the Netherlands, United Kingdom, Italy, Sweden, Canada, Denmark, and Norway. Beyond the donor agencies, the "international development community" as a whole also includes a vast number of nongovernmental organizations (NGOs), private firms, research institutes, academics, and "development practitioners." Violent conflict demolishes the work of this community. Needless to say, it is the noncombatant populations of the developing countries who bear the greatest costs of violent conflict and who reap the greatest benefits when conflict is prevented.

Notes

1. *Far East Economic Review*, June 15, 2000, p. 79.
2. From Horowitz, 1985, pp. 52–53.
3. See Little, 1994, pp. 16, 26–30.

Acknowledgments

It is twelve years since I was first drawn to thinking about the problems of failed states and violent conflict in developing nations. After a career that included long sojourns in countries blessed with relative social stability and improving welfare, I was asked by John Eriksson in 1989 to contemplate the problems Cambodia would inherit if the ongoing peace negotiations were to succeed, and what challenges the international development community would face in the effort that would follow to reconstruct an economy and society emerging from such a horrific experience. One thing led to another, especially an assignment from Robert Picciotto to explore the role of the World Bank in postconflict reconstruction. It was a short step from working on reconstruction to thinking about prevention as vastly to be preferred, and about what the development community could do to help their "beneficiaries" avoid resorting to violent conflict to resolve their internal differences. Although I owe Eriksson and Picciotto a special debt (I will not say special thanks; to move from working on countries making progress to countries tearing themselves apart is not exactly a felicitous career change), there have been many others who, in the course of work or casual rumination, knowingly and unknowingly contributed to my education on these problems over these years.

I am especially grateful to John Eriksson, Ronald Ridker, Milton Esman, Donald McClelland, Michael Cernea, Colin Scott, Nat Colletta, and William Renison for reading and commenting on the manuscript in draft. They provided encouragement, saved me from numerous errors, and made valuable suggestions regarding things overlooked. Kevin P. Clements gave a major assist by taking me on as a visiting fellow at George Mason University's Institute for Conflict Analysis and Resolution (ICAR), where he was director at the time. The book would not have been possible without the access to ICAR's research materials and the university library. I also owe thanks to Deborah A. Brautigan, Ramish Chander, Eric Griffel, Ronald J. Herring, Devesh Kapur, Princeton Lyman, Michael Lund, C. Robless, Leo E. Rose, Stanley W. Samarasinghe, Townsend Swayze, Norman Uphoff, Joseph Wheeler, and Maurice J. Williams, and to James Lavelle and Richard Mollica. Donald Snodgrass is due particular thanks for providing me with his manuscript on Malaysia. I am also indebted to E. Wayne Nafziger for sharing with me his draft manuscript, "The Political Economy of Preventing Humanitarian Emergencies."

Part I

Conflicts, Causes, and Economic Development

1. Introduction

Conflict and the International Development Agencies

Our age has been both remarkable and dreadful, the best or worst of times depending on where one lived and when. With the development of enormously destructive military technologies, the mobilization of entire populations and economies for warfare, and the astonishing power of cruel leaders and lunatic ideologies over the minds of large populations (some more educated than in any previous era), wars between states and against peoples have surpassed previous human history in their casualties, viciousness, and destruction. One estimate puts the number of people killed by armed conflict in the twentieth century at over 100 million, with another 170 million deaths from political violence not associated with warfare.[1] Over this same period, increasingly in the second half of the twentieth century, advances in science and industry, public health, economic activity, and the arts of governance have brought to the populations of many nations an unprecedented rise in longevity and material wealth. There has also been a widening acceptance of the norms of an open, humane, and democratic society as the birthright of the citizens of a modern state. The flow of capital and technology from rich to poor nations has enabled some of the less developed countries—those that have adopted development-enhancing economic policies, and that have maintained nonviolent politics—to reduce poverty and transform their economies and living standards at a faster rate than ever was achieved by the world's now rich economies.

In a fundamental turn in history, interstate war erupting in Western Europe or emanating from Japan now appears as unthinkable as war in North America. In five decades of peace among them, the industrially advanced, democratic states have developed highly interdependent security arrangements and economic systems. They have created a panoply of treaties and interstate institutions to manage problems among themselves. They maintain constant dialogue at many levels in regular search for accommodation and positive-sum solutions. Since World War II the network of U.N. and other international security systems has permitted very few cross-border invasions to succeed, despite the global reach of the Soviet–U.S. rivalry and the postcolonial proliferation of new and fragile sovereign states. A cautiously optimistic view on the future of interstate warfare has become credible. As framed by Stremlau and Sagasti,

> It is now safe to conclude that the age of imperialism has finally passed. Never before has so large and diverse a constellation of sovereign states, covering all of the world's habitable territory, coexisted so peacefully. If current trends hold, historians may one day mark the second half of the 20th century as the beginning of the end for significant interstate wars, fulfilling the dream of statesmen since the Treaty of Westphalia (1648).[2]

It may also be safe to conclude that the age of totalitarian ideology is winding down. The worst scourges of the last century, perhaps the worst in all recorded history, have been the vast ideologically motivated debacles of the Nazi, Soviet, Maoist, and Khmer Rouge regimes.

Though both ideological and utopian fervor have virtually disappeared as sources of large-scale state-sponsored violence (whether or not state-sponsored Islamic fundamentalism is emerging as a continuing exception remains to be seen), the large number of ongoing or recent domestic conflicts of a religious or ethnic character demonstrate that the world has far to go before a similar statement regarding the waning of internal violent conflict might also be credible. Despite the fact that the combatants in most if not all these internal conflicts define themselves, and their opponents, in ascriptive or cultural terms—language, religion, history, common descent, and so forth—many of the conflicts tend to contradict rather than support Samuel P. Huntington's thesis that the world's principal conflicts after the Cold War have been, and will continue to be, between entire civilizations—Western, Islamic, Confucian, Hindu, Slavic–Orthodox, and others.[3] In many African conflicts especially, the combatant groups have been co-members of a common larger culture, much closer to each other linguistically, religiously, and culturally than to any other outside groups. In some cases, such as in Sudan or New Guinea, some of the combatants have been animists, outside any of the main "civilizations." Turkey is an example of a heterogeneous country that does not fall neatly into one "civilization" or another, nor would the Kurdish insurgency illustrate an intercivilization fault line.

The international responses to some of the conflicts have also crossed "civilization" lines. In Bosnia, predominantly Christian and "Western" countries supported the Muslim center, which fought against Eastern Orthodox and Catholic opponents. (The most active proponent of civilization clash, Osama bin Laden, ignored the Bosnian intervention and the West's interventions in Kosovo and Kuwait, events inconsistent with his proclaimed worldview.) During the battle in Chechnya in the fall of 1999, between local and Russian forces, the president of Chechnya decried the absence of foreign Muslim support and called for help from Christian nations.[4] Aside from its critics who see the thesis as glossing over the complexities of the post–Cold War world, Huntington's paradigm is (paradoxically) too narrow an explanation of the conflicts with which we are concerned here.

Nevertheless, "ethnic" fault lines (often separating differentiated groups within Huntington's large "civilization" categories) have been central to Third World internal conflicts, to a lesser extent in Central American conflicts than in Africa and Asia, and will be at the center of this book. Ethnicity remains important in modern Western nations, even in their politics, but differs substantially from ethnicity in developing countries. As Martin O. Heisler points out, the fact that almost all societies are multiethnic often leads to a view that ethnic boundaries are everywhere sharp and that ethnicity should everywhere be a fundamental category of sociopolitical analysis. To the contrary, the classic anthropological paradigm, drawn from study of small, premodern societies, bears little resemblance to the nature and function of ethnicity in complex, modern societies. In the former, ethnic groups "form whole social systems and comprise the basic social, political and economic environments for their members' lives." In the latter, "instead of such integrity and comprehensiveness, we find predominantly symbolic or utilitarian modes of ethnicity." In the former, the individual is molded completely into the inherited ethnic identity from childhood; in the latter, the individual has the social freedom and mobility, and educational exposure, to modify or reject adherence to worldview, religious, esthetic, linguistic, marital choice, or other characteristics (or "markers) denoting the identity impressed during childhood. In the latter, ethnicity is vitiated for functions outside the cultural and esthetic. Identity becomes shaped by a complex of interests and associations—economic class and function, profession, political conviction, leisure preferences, and so on. Ethnic frictions are better described as competition and contention rather than conflict, although there remain some obvious exceptions (e.g., Northern Ireland, the Basque provinces of Spain, fringe xenophobic groups elsewhere).[5] For the most part, the developing nations are in transition between the "anthropological" and "modern" paradigms. We will return repeatedly below to the problems of identity-based conflict and their implications for preventive interventions.

Although the threat of interstate war has diminished, potentialities for such conflicts (and associated terrorism) remain. Some regions contain more sources of potential interstate violence than others, especially the Middle East, the Asian subcontinent, the Caucuses, central Africa, and Northeast Asia. Some of the nations involved may resort to military force to defend or advance perceived vital interests. One might plausibly argue that conventional interstate military aggression is becoming a less viable option with each demonstration that the international community is moving, however haltingly, toward norms of acceptable intervention and willingness to mount conflict-avoiding and peacekeeping initiatives. Conversely, the willingness of the permanent U.N. Security Council members to sanction such interventions, or to incur the risks and costs of military undertakings, has varied case by case.

Repeated demonstrations of how difficult it is for the international community to develop a joint policy and put together an effective intervention coalition may actually encourage some future potential aggressors to discount the probabilities of such intervention should they decide to resort to force. The current international fundamentalist terrorism to promote apocalyptic visions of global rearrangement appears to be a special case; rational weighing of the risks of potential response and considering the probabilities and implications of success or failure appear to have been of little consequence.

Unfortunately, while there has been a decline in interstate warfare and an increase in the effectiveness of international (and some regional) peacekeeping norms and institutions, and of multilateral action, to prevent or contain international conflict, the post–Cold War period has also seen a sharp rise in violent conflict *within* states. By one count, during the post–Cold War years of 1989 to 1996 there were 101 armed conflicts of which 95 were intrastate.[6] These internal conflicts have varied in their intensity, from low annual casualty levels to "ethnic cleansing" and genocide. Some have spilled over borders and brought on, or exacerbated, violent conflict in neighboring countries. Many have generated large cross-border movements of refugees and internal population displacement. As a first step in recording and monitoring these problems, conflict watchers commonly distinguish between levels of violence. One source records four levels: political tension involving fewer than 25 political killings a year; violent political conflict—under 100 political fatalities a year; low-intensity conflict—between 100 and 1,000 fatalities; high-intensity conflict—more than 1,000 a year.[7] Under these definitions there were 17 high-level conflicts under way in 1997, 70 low-intensity conflicts, and 74 violent political conflicts, for a total of 161. All but 11 of these were internal. Because some large nations (e.g., Ethiopia, India, China) recorded several separate internal conflicts, the number of countries involved was less, about 110.

In 1997, high-intensity conflicts occurred in Congo (formerly Zaire), Afghanistan, Algeria, Congo Republic (Brazzaville), Rwanda, Sudan, Sri Lanka, Turkey, Colombia, Albania, India–Pakistan, Burma, Burundi, Iraq, India (Assam and Bihar), and Tajikistan. Among the lower-intensity conflicts were several that subsequently escalated, causing high casualty rates and/or population displacement, including Chechnya, Angola, and East Timor. Kosovo had not yet appeared. The list changes year by year as some conflicts diminish or are resolved, while others erupt or escalate from previous low-intensity or violent political conflict. Because many of these conflicts have been fought with cheap, low-technology weaponry, even with much individual slaughter effected with knives, the struggles can continue for years with neither party gaining a decisive advantage.

These conflicts have had appalling consequences. Millions have died: in Bosnia 150,000, Rwanda 800,000, Sierra Leone 130,000, Sudan 800,000. The United Nations Children's Fund (UNICEF)[8] estimated 850,000 child deaths in Angola and Mozambique between 1980 and 1988 from combat and from the breakdown of food production and health services. Millions of land mines that will take decades to remove continue to claim victims and keep substantial agricultural land out of production. Vast numbers of non-combatants have been forced to flee their homes; in 1997 there were over 35 million refugees and internally displaced persons. There has been massive destruction of economic infrastructure, housing, and productive facilities; further deterioration of infrastructure from wartime suspension of maintenance; loss or virtual collapse of economic output and concomitant slumps in per capita income; and years of development aborted.[9] Calculations of what might have happened had conflict been avoided are obviously illustrative rather than empirical. In the case of Sri Lanka, one study estimated that the opportunity cost of the civil war during the years 1983 to 1988 was $1.5 billion, equivalent to over 20 percent of 1988 gross domestic product (GDP).[10] In Rwanda, GDP fell to an estimated 46 percent of its preconflict peak, whereas in Bosnia it fell to 27 percent and in Lebanon to 24 percent.[11] An estimate of the output Mozambique lost during the civil war years of 1982 to 1992 provides another example:

> Production losses [of an estimated $20 billion] were due to the deaths of some 1.5 million people and the removal of over half the population from customary sources of livelihood (1.5 to 2 million were international refugees displaced into camps or resettlement schemes, 2 million were displaced but not into formal settlements, and more than 1 million were living in the vicinity of their ruined villages but were socioeconomically or psychologically displaced). The war also inflicted direct damage on markets, communications, public health services, and other infrastructure. Destruction of capital stock led to continuing losses of output with difficult-to-calculate impacts on income flow and multiplier effects.[12]

The economic costs of the civil war in Mozambique illustrate what has been a widespread problem in sub-Saharan Africa. Much attention and analysis have been devoted to understanding the relatively poor performance of sub-Saharan economies compared with other regions comprised largely of developing countries. Nobel economist Amartya Sen has stressed the importance of civil war and other "destructive political forces" as reasons for the economic regress across the region. "In the list of worst (1960–1985) performers . . . the association is hard to miss. If, for example, we pick the five worst performers in economic growth and the five worst in mortality reduction . . . we get eight that are sub-Saharan countries, and six of these have had major civil wars." These conflicts have implications for long-run regress; they "not only affect capital and output; they also disrupt trade and commerce, discourage investments, and . . . distance the political leadership from the economic hardships of the population." These wars also have "spread" effects, "reducing *regional* trade and, in neighboring countries, causing political instability, weakening the climate for economic investment, and inducing diversions of economic resources to military purposes."[13] Looking at these conflicts through their effects on a population's food status, Ellen Messer identified forty-three developing countries that underwent "food wars" between 1970 and 1990, that is, conflicts resulting in reduced food production and substantial food deprivation, including cases where hunger was deliberately induced as a form of weapon.[14] In cases such as Afghanistan's long-running civil wars, where in 1998 25 percent of all children aged six to thirty-six months of age were found to be wasted (severely underweight for height) and 52 percent stunted in their growth, an entire generation can be exposed to physical and intellectual impairment.

Civil wars leave a legacy of torn social fabric, and of lingering distrust and hatred among the surviving antagonists, who must create a new polity after the conflict has been resolved. The often vicious character of ethnic conflicts, in which the armed combatants of one or both ethnicities deliberately victimize the noncombatants of the opposing ethnic group, can cause lasting psychosocial impairment of victims of war trauma. Extended conflict and victimization can produce a culture of criminal impunity and violence, quite apart from the special problem of violent behavior of unemployed demobilized soldiers.[15] The psychosocial effects on individual victims have been well studied in several populations, from Holocaust survivors to Cambodian survivors. In recent years, postconflict reconstruction programs have included assistance for the creation or strengthening of mental health services and projects attempting to encourage ethnically mixed communities to reach accommodation, and ultimately reconciliation.

The Focus of International Attention: Full-Blown Crises and Their Aftermath

The relative neglect of precrisis conflict prevention is apparent from the concentration of international efforts, and scholarship, at the eleventh hour and after—namely the periods of acute crisis, conflict resolution, peacekeeping, and postconflict reconstruction. It is not surprising, of course, that the advent (rather than the threat) of hostilities, mass population dislocation, ethnic cleansing, and outright slaughter has commanded international attention, along with the needs for immediate postconflict resettlement, including care for the victims and restoration of essential security and economic and social services. In addition to the established humanitarian agencies of the U.N. system (U.N. High Commissioner for Refugees, the World Food Program), and the various refugee and rehabilitation organizations created in the wake of World Wars I and II, large numbers of intergovernmental and nongovernmental agencies have been founded. The development aid agencies have had to devote increasing amounts of their resources to these crises. One estimate put international spending on emergency and disaster relief during the period 1990 to 1994 at $6 billion, about 10 percent of total official development assistance. The annual cost of providing for ex-Yugoslav refugees in Germany was more than the entire German aid budget.[16]

A large literature is emerging from practitioners and scholars studying the many ethical, technical, and managerial problems of "complex humanitarian emergency" response.[17] These emergencies pose unique problems of children's health, women's reproductive health, psychosocial trauma, refugee camp management and security, preservation of human rights in situations of chaos, family reunification, care of orphans, rehabilitation of victims of mines and unexploded ordnance, and postconflict social rehabilitation. To help meet the special technical, management, and ethical training needs these problems raise for professionals in the health, psychiatric, disaster management, and other fields, many agencies and universities have developed new short-course and graduate academic programs.[18]

There have been many criticisms of the performance of these agencies, along with debates among them over issues of mandates and coordination. The debate over whether humanitarian agencies should continue to succor refugees when significant amounts of the food and other aid are being diverted to combatants (in the case of Rwanda, to perpetrators of the genocide) has been particularly sharp. Another idea that has captured much attention is the so-called relief-to-development continuum, the notion that the sharp separation between the humanitarian work of relief agencies and the reconstruction/rehabilitation work of the development agencies was artificial and detrimental to the recovery process. Because resistance to a call for improved coordination, in a search for ways to realize any potentiality of this continuum, would have been unseemly, the notion has spawned a certain amount of exploration and agency interaction. Though some emergency relief activities have development potential (e.g., preparing refugees to be able to resume economic activity upon repatriation), the continuum concept has yet to achieve significant realization.[19]

The long-term consequences of psychosocial impairment for social and economic reconstruction, when significant numbers of the youth and the workforce adults have been traumatized in the course of a conflict, are not well understood despite their apparent importance. Besides capital flight, other problems exist: mistrust of everyone outside the immediate family, withdrawal from cooperative functions like village labor exchange, mistrust of arm's-length contracts, refusal to put money into banks, a high future discount rate that depresses savings or investment behavior—all these can be widespread, impeding both social and economic recovery.

Even in countries where social conflict has not risen to high-intensity violence, the existence of lower-level social conflict can impede the functioning of the economy. One quantitative study has found significant negative correlation between social conflict and the ability of economies to recover from external shocks such as the oil price hikes of the 1970s:

> [L]atent social conflicts and the institutions of conflict management matter to the persistence of economic growth, . . . their effects are measurable. This is an important conclusion not only in retrospect—as we try to understand what went wrong in so many countries after the mid-1970s—but also prospectively. An increasing number of developing countries are integrating themselves with the international economy. As the Asian financial crisis demonstrates vividly, this will increase their exposure to shocks. Therefore, it will be all the more important to develop institutions that mediate social conflicts. The results of this [study] . . . indicate that participatory and democratic institutions, the rule of law, and social insurance are all components of a strategy to enhance resilience to volatility in the external environment.[20]

The Search for More Effective Prevention

During the Cold War, internal conflicts in countries with economies marginal to world trade and investment, relatively small populations, locations of little strategic importance, and few historic or emotional ties to major powers, could still induce the major powers to intervene or to use development assistance as a lure to become a client state in a global competition. However, since the end of the Cold War, these same powers have shown much less inclination to intervene when vital national interests no longer appear to be at stake, despite the fact that few if any such interventions would entail credible risk of major-power confrontation. For a variety of reasons, the international community has had great difficulty developing effective responses to these internal conflicts. The countries capable of unilateral action or of joint response under U.N. or regional auspices must make judgments in each case regarding the applicable international law, all the regional or global implications of action or inaction, and the implications for their domestic public opinion and support.

In the case of small countries with little geopolitical weight—such as Rwanda—the United States and other Western powers have been reluctant to intervene. The earlier failed intervention in Somalia demonstrated the complexity and risks even for great powers with vastly greater military capacities. Even in the Yugoslav breakup and its attendant massacres, the diplomatic and military pressures succeeded in imposing a peace only after three years of warfare and "ethnic cleansing." Despite the recurrent protestations that lessons have been learned from each delayed and flawed response, the international community is still far from having a reliable response capability. Kosovo and East Timor were recent examples of sluggish financial, administrative, and security crisis-responses that, although ultimately successful, were inadequate to prevent heavy bloodletting, massive population displacement, and extensive destruction. It remains to be seen if the current campaign against "international" terrorism has any sustained effects on the international community's interest in, and response to, internal warfare where one or both parties employ terrorist methods.

Although the international community might be seen as haltingly moving in the direction of increased willingness to intervene against gross human rights violations (often in the form of regime terrorism against domestic opponents), important countries such as China and India have objected strongly to the proposition that human rights conventions might dominate over the principle of sovereignty as a justification for intervention. The action by the North Atlantic Treaty Organization (NATO) in the Kosovo crisis without U.N. Security Council sanction was a striking example of illegal intervention in the eyes of countries wanting to keep their own separatist threats (e.g., Tibet in China, Kashmir in India) from becoming internationalized on similar grounds. This case was especially striking because the intervening powers insisted that Kosovo was still within (rump) Yugoslavia's jurisdiction. Without seeking explicit Security Council sanction, the NATO powers thereby implicitly asserted that the U.N. human rights conventions trumped the U.N. Charter's provisions regarding inviolability of national sovereignty.

In his opening address to the 54th session of the U.N. General Assembly in September 1999, Secretary-General Kofi Annan pointed to the contradiction between the international norms regarding sovereignty and gross humanitarian violations. He argued that a credible, more aggressive Security Council stance would serve as a deterrent to government leaders who would know that they could not expect sovereign immunity if they committed crimes against humanity. Because the permanent members of the Security Council are not unanimous in supporting the idea of humanitarian intervention, the secretary-general called on U.N. members to define a new paradigm for intervention that would enable the international community to respond more swiftly and effectively to future Rwandas. (Those who advocate bringing gross human rights violators to justice also believe that international tribunals can act as a deterrent by demonstrating that sovereign immunity is no longer a protection for criminal behavior.) Annan's call may be seen as another step in the efforts to establish human rights as an overriding international norm.

Acceptance of this norm is not a foregone conclusion, nor are its operational implications clear. The idea that the world as a whole, through joint action under international conventions, should no longer tolerate *gross* violations of human rights wherever they occur may seem a utopian objective for a species many of whose members behave in much the same fashion as humans did in earlier Hobbesian ages. Many of the incentives, responses, and justifications for violent conflict today closely resemble the conflict behavior of medieval Europe, to take just one period and place. Religious antagonism pitted Catholic Western Europe against the Islamic world in a continuous state of war for centuries. Catholic Venice, however, traded commodities and young Slavs (i.e., slaves) with Islamic states despite papal threats, rationalizing their policy by citing its success as a demonstrable heavenly reward for their veneration of the relics of St. Mark's. The cultures of some peoples were more warlike than others. In the ninth and tenth centuries the Danish and Norwegian Vikings sustained their living standards by frequent looting raids on the British Isles and the Carolingian empire; their victims were less warlike, defending but not retaliating.

Long before the arrival of nation-states, ethnic group hatred could be mobilized to carry out general slaughter of noncombatants—what we would now call gross violations of human rights or terrorism. In 1182, the Byzantine emperor tried to loosen the grip of the Italian city-states over eastern Mediterranean commerce by allowing Byzantium's populace to massacre the resident foreigners, the Pisans, Genoese, and Venetians. Unemployed young Normans of the lesser nobility were readily recruited for violent assaults on other societies—southern Italy, England, and the first Crusade to the Holy Land. Class conflict also spawned horrific violence. Between 1323 and 1328 the peasants of Flanders, burdened by heavy taxation, rose up against the nobility and the Church in an effort to bring about a social revolution. Both sides fought with great cruelty. After the French knighthood crushed the peasantry in a climactic battle, they urged the king, Philip VI, to put the country to the torch and to decimate the peasantry, man, woman, and child. (He confiscated the peasants' assets instead.) Economic competition among the Italian cities was seen as a maximalist, negative-sum struggle, requiring constant warfare designed to utterly ruin rivals. That an alternative nonviolent solution was possible was demonstrated by the North Sea and Baltic ports that joined together to form the Hanseatic League in 1230 as a common front against the kings of Denmark.[21]

The idea that has been gathering strength, albeit haltingly, in recent times—that all nations should participate in a system of rules and international institutions with the overriding objective of avoiding violent conflict, both between and within sovereign states—is a radical departure from previous human worldviews. Up until the late tenth century the only European concept of unacceptable conflict was a narrow one developed in France by the Roman Catholic Church. Conflict was justified only if undertaken to protect the helpless and the Church. Because the elimination of violent political conflict was not feasible, the Church developed the notion of the "Peace of God," specifying brief periods during the year when fighting was forbidden on pain of excommunication. The attempt to limit warfare among Christians was not seen as inconsistent with the idea of "just" conflicts (the Crusades, for example), a concept with a long history among many religions.

In our time we appear to be moving, at times slowly, toward diminishing tolerance of interstate and internal warfare or of leaders and governments that violate human rights with impunity, and toward a definition of rights that incorporates group as well as individual rights. At the Istanbul summit in November 1999, the members of the Organization for Security and Cooperation in Europe (OSCE) adopted a new treaty that legitimates possible intervention in conflicts within states, even before such conflicts have reached the point of open warfare. Although the treaty in effect opens the door to intervention in unstable areas only in Europe, the principle is a far-reaching extension of the primacy of gross human rights violations over the inviolability of sovereignty.[22]

Difficult questions remain that make the response of the international community in individual cases uncertain and of varying effectiveness, quite apart from questions of Realpolitik and of achieving a legitimating consensus for action. Under international law the principles of sovereignty and self-determination often conflict with principles of universal human rights and with U.N. Charter provisions that permit Security Council action in internal conflicts deemed to constitute a "threat to peace." The development of international legal principles that would legitimate and facilitate more timely and effective international responses has some distance yet to travel.[23] It has also been argued that establishment of a principle of international intervention in cases of massive human rights violations would be a "dangerous crusade" because the frequency of such horrors could mean a commitment to virtually endless warfare. In this view, regional arrangements based on the willingness of one intervener to take the lead would be more feasible and less open-ended.[24]

There are also obvious practical difficulties that would face any system of formal, institutionalized, preconflict intervention. It is difficult to predict if tension at a particular time and place will evolve into violent conflict. It is difficult to predict if scattered, low-level violence will escalate into general conflict. Several efforts have been made (which we discuss further below) to develop "early warning" models, sets of indices that (based on past experience in many countries) would presage a descent into violent conflict. These approaches can be elaborate, even rather obvious after the fact, but for various reasons (including the fact that they are still "works in progress") appear thus far to have had little practical application. Conflicts between massed ethnic groups where government serves as nonpartisan conflict manager are very different from conflicts where one group controls the state and uses state power preemptively against other groups, or where one group dominates state institutions and state power and a violent challenge to the state is initiated by rival or disaffected group(s), or where the challenge arises from (or is realizable only from) external manipulation rather than from indigenous political dynamics and resources, or where rival groups are essentially (perhaps reluctantly) clients of warlords engaged in winner-take-all power struggles. Just as the wide variation among deeply divided societies prone to conflict has made it difficult to develop a truly general theory of conflict, so the relevant indices of early warning must and do vary widely from one situation to another.

In a recent paper discussing yet another form of large-scale internal conflict, mass movements of ordinary citizens against an incumbent regime, Tony Oberschall (1999) sets out a collective action theory to capture major variables that appear to determine whether or not a mass challenge emerges. Despite the clarification a collective action perspective may provide for an understanding of the necessary and sufficient conditions for mass challenge, Oberschall notes that different scenarios may result in any case, and that "prediction of path and outcome of confrontations are difficult. The uncertainties in the theory are not deficiencies of the conceptualization, but express the uncertainties of the real world of challenge and confrontation."

According to Oberschall, even in a situation where theory may indicate high potentiality for conflict, "The decision maker has limited information and has to anticipate the likelihood of future events determined by the choices of thousands of ordinary citizens and by the authorities' countermeasures.

The authorities themselves make guesses about how the challengers will respond to social control and to conciliation, and may be uncertain about how their agents, the police and army, will conform to their commands. Thus to chart a protracted conflict and predict its outcome is a demanding task [even though] collective action theory has provided a start." Oberschall also emphasizes the speed with which unanticipated events might unfold. "What looks like a stable equilibrium can unravel rapidly, and it astonishes both the regime and the security forces and the academics and national security advisers." The conflict following the August 30, 1999, referendum in East Timor presents a striking example of poor predictive powers. Although East Timor had been simmering with violence for years because of its population's refusal to accept Indonesia's imposed sovereignty, an assessment of world conflict potentialities, issued that same month by the U.S. National Intelligence Council (1999), made no mention of East Timor and rated the situation in Indonesia generally as likely to improve. According to the author of the report, the assessment was based on "the coordinated views of analysts and experts from agencies across the Federal Government."[25] In a final gloomy observation, Oberschall reminds us that even where, as in Rwanda, Bosnia, and elsewhere, the world did have fairly clear indicators and warnings of impending massacre, advance knowledge was of no avail in the absence of international political will.

There is probably no better witness to the advance knowledge available in Rwanda than Lt.-General Romeo A. Dallaire, commander at the time of U.N. forces on the ground. On the problem of international will and the immorality of preventive inaction, he has written that the experience in Rwanda

> was seen as too difficult and not of sufficient interest and value to prevent the outbreak of violence, and once violence had broken out, it was still not of sufficient interest to warrant the expense of resources and risk of more casualties to stop the violence from spreading. . . . Like the crisis at the time, the need for a response mechanism and the consequences of not looking for solutions are guaranteeing the recurrence of other humanitarian catastrophes now and into the future. . . .
>
> I remain mystified that human life, the security of noncombatants, and the prevention of such horrors as the genocide in Rwanda are, sadly, not sufficient to act as a catalyst for a swift and determined response from the international community. . . . It would be immoral if not outright criminal to allow another tragedy to occur by failing in our collective responsibility to humanity at large. . . . The killings could have been prevented if there had been the international will to accept the costs of doing so. The looming threat of overwhelming international retribution is still required to keep in check some of the impulses of hate-filled elements.[26]

Even if lack of political will, or the great variance from one conflict to another in the geopolitical importance of the countries involved, did not pose such difficult obstacles to timely and effective international intervention, the development of effective interventions becomes increasingly problematic as the stakes, tensions, and violence escalate toward a general resort to internal resolution by force. Beyond some point of breakdown in mutual trust, some point of accumulated violent acts and extremist rhetoric, room for compromise and third-party mediation may diminish to zero. Ironically, the longer one goes back in time when the parties still have flexibility, before political rhetoric has deteriorated, and while there is still (perhaps ample) room for policy adjustment and trade-off, the less alarming are the "early warning" indicators, the fewer are the apparent reasons or justifications for international development agencies to concern themselves over conflict (exacerbation or amelioration) implications of their programs. In short, during the preconflict years when there may still be ample scope for conflict-avoiding initiatives, international consciousness and attention regarding such potentialities are normally dormant. There is a parallel incongruence between international intent and effectiveness: the more violent, the more vicious an internal conflict becomes, international intent to intervene strengthens (not in the case of Rwanda!) while the scope for effective (nonmilitary) prevention or resolution diminishes.

This weakness of eleventh-hour measures has dogged the attempts during the 1990s to use economic sanctions as a punitive instrument for forcing governments to cease policies deemed to be violating international norms, such as external aggression or support of terrorism. Several of the sanctions cases that were aimed at governments fomenting *internal* conflict through serious human-rights abuses or aggression against victimized ethnicities were backed by U.N. mandates: Burma, Rwanda, ex-Yugoslavia, and Sierra Leone. More economic sanctions were initiated by individual countries (primarily the United States, Western Europe, and the USSR/Russia) than by U.N. action. Although the main sanction instruments have been restrictions on international trade, travel, and investment, they have also included aid cutoffs (except for refugee and other humanitarian assistance). The U.N.-mandated economic sanctions generally entail suspensions of World Bank and other multilateral development bank activity. Because sanctions have been employed only to force suspension of *ongoing* conflict or abuse, not as a prevention tool, they are, in our perspective, too late. Their application has been a clear sign that preventive diplomacy or earlier prevention measures, if any, have failed. Although the report of the Carnegie Commission on Preventing Deadly Conflict[27] supports a continuing role for economic sanctions, especially if their design is improved, the literature evaluating the effects of sanctions has been very critical. Most analyses have shown that sanctions are ineffective and have undesirable unintended consequences. While seldom unhorsing their target regimes or achieving the intended change in policies, they often cause hardship for target country populations.[28] In short, as an instrument for conflict prevention or resolution, economic sanctions have been neither quick nor effective. We will reconsider sanctions below, in the context of early prevention efforts.

During the years when internal socioeconomic and political conflicts are still relatively nonviolent, still too ordinary as a universal feature of human society, there is a presumption that management or resolution of such conflicts is the responsibility of the local political and juridical institutions and processes. It is only when the local processes are failing and conflict turns violent that international conflict-resolution efforts assume legitimacy and get started. In fact, with the explosion of internal conflict in the decolonized countries, conflict resolution has emerged as a new specialization—indeed, a subject for academic research, international mediation organizations, professional associations, and professional training at the postgraduate level in a number of universities. Kevin Avruch writes, "By the late 1980s some practitioners would advertise themselves with 'Have Process, Will Travel.' Conflict resolution had become a commodity. By the early 1990s, after the collapse of the Soviet Union and the opening of Eastern Europe, it also became an exportable commodity."[29]

Conflict scholarship has ranged over the whole gamut of conflict sources and triggers, from the perceptual, psychological, and symbolic, to the hard issues of material and security interests. Conflict resolution theorists have tended to fall into two camps, reflecting the opposite ends of this gamut. Their contrasting concepts and approaches have required the use of terminology that differentiates between different degrees of "resolution." Avruch describes the two concepts:

> The first one reflects colloquial usage; it is inclusive, encompassing virtu-ally any strategy or technique that brings a dispute to an end, or even stops the violence. The second, what we have called the restricted sense of con-flict resolution, is specialized and exclusive. Rooted in . . . Lederach's notion of "conflict transformation," the restricted conception seeks to get at the underlying root causes of the conflict, to solve the problems that led to it in the first place. Following the logic of this sense of conflict resolu-tion usually means contemplating profound, even radical structural changes to the sociopolitical system that gave rise to the conflict in the first place. The restricted conflict resolutionists are unwilling to grant the broad or inclusive view of conflict termination the name "resolution." [Resolution] is regulation, settlement, or mitigation. It consists of bargaining and com-

promise, of interest-based negotiation, of mediation, good offices, facilitation or—very close to the edges of talk at all—"coercive diplomacy." It
may well result in signed agreements, cease-fires, demilitarized zones, truces
and armistice lines; it may even stop the violence and killing *for now*. But
unless it gets to the causes of the conflict, to repressive institutions or the
unequal distribution of social goods and resources, for instance, the agreement will be broken . . . and the violence and killing will assuredly start up
once again.[30]

The term "preventive diplomacy" has been coined to define a spectrum of
international activities that acknowledges the need to address radical structural changes but that in practice has focused on bargaining, interest-based
negotiation, and good offices, the tools of the diplomatic trade. Our interest
is in prevention rather than resolution—that is, in managing or mitigating
conflicts before they reach the stage of urgent need for diplomatic intervention or, worse, high-intensity violence that triggers interventions by force.
Nevertheless, prevention (in a postconflict situation, prevention of conflict
resumption) is the key to the difference between the two concepts of resolution. Avruch's "restricted" or more fundamental concept of resolution is obviously preferable. By definition, it goes beyond immediate cease-fires,
interim or transitional arrangements, and accommodations that may be su-
perficial and face-saving, even accepted (as in the case of Bosnia, for example)
only under duress, to the presumed heart of the matter between the protagonists. Unfortunately (as Bosnia also demonstrates), securing resolution of
fundamental differences *after* the protagonists have been at each other's throats
is very difficult. The notion that resolution practitioners should strive for
fundamental transformation has apparently run up against this hard reality.

> The hopeful viewpoint is that, given enough time, perhaps even a more
> demanding . . . restricted sense of conflict will prevail, one based on con-
> flict *transformation*, aimed toward a profound restructuring of society and
> polity. But other evidence does not point to this at all. In the mid-1980s
> there was much talk about (restricted) conflict resolution as a "new para-
> digm" for theory and practice. By the mid-1990s, however, it appeared
> that the new paradigm was not so much still untried, awaiting birth (the
> hopeful view), as already declared too radical, utopian, or unworkable—
> and disposed of in the counterrevolution of pragmatism and "realism."[31]

In those cases where internal conflict has been terminated by international military intervention, the third parties may be in position to design a
settlement that includes the immediate installation of what appear to be elements of both concepts of resolution, that is, the immediate military stand-

down (sustained by international peace-monitoring or peacekeeping) and the creation of a new political structure designed to contain if not transform the political and power relations among the antagonists. The record is not yet encouraging. For example, the Dayton Peace Accords of 1995 successfully terminated the conflict in Bosnia while purporting to gain acceptance by the three parties—the Bosnia Muslims, Croats, and Serbs—of a completely new set of political relationships and institutions. The presence of U.N. forces has kept the peace thus far. However, between the deep mistrust, the continuing leadership of the same parties that fought the war, the determination of the dominant Bosnian Croat and Serb parties to undermine the Dayton Accords by refusing to implement many of its critical features (abetted until recently by undermining policies of the neighboring states of Croatia and Serbia [ex-Yugoslavia]), the political structuring has been deeply flawed in conception and implementation and may require a complete overhaul to avoid a recurrence of conflict.[32]

The Many Forms of Internal Conflict

This study is not concerned with violence that is interpersonal or criminal. Both these forms of violence are ever present in all societies, rising and falling in frequency from time to time, and occurring at differing levels of intensity in different societies. High levels of violent criminal behavior are often found in countries that are also burdened with extensive public-sector corruption and weak or compromised judiciary systems. Because extensive criminality and weak rule of law are known to damage the growth process by undermining personal security and property rights, development scholars and agencies have been giving these problems increasing attention. Without intending to diminish the importance of these aid-assisted efforts to reduce lawlessness, we focus instead on the problems of preventing violent conflict between population subgroups, conflict that commonly erupts on (or rises to) a scale that threatens social and political stability and economic activity on a national level, conflict that typically involves organized armed (military or paramilitary) forces that represent (or claim to represent) defined constituencies.

Violent internal conflict takes many forms, some of which are unlikely to be preventable by any outside interventions, either diplomatic at the time the violence actually breaks out, or by international development agencies through societal changes induced by economic development, except perhaps in a very long run. (Examples might be warlord rivalries, as in Sierra Leone, or the hegemony civil wars of the hermetic Burmese regime.) Large-scale internal conflict commonly is dubbed a "civil war." Analysts typically use a violence threshold to distinguish civil war from low-level violence or civil insecurity: a country moves into the civil war column when its annual count of fatalities passes the 1,000 mark. Also most commonly, the struggle is between the state (government) and the population group(s) aligned with the state on the one side, and groups challenging the state on the other. In some cases the challenging side aims to take over the government. In other cases, it wants to secede from the state. In yet others, severe violence breaks out between two population groups, with the state attempting to maintain order, not siding with either group. A civil war may rage localized for years without destabilizing the state or the bulk of the economy, or it may cause the state to collapse and the institutional framework of the economy to disintegrate. The roots of these conflicts, which we examine below, have comprised varying mixes of fears, hegemonic ambitions, and grievances over economic, political, and cultural differences and rivalries. In the worst intrastate cases of mass violent death this past century (apart from famines caused by government policies), the state has initiated slaughter of noncombatant population groups deemed to be ethnic or class enemies, and/or tools of a threatening foreign power.

Some recent research (especially the quantitative) into the causes of civil wars has excluded, by definition, conflicts where one side is not responding with organized fighting. The violent aggressor side (or the state) attacks another population group that, unable to mount an armed defense, must flee to seek refuge haven elsewhere. These are pogroms or "ethnic cleansing" campaigns rather than "warfare." Also excluded by definition are the conflicts where violent aggression is chronic but the level of fatalities falls below the 1,000-per-year threshold. Under these distinctions, civil wars in developing countries are a subset of the wider general problem of internal violence. As some of the problems underlying the cases that fall outside the conventional definition of civil war are similar to the root causes of the conflicts excluded by these definitions, we will not limit ourselves here to "civil war" cases.

Internal conflicts have varied by scale, by the extent of geographic coverage, by the extent of noncombatant casualties, and by the extent of resort to cultural destruction and sometimes horrific tactics to terrorize the opposing, or victim, population group(s). In turn, these and other characteristics of a conflict will affect how the struggle, after settlement, will enter into the historic memories of each side, shaping both the near-term chances for avoiding resumption and the nature of their long-term relationship. Some conflicts may be small running sores in terms of the numbers of combatants challenging the state and/or the proportion of the disaffected population group that actually favors an extra-legal challenge to the state or supports an insurgent force. Some conflicts may remain well below the civil war threshold for long periods because the insurgents are unable to acquire enough finance and weaponry to challenge the security forces of the state. Even below-threshold, running-sore conflicts have proven extremely damaging to economic development and the general welfare. Obviously, our sketch of conflict characteristics is not intended as a full treatment of the factors determining whether or not a conflict escalates into a major challenge, a civil war, or a major economic drain on the state. It should serve, however, to underscore the point that the conflicts within developing countries in recent decades have been far from uniform in their etiology or their characteristics.

International Terrorism

At this writing it is only weeks since the suicide attacks of September 11, 2001, on the World Trade towers and the Pentagon, and the responding war in Afghanistan against the Al Qaeda organization and its Taliban host. At the U.N. General Assembly session in mid-November, virtually every nation in the world condemned international terrorism and concurred in the necessity of protecting the world against this threat.

This conflict is obviously very different from the conflicts this book is concerned with. It is international rather than internal. According to the announced, and presumed, aims of the Al Qaeda and Taliban leadership, their fundamentalist objectives are so extreme as to be apocalyptic and completely infeasible. Under the broadest interpretation, they seek to change, indeed roll back, the course of history, which they see as a long struggle between Islam and Christianity. To accomplish this goal, they created a worldwide network to intervene in internal conflicts (such as in the Philippines) where one side was (perhaps among other characteristics) Muslim. In countries already largely Muslim they opposed the intrusions of modernity into their vision of the theocratic world demanded by Islam, allying with local fundamentalist groups to help overthrow regimes seen as corrupt and as having departed from true Islamic orthodoxy. A narrower goal is to roll back, by terror and mass uprising, the power, influence, and presence of the United States, especially in regions and countries largely Muslim. The fact that Osama bin Laden came from Saudi Arabia, as did most of the suicide hijackers who carried out the September 11 attacks, gave credence to the view that a core Al Qaeda objective was the overthrow of the Saudi royal family.

Though some of the parties in the internal antagonisms we are concerned with have employed terrorist tactics after the unresolved enmities had reached the stage of violent confrontation, few have extended such tactics to outside countries. In contrast, Al Qaeda and some of the (Egyptian, Palestinian and other) fundamentalist organizations with which it is allied (possibly also linked to one or more regimes making opportunistic use of these movements) are "international" in the sense that they embrace cells operating in, or out of, many countries. The goals of most of the antagonists discussed in this book include concrete economic and political changes that are in principle negotiable, or resolvable in some cases by secession. Long before the resort to violence, such goals can be affected by the processes of change inherent in economic development, and often by the international agencies helping to finance and assist such development. Religion is often a factor in these conflicts, but seldom the essential root cause. The relative material disadvantage of some antagonists is frequently a critical motivation when aggrieved groups see no other recourse short of violence.

In contrast, the fundamentalist program can become entirely consumed with power and cultural-religious cleansing, and be disinterested in poverty. Much of the sympathy Al Qaeda and the Taliban have evoked among co-religionists in the Middle East and elsewhere has been reported as arising from deep wellsprings of resentment over the material and technological gulf between the West and much of the Muslim world. Some scholars have cited frustration and humiliation over the long stagnation of the Islamic heartland and the failure, thus far, of Islamic intellectual and religious leadership to reinterpret Islam, and its role in relation to the state, in the light of modern realities. If the utopian designs of the extreme Islamic fundamentalists currently on the stage are represented fairly by the policies promulgated in Afghanistan, a country where they have had the opportunity for relatively unhampered governance, it is clear that the fundamentalists view as anathema some of the basic requirements for modern development. They deny education or employment for the female half of their labor force. They deny education of youth that prepares them with secular skills and habits of critical thinking. They oppose an open economy that draws in technological learning (beyond the arts of terrorist destruction), that has close trade relations with outside economies, and that seeks foreign investment to build domestic productive capacities. They are against the idea of government that is responsible to a constituency and open to change and evolution; and they oppose the concept of a pluralistic civil society comprising independent institutions and interest-group and citizenry organizations. In such a worldview the international development agencies must be seen as part of the problem, not the solution, as instruments for advancing the very values and societal characteristics to which the fundamentalists are deadly opposed.

This incompatibility between the extreme fringe of Islamic fundamentalism and the worldview of the international development "community" is illustrated by a response to the events of September 11 from a group of senior World Bank officials.

Poverty in the midst of plenty is the challenge of our times. It was true before September 11. It is even more so today. When the promised benefits of globalization remain elusive for many of the poorest citizens of our planet, when hope falters and young people cannot imagine the future, when the gap is too wide between words and action, the voices of extremism find a responsive echo.[33]

They assert that while growth remains essential, the "quality" of that growth matters, and that "quality growth" is "an effective way to prevent conflicts." Their definition of quality includes notions that are basic to the international development paradigm but diametrically opposed to the fundamentalist agenda: responsiveness ("listening to many voices" in the development process), local empowerment, working with nongovernmental civil society, utilizing research and technology, expanding trade relations, and drawing benefits from the globalization of science, communications, and information.

Although the international terrorism conflict differs from the conflicts that are the subject of this book, the events of September 11, 2001, have demonstrated that international terrorism has major capacities to affect the fortunes of developing countries, their exposure to internal conflict, the significance of underdevelopment for the more advanced and wealthy countries, and the need for the wealthy countries to reconsider the policy framework within which they address underdevelopment. First, the fact that the feasibility of threats of such a scale (both what has been perpetrated and what further seems feasible) has now been demonstrated calls into question the traditional bases for judging the relative geopolitical importance of individual states. Afghanistan is remote from Europe and the Western Hemisphere; it is a country of little economic importance, extremely poor, with no industrial capacity. After the withdrawal, and then collapse, of the Soviet Union, Afghanistan was seen as having only local region importance, certainly not as a country that could be the source of an effective attack on Western vital interests. Afghanistan has demonstrated to the wealthy nations that turbulence and deep grievances in developing countries can no longer be left to benign neglect under the mistaken assumption that such turbulence can have no unpleasant international consequences.

Second, the short-term shock effects on the world economy are very damaging to developing nations. Many of them will suffer income declines and increased unemployment due to the depressing effects of these events (reinforcing the already widespread sluggishness and recession of the industrialized economies) on tourism, foreign investment, and export earnings. For many developing countries the overall effects on national income will be very substantial. This can only deepen internal competition and raise the levels of tension between antagonistic groups in deeply divided societies.

Third, while the initial U.S. commitment of substantial economic aid to Pakistan ($600 million) is drawing on a supplementary attack-response budget of $40 billion provided by the Congress shortly after the September 11 events, a general donor focus on the regions and countries at immediate risk to direct destabilizing could have the perverse result of diverting aid resources away from other poor countries at risk of internal instabilities. It would also be unfortunate if aid agencies lowered their standards for project design or government reform commitment because of political pressures for rapid disbursement or for providing financial support to regimes not committed to improving the welfare of their populations.

Fourth, and perhaps most seriously for the long term, the fundamentalist extreme, if not countered by the Islamic mainstream and the positive sociocultural effects of economic growth and modernization, could radicalize Muslim groups and the general Muslim worldview in the swath of countries (across Africa, Central Asia, and Southeast Asia) with mixed Muslim and non-Muslim populations. Antagonisms in which religion has been only one factor could be deepened through a rising salience of religious identity as an overriding and exclusivist issue.

All these effects and potentialities have added urgency to the need for a reexamination of the role and scale of foreign aid. In fact, within weeks, if not days, after September 11, there was already much scurrying around in development circles to initiate such reexamination. Task forces were formed (in the World Bank and USAID, at least) to identify the implications for these agencies and to search for greater coordination.

In my view, it is impossible to escape the conclusion that the United States and other donor countries—for their own self-interest, and to be faithful to their own humanitarian values—must revise their foreign economic policies in ways that greatly enhance the pace and opportunities for poverty reduction and economic growth of the developing nations. The advent of the Cold War in the late 1940s provided the first grand impetus for foreign aid and for the promotion of trade and investment as instruments for driving the economic advance of the developing countries. The advent of international terrorism, with the finance, powerful methods and weapons, and suicidal determination to exploit the very open society the terrorists despise should provide a second grand impetus. However, as vital as a generalized, reinvigorated attack on poverty will be, the development agencies will also need to address with greater subtlety and sharper focus than has been the case in the past the core problems of group imbalances and antagonisms.

The Scope for Early Prevention

The search for ways to avoid impending conflicts is hardly a new function of diplomacy. Nevertheless, both the modern development of international and multinational institutions for dispute management and the end of the era of Cold War proxy conflicts have led a school of practitioners and scholars to carve out "preventive diplomacy" as a new category of study and practice. While some use this term to embrace everything from root-cause ameliora- tion (poverty, environment, etc.) to crisis management methods (diplomatic, people-to-people, mediation, etc.), to postconflict reconstruction, the concept is more useful when used to focus on diplomatic processes and on the period when "violence is imminent or early but still short of mass deadly conflict," as Bruce Jentleson suggests in his recent review of experience and the state of the art.[34] By this definition, the start of preventive diplomacy in any situation spells the end of the period when root-cause prevention might have been attempted, and confirms root-cause failure. Such failure is even more complete when pre- ventive diplomacy comes to naught and the only remaining preconflict interna- tional option is preemptive military intervention. Jentleson calls this last option "coercive prevention" in a second recent paper that focuses on the situations of irreconcilable antagonists hurtling toward violent conflict.

Jentleson challenges the prevailing arguments against preemptive mili- tary actions. First, he describes how international conventions and norms have been moving in the direction of defining sovereign legitimacy as based on state responsibilities in addition to the classical state right of noninterven- tion, a movement that still has far to go. He notes that, "The scope of a state's right to sovereign authority is not unconditional or normatively superior to the right to security of the polity. Until and unless this conception of respon- sibility gains international legitimacy, international conflict prevention strat- egies will continue more often than not to be too little, too late."[35] Second, Jentleson argues that the common explanation (mainly in the United States) for inaction or for intervention—whether or not a "CNN effect" has aroused public opinion—overstates public reluctance and understates the opinion- molding power of presidential leadership in international affairs. He also objects to the superficiality of the common assertion that in the post–Cold War world few of the recent intrastate conflicts have threatened U.S. "vital interests." "Although it may be true that many of these issues and places have limited intrinsic importance, the more the conflicts intensify the more important the issues and places often become. Initial assessments . . . often fail to account for the dynamics of spread and escalation by which the risks to the interests of outside parties become greater. . . . [T]he damage to major power and other international interests often proves greater than anticipated because the assessment of the conflict's limited importance results in inaction or inadequate action."[36] He also notes that even where interests are of only limited importance, intervention may be a rational policy if a proportionately limited force commitment is sufficient to be effective. Third, Jentleson makes the case (concurred in by numbers of country experts) that early use of sufficient international force, and/or credible threats to apply such force (supplemented, of course, with appropriate diplomatic, economic, and other actions), would likely have prevented the bloodbaths in Bosnia, Kosovo, East Timor, and Rwanda.

Unfortunately, even if all the difficulties that face mobilizing the necessary political will and practical implementation arrangements can be overcome, leading to the sanctioning and establishment of standing international coercion capacity, preventive coercion will remain an eleventh-hour response. The coercive introduction of international forces is likely to be feasible only if conflict is incontestably imminent. Early in this context is very late indeed.

Although prevention at the moment of extreme crisis is not the focus of this study, Jentleson makes a number of points worth noting in our "early early" context. First, for outside powers the risks of preventive efforts are much less than the risks created by conflict: "When there is no prevention, the real estate in question risks getting bigger. Whether because the conflict then takes in areas that are more strategic or simply because a larger area is in conflict [through contagion effects], outside powers can find their interests much more at risk." Second, a "wait-and-see" attitude risks a narrowing of options as a conflict deepens and as resolution becomes increasingly difficult. Again, efforts to prevent conflict should ideally start while options remain open, before the party(ies) resort to violence. Third, the financial cost of preventive military action is likely to be much less than the cost of midconflict intervention to bring a civil war to a halt and the humanitarian aid cost of the refugee flows that these conflicts usually entail.

The case for preventive "intervention" by the international development agencies—where their actions may be relevant and salient—is stronger than the case for coercive prevention, for obvious reasons. First, the development agencies are on the ground, usually years before conflicts have turned violent, long before any need for the instruments or agencies of international diplomatic or military intervention. Their presence is usually welcomed as the dispensers of international transfers and facilitators of economic and social progress. The international development system is well established and is operating in virtually every developing country. It needs no ad hoc invention under crisis conditions.

Second, a conflict-prevention role for the development agencies should be very much less costly than eleventh-hour coercive prevention. Effective prevention through the addressing of root causes in countries at conflict-risk may require a greater resource input than the development system as a whole is now providing. However, the extra cost of a (successful) preventive strategy is virtually certain to be less than the huge costs of coercive intervention and/or postconflict reconstruction.

Third, in difficult cases, development agencies may have to use strong persuasion or exert heavy "conditionality" pressures. However overbearing such actions might be, they would not have the character of coercion by force; they would be largely integral to the development assistance activities the agencies are already conducting as a normal course, and they may be justifiable in world opinion as essentially humanitarian in nature and purpose.

Fourth, for many years the mandates of the development agencies have been moving away from their earlier focus on bricks-and-mortar investment and dominance of economic criteria for project choice and design and toward creating institutional frameworks and promoting development-enhancing governance. Many of the bilateral development agencies have been providing financial and technical assistance designed to strengthen not only democratic processes but also formal judicial systems and civil society conflict-resolution organizations. Thus, deliberate incorporation of conflict prevention as an objective—preferably the *principal* objective in countries at risk—is likely to involve new initiatives, and changes to ongoing programs, that are incremental, technical, and unnewsworthy, compared with the drastic nature of coercive prevention.

Fifth, mobilizing "political will" for development assistance that is oriented for conflict prevention should be easier than the task of mobilizing such will for military interventions.

In the United States in particular, a coherent prevention strategy, one built upon development assistance that addresses economic and social root causes of post–Cold War conflict, might conceivably create a public understanding and support base that would be wider than the collection of relatively narrowly defined groups (such as those interested in child health, HIV/AIDS, the environment, and NGO financing) that for some time has provided the only active support for foreign aid. The previous USAID administrator, J. Brian Atwood, made such a bid for the role of foreign aid in an op-ed article in 1994. He asserted that the Clinton administration had "made crisis prevention a central theme of its foreign policy." Noting Secretary-General Kofi Annan's call for preventive diplomacy, Atwood wrote:

> Our common objective is clear: to help societies build the capacity to deal with the social, economic and political forces that threaten to tear them

apart. . . . Some of the components are clear. We cannot prevent failed states with a top-down approach. No amount of international resources or organizational capacity can serve as a substitute for building stable, pluralist societies. . . . Technology should be better exploited and shared to empower individuals and enhance the networking of nongovernmental groups, increase food supplies, slow population growth and preserve natural resources. Sustainable development that creates chains of enterprises, respects the environment and enlarges the range of freedom and opportunity over generations should be pursued as the *principle* [*sic*] *antidote* to social disarray.[37]

The current administrator of USAID, Andrew Natsios, recently incorporated conflict prevention as one of the three main objectives of U.S. foreign aid, the other two being health, and economic development and agriculture. Presenting USAID's 2002 budget proposal to the Congress, Natsios asserted that USAID "must improve its ability to promote conflict prevention." To accomplish this, USAID "will undertake a major new conflict prevention, management, and resolution initiative." While this policy stance sets the stage for new approaches to prevention, the core concept appears to be a continuation of the agency's ongoing reliance on the spread of democracy (an approach we examine below).

This initiative will integrate the existing portfolio of USAID programs with new approaches to crisis and conflict analysis, and new methodologies to assist conflicting parties to resolve their issues peacefully. Our experience has proven that by promoting and assisting the growth of democracy—by giving people the opportunity to peacefully influence their government—the United States advances the emergence and establishment of societies that will become better trade partners and more stable governments. By facilitating citizens' participation and trust in their government, our democracy efforts can help stop the violent internal conflicts that lead to destabilizing and costly refugee flows, anarchy and failed states, and the spread of disease.[38]

Major obstacles will have to be overcome, however, to turn U.S. foreign aid into an effective instrument for conflict prevention. As explored in a recent conference sponsored by USAID and the Woodrow Wilson International Center, these obstacles include (1) the need to redefine what comprises national security in the post–Cold War world, to embrace a spectrum of political, economic, and social issues that is broader than the narrow, threat-centered, paradigm of the Cold War decades; (2) traditional problems of poor coordination among different arms of the U.S. government responsible for varying aspects of foreign policy and international programs; and (3) the need for overhaul of the foreign aid legislation. The USAID's current legislative mandate and funding structure are a particularly severe constraint on the agency's ability to address conflict prevention. The agency's operating and performance evaluation systems are also too mechanical and quantitative for a conflict-prevention objective: the ultimate "measurement" of program outcome would be events (i.e., conflicts) that do not take place.

> The basic foreign aid act is very much in a child survival and humanitarian mode at present. Can this shift in Congress and with the American public to a structural prevention focus? If so, at what loss and gain of votes and support? Much of the USAID process is now geared to "Results" packages; can USAID and Congress shift to measuring aid success with institution-building indicators, instead of more understandable birth, death, disease, health, election, etc., indicators?
>
> It will be a difficult policy change from poverty reduction to [conflict-management] capacity development for Congress, the media, the public and especially the multitude of special interest groups that have influenced budget earmarking and directives. This use of directives and earmarking has been carried out to the extreme, resulting in very little [program expenditure] flexibility. . . . [T]here is such a history now of these special interest groups and Congress directing from America where development assistance should go that the present budget structure leaves little flexibility to respond to local requirements.[39]

The limited room for matching resources to the high priority that Natsios has assigned to conflict prevention is evident in the USAID budget for 2002. The posture of the Bush administration and the Congress regarding foreign aid and developing-country crisis prevention—will they reorient the legislation to sweep away the legislative constraints on USAID's flexibility? or incorporate conflict prevention in the legislation in a manner that translates into funding levels commensurate with prevention's importance?—is not clear at this writing. Can the NGOs and other groups that support foreign aid's humanitarian purposes (and whose field programs depend on USAID's budget) be brought around to support conflict prevention as a humanitarian objective that may override their particular activities? Can foreign aid's humanitarian supporters accept a more comprehensive prevention paradigm, a wider concept of humanitarian prevention that goes to the prior roots of disorder rather than absorbing such large aid resources in conflict alleviation and repair? A positive answer to such questions would greatly enhance the ability of American development assistance to adopt the orientation and program specifics we will illustrate and propose below.

Returning to Bruce Jentleson, his conclusion to his case for the realism of coercive prevention is even more apt when applied to the potential preventive role of development assistance:

> [W]e currently suffer from being too often caught in the middle. We seek to do as little as we can, or at least avoid squarely facing up to the issues until they press themselves upon us so intensely as to be undeniable. We then end up with commitments that last much longer, cost much more, and accomplish much less than promised. No wonder that not just isolationists but serious strategic thinkers counsel doing less. Yet as argued from the outset, the interests at stake and the costs of inaction are too great for those arguments to stand up to analysis. Conflict prevention strategies of doing more and sooner truly are the best option—or the least bad in the Churchillian sense. . . .
>
> Even if just one or two of the next wave of Bosnias, Rwandas, Kosovos, and East Timors can be prevented, that would be a major contribution to making the second decade of the post–Cold War era more peaceful and principled than the first. And perhaps we can do better than that.[40]

I believe the development agencies can do even better. Their activities are often relevant, sometimes salient, to the underlying tensions, disparities, and policies that ameliorate or exacerbate internal divisions. Examination of these relevancies and how the agencies' contributions to conflict amelioration might be strengthened is the subject of this book. Chapter 2 cites examples and case studies to illustrate dynamics of conflict avoidance and failure, and to give examples of how the international development agencies have either exacerbated internal conflicts, ameliorated them, or missed opportunities to foster prevention. Chapter 3 explores the causes of violent conflicts in developing countries. Part II reviews conflict-prevention activities and options of these agencies in some detail. I will show how these activities might help to prevent violent conflict or at least avoid making things worse. Chapter 4 introduces the subject and the need for risk assessment as the context for considering program and policy specifics. Chapter 5 looks at external efforts to change political and intercommunal behavior directly through political engineering and development of civil society. Chapter 6 examines the conflict implications of specific policies and projects that are the bread and butter of international development assistance; Chapter 7 considers the work of the development agencies as intellectual influences and as wielders of various kinds of suasion and pressure.

There are certainly conflict situations where the international agencies' activities are unlikely to be salient enough or even relevant to have any preventive influence or effect. However, paralleling Jentleson's bottom line for the effort that would be required to create a coercive prevention system, the effort required to orient the international development agencies toward early conflict prevention would be completely justified, and would make a major contribution to the post–Cold War world, if the agencies' activities succeeded in preventing even one or two conflict catastrophes.

Mandates and Competence for an Overdue Responsibility

But do the development agencies have the mandates and competence to concern themselves with conflict prevention? The merits of international development agencies taking conflict potential and prevention into account in their programs and policy advice would seem beyond question. The prevention of a single Rwanda or Sri Lanka would mean the avoidance of massive loss of life and injury. Prevention would also reduce the volume of aid funds that must be diverted each year to humanitarian relief and to reconstructing lost assets and making up for lost ground. In the period between 1980 and 1988 the World Bank allocated $6.2 billion in loans to assist eighteen postconflict countries make up this lost ground. Even on prudentiary grounds the arguments for development agency attention are strong. The conflicts often destroy infrastructure that had been financed by these same agencies. The descent into violent conflict may weaken or destroy a country's ability to service its official and private bank debt. Funds allocated to activities that help prevent a conflict that otherwise would have likely broken out must have a benefit-cost relation that greatly exceeds the rate of return of all alternative investments.

Although this proposition cannot, by its contrary-to-fact nature, be empirically demonstrated (and rests on the assumption that development agency activities may have the power in some cases to tip the balance, an assumption we will have to explore below), the case of Mozambique can serve as an illustration. From 1978 to 1987 Mozambique received a total of $2.6 billion in aid ("official development assistance," or ODA), an average of only $260 million a year. In 1994, two years after the peace agreement, one-year postconflict aid amounted to about $1.3 billion (equal to 100% of the country's GNP), much larger in real terms than past aid volume but only a fraction of the resources Mozambique will need cumulatively to make up for the estimated $20 billion of lost production stemming from its conflict.[41]

It may seem that social and economic reengineering for the purpose of improving the effectiveness of conflict-resolution processes, and reducing underlying inequalities and other sources of intergroup hostility, goes beyond the mandates of these agencies. The mandates of bilateral development agencies are set unilaterally by the governments of these donor nations. The question of the acceptability of these mandates rests with the recipient countries. If a recipient government prefers that a donor agency not work directly with local NGOs to strengthen the country's civil society, or not assist local independent journalists or human rights activists, or not deliberately shape a development project to widen the participation and distribution of benefits to a generally excluded ethnic group, it can exercise its sovereign right to reject such agency initiatives. In fact, some bilateral agencies, as we shall see below, are undertaking open and publicized activities of social and political reengineering with the concurrence (or toleration) of the local authorities. A social engineering activity that is viewed as benign in one country (e.g., assistance to women's NGOs as a means of increasing women's empowerment) might be viewed as unacceptable intervention if proposed in a more conservative country.

The multilateral agencies are a different story. Their original mandates were set in articles of agreement among the founding member governments. Change or expansion in the scope of their activities has to be approved by their boards of executive directors, representing the member governments. The World Bank has been especially important, compared with the regional development banks (the Asian Development Bank, African Development Bank, the Inter-American Development Bank, and more recently the European Development Bank), for its intellectual leadership in development policy and its global reach. In practice, the World Bank's executive directors have reinterpreted its mandate recurrently to legitimate its concern and involvement with subjects that are departures from its earlier narrow focus on economic growth as embodied in the expansion of material output. Although subjects such as the participation of women in development, protection of the environment, "sustainable" development, corruption, the quality of governance, and adherence to international norms concerning human rights may appear prima facie as noneconomic and be forced upon the World Bank by pressures from public opinion and nongovernmental organizations (NGOs), they have been incorporated into a larger economic paradigm that takes into account the relationships, quantitative and institutional, between economic expansion and such related or component processes and factors.

The extension of the paradigm to include the relationships between development and violent conflict has started only recently but has already become legitimated by the World Bank's management and by U.N. Secretary-General Kofi Annan. In an address to the World Bank staff in October 1999, Annan noted that "postconflict peace-building" was a "major innovation of the 1990s, and something of a growth industry." He added:

> But how much better it would be . . . if we could prevent these conflicts from arising in the first place. . . . [M]ost researchers agree that it is useful

to distinguish "structural" or long-term factors, which make violent conflict more likely, from "triggers" which actually ignite it. The structural factors all have to do with social and economic policy, and the way that societies govern themselves. It is here that the link between security and development policy is most obvious. . . . So the fact that political violence occurs more frequently in poor countries has more to do with failures of governance, and particularly with failure to address "horizontal" inequalities, than with poverty as such. . . .

If I could sum up my message this afternoon in one sentence, it is that human security, good governance, equitable development and respect for human rights are interdependent and mutually reinforcing. If war is the worst enemy of development, healthy and balanced development is the best form of conflict prevention.[42]

Annan said that he welcomed "Jim Wolfensohn's call for the World Bank and its partners to start asking hard questions about 'how we can best integrate a concern for conflict prevention into development operations.'"

But why has such a call been so long overdue? In the five decades during which the development organizations have been at work, there has been no dearth of internal conflicts undermining if not destroying their projects and hindering if not reversing altogether the development process. In fact, as some of the World Bank's and other development agencies' country experiences that we will review here demonstrate, conflict prevention has been an occasional agency objective, and the relevance of development assistance activities to incipient or actual conflict has been obvious and not unnoticed. These agencies have always had among their staffs many sophisticated practitioners of development diplomacy and the development professions. It is remarkable, then, and indeed reprehensible, that it has taken so long to reach this recognition that conflict prevention must be integrated into development operations.

The most commonly heard explanation, by the development practitioners themselves—and in the case of the World Bank, by the "strict constructionist" defenders of the bank's original charter—is that their mandates have dictated a focus on the economic and the technical problems of development. The strict, and artificial, wall erected between economics and domestic politics very broadly defined is evident from the World Bank's earliest work on two of our deeply divided case countries, Sri Lanka (formerly Ceylon) and Malaysia (formerly Malaya).

In the 1950s, the World Bank sent technical missions to many developing countries to analyze their conditions and design initial development programs. These were influential studies, commonly the first comprehensive, development-oriented examinations of these economies. The studies reflected the World Bank's rigid stance against any (public) discussion of the internal political affairs of these countries (or countries-to-be). Even granting the appropriateness of this constraint at the time (in contrast with the Bank's growing frankness on internal social and political issues in recent years), it is striking how sanitized the studies read today. They are silent on the key intergroup distribution questions that were already salient then, and that have dominated their politics and economic development ever since, including whether the country avoided or fell into civil war.

As an example, the report on (then) Malaya said nothing about income distribution or the potential effects of development on the central issue of the ethnic sectoral distribution of the labor force.[43] The 1953 report on (then) Ceylon reflects the optimism over interethnic relations in that country soon after independence, describing the different groups as "living side by side with an unusual degree of communal tolerance." There is a hint of awareness of significant ethnic difference and stereotyping in its one sociological, as it were, observation that the Tamil were "a particularly hard-working and energetic people," a compliment not given to the island's other ethnic groups. The study's extensive discussion of education omits any mention of the Tamil overrepresentation (in proportion to their population) in the schools, professions, and (as a result) the civil service. A reader not knowledgeable about Ceylon would have come away from the World Bank study with no inkling that ethnic conflicts were already brewing with respect to language, education, and other subjects relevant to the country's economic development.[44]

The development practitioners might also argue, with some justification, that getting the economic and technical aspects right is difficult enough. The accumulation of additional subjects that the agriculture, infrastructure, education, or other project designers must "take into account"—such as environmental impact, effect on poverty, institutional context and relation to governance reform, impact on women, participation of beneficiaries and NGOs in project design and implementation—has added greatly to the complexity of their work and to the interventionist character of much policy dialogue with governments. Postconflict reconstruction is only the latest of this accretion of objectives and tasks. There is always a danger that the formal addition of conflict prevention as a new subject—with its additional bureaucratic baggage in the form of assessment requirements, project annexes, new appraisal criteria, staff reorientation sessions, and additional exposure to evaluation—will be received by an agency's staff as just one more burden, one more challenge to overcome with creative boilerplate.

More fundamentally, the institutional unreadiness to grapple with conflict prevention, whether in postconflict situations or where violent conflict may be a potential rather than actual problem, has been a major conceptual difficulty. Reflecting the nature of their mandates and objectives, the development agencies' intellectual paradigms have been essentially economic. The agencies began to employ social scientists other than economists only in recent years, mainly anthropologists and political scientists, but these were few in number compared with the historic dominance of the economists. Economics has been *the* discipline for analyzing country circumstances, for framing the policies to be promoted, and for evaluating the suitability of individual projects for agency support. Over the half-century the international development system has been in existence, great advances have occurred in the conceptual and analytic armory that economics can bring to bear to diagnose development problems, design policies and programs, and evaluate interventions and their outcomes. The economists and statisticians of the international agencies labored for years to help developing nations establish domestic data-gathering and research institutions. A global professional network now exists that has produced a vast quantity of information and analysis. The accumulated literature of "development economics" is enormous. The boundaries of economics have also expanded in new directions, useful for analyzing the development process. Beyond the traditional attention to macroeconomic issues, trade policy and exchange rates, monetary and inflation management, public-sector finance, and so on, economics has branched out to explore institutional problems, such as the dynamics of bureaucratic behavior, collective action, corruption, and alternative modes of governance.

The conceptual difficulty is that this foundation discipline for the development agencies has had a major blind spot that has kept its practitioners from applying their tools to the relationships between development and conflict and to the ethnic and cultural phenomena that are at the heart of much Third World conflict. One economist who has written on these problems, Robert Klitgaard, describes the ethnicity blind spot as a deliberate self-imposed handicap, a topic that has been "overlooked or suppressed in the practical literature on economic and political development." He cites one eminent Nobel economist's view:

> Jan Tinbergen reflected on the subject . . . in his review of three decades of work on economic development. Among the determining factors of development were "racial differences."
>
> "Objective treatment of this subject is obstructed, however, by the emotions aroused by two extreme views: one assumes a priori that the subject is taboo; the other, that whites—and even more particularly—German-defined Aryan people—are superior in all respects. . . . I do not think research on these questions has a high priority."[45]

Writing in the early 1990s, Klitgaard went on to note that the concepts of race and ethnicity are "analytically slippery" and that relevant developing country data are scarce. "Most people interested in economic and political development are untrained and perhaps afraid of the anthropological and biological fields that might throw light on ethnic differences. . . . Presumably, ethnic inequalities are affected by public policies toward education, employment, infrastructure, markets, and affirmative action. I believe an important challenge is to understand how and how much, and under what circumstances."[46] Klitgaard also cites a review done about 1980 of twenty-two course syllabi on economic development in U.S. universities, none of which mentioned ethnic issues. Tinbergen and Klitgaard overstated somewhat the narrowness of the profession. For example, race and ethnicity figure prominently in studies of the structures and functioning of Southeast Asian economies and their racial/ethnic divisions of labor, and in economic and political scholarship on the ethnically tiered societies of European colonies in Africa.[47] Nevertheless, their point is generally correct for quantitative or empirically based policy research. It was only in the late 1990s that World Bank and academic economic research began to nibble at these issues.

The reluctance of the World Bank to engage the issues surrounding race and ethnicity stems from the institution's traditional hesistancy to be drawn into "sovereignty" questions and the traditional resistance of the World Bank's clients to what they deemed unacceptable intrusion into areas of their sovereign domestic realm. Beginning in the early 1970s, the long struggle over incorporating the environment as a proper and integral part of the World Bank's responsibilities has illustrated the difficulty faced by any expansion in its scope that appears to contract the area of sovereign policy not to be trespassed. The promoters of concern over the environment, within and outside the World Bank, also faced considerable opposition by Bank staff who resisted injection of environmental criteria into project work and the creation of a new unit in the organization to introduce environmental review and perspective into Bank operations. Intrusion into "sovereignty" issues followed naturally, but not easily, as the World Bank began to be pushed to take account of the rights of people who would be forcibly relocated under Bank-financed hydroelectric and other projects. A perspective that now appears unassailable was long resisted as excessively intrusive.[48]

During the 1990s, the area not to be trespassed contracted dramatically. Arguing that the character of government was relevant to the success of economic development, the World Bank undertook new activities to reform and strengthen "governance." It defined governance as the "manner in which power is exercised" in managing resources for development. It argued that the institution's concern for open and "enlightened" policy-making, "professional" bureaucracy, executive accountability, civil society participation in public affairs, and the rule of law was legitimate under the World Bank's mandate.

> The Bank's Articles of Agreement explicitly prohibit the institution from interfering in a country's internal political affairs and require it to take only economic considerations into account in its decisions. Thus, the Bank's call for good governance and its concern with accountability, transparency, and the rule of law have to do exclusively with the contribution they make to social and economic development and to the Bank's fundamental objective of sustainable poverty reduction in the developing world.[49]

In practice, the World Bank's involvement with governance issues takes it into such areas as public-sector management (civil service, public investment, "strategic planning," economic management, etc.), a country's legal framework, and military expenditures. Human rights are also said to benefit from Bank programs that reduce poverty and unemployment. As we will argue in some detail below, in deeply divided societies at risk to conflict an effort to sustain a final wall between the World Bank and the "political" would be highly artificial. The ethnic–political roots of conflict in many of these societies are intertwined with virtually every aspect of governance the Bank accepts as legitimate for its attention.

Finally, there are those who question the *competence* of the aid agencies. The message of this book is that these agencies should be charged with helping to ameliorate root causes of internal conflict in developing countries. Have they demonstrated the capacity to initiate and support substantial socioeconomic change? Does aid work? This question has been examined many times over the years. The findings of most independent scholarship have concluded that aid has had a satisfactory (albeit certainly not 100 percent), record of accomplishing its objectives. One example is the conclusion of a major study from 1986, by Robert Cassen and colleagues, appropriately titled *Does Aid Work?*, namely, that *"the great majority of aid succeeds in its development objectives."*[50]

> In the broadest sense, this study finds that most aid does indeed "work." It succeeds in achieving its developmental objectives (where those are primary), contributing positively to the recipient countries' performance, and not substituting for activities which would have occurred anyway. That is not to say that aid works on every count. Its performance varies by country and by sector. . . . And there is a substantial fraction of aid which does not work—which may have a low rate of return, or become derelict shortly after completion, or never reach completion, or have positively harmful effects.[51]

Citing the extensive evaluation literature on aid activities that records "high" rates of good or acceptable results, the Cassen study notes the difficulty of setting a meaningful standard for the overall performance of the aid enterprise.

> [T]here have been a significant number of failures. The exact proportion is not known; but supposing it proved to be a quarter or a third of all aid, would that be considered "good" or "bad"? . . . A record showing only the achievement of high rates of return would be evidence that the challenges of development were not being addressed. . . . Some failures, then, are inevitable and not objectionable. But what would be a tolerable proportion? One approach would be to compare investment under aid with other types of investment. If x per cent of aid fails, what percentage of private investment fails? Or of public investment other than aid? Unfortunately, x is unknown both in aid and in most other spheres.[52]

A more recent paper on the efficacy of the World Bank's influence on recipient country policies noted "the key role that the World Bank and its staff have played in the promotion of better economic policies at both the macro level and the sectoral level. Through the numerous missions, policy dialogues, and evaluations of specific projects, the Bank has provided a tutelage function in promoting sound economic analysis. This has had an enormous impact on the type of economic policies pursued by countries and, ultimately, on the performance of their economies."[53] Needless to say, the impact of this influence has varied tremendously from country to country and from time to time. (A recent study of aid influence on economic policy reform in ten African countries in the 1980s and 1990s, commissioned by the World Bank, reached mixed conclusions regarding aid efficacy and the policy outcomes.)[54] The obstacles to effective influence on economic stabilization policies (such as exchange rate reform) are not nearly as great as those facing efforts at fundamental changes in the economic role of government or policies that would weaken the position of powerful vested interests. Policy changes at the project or micro level are generally easier to bring about than across-the-board institutional change. The effectiveness of donor influence may also vary (1) according to what aid instruments are employed—technical assistance, investment projects, general financing for budget or balance of payments support, (2) the volume and timing of the aid offered, (3) the degree of coordination of influence among the donors, and (4) the nature of the relationship between donors and recipients. We return to these issues below, in the context of the conflict-relevance of the donor agencies, rather than their development or economic management impact per se.

Except for the efforts to affect political institutions and processes in developing countries, where bilateral development agencies predominate, the World Bank will figure prominently in what follows. This is because the Bank has long been the leading source of ideas and advice to policymakers in developing countries. It attained this intellectual role by developing a larger staff of highly qualified policy analysts and development professionals, covering virtually all sectors, than any other international development agency, by conducting extensive research into development problems, by publishing statistical journals and development studies that have attained worldwide readership, and by being able to hire consultants from the worldwide pool of development academics and experienced practitioners. Although the World Bank has not been a primary source of intellectual innovation, compared with academic contributions to development management and economics, it has served as the leading "conveyor belt" for ideas about development policy.[55] Though not free of bureaucratic and operational problems as it grew in size, the Bank has had the ability to absorb new ideas and adjust its emphases and operations to changing conditions over time.

The World Bank began with a focus on project soundness and factors determining borrowing-country creditworthiness, such as government budgets, tax systems, and monetary stability. To these "were added in the 1950s the need for national development plans. The Bank began to stress the role of the private sector during the 1960s, and of rural development and population policies in the 1970s. The 1980s in turn were the decade of 'structural adjustment' and 'outward orientation.' One implication of this is that conditionality was part of the Bank's approach to lending from practically day one. Bank money always came with ideas and advice attached."[56]

The Bank's role as the preeminent source of development policy advice was enhanced by its formal position of convener and analyst for many of the country aid-coordination groups, commonly called Consortia or Consultative Groups (CGs). Between the emergence of postconflict reconstruction as a distinct subject for Bank policy, and its establishment of a Post-Conflict Unit (recently renamed the Conflict Prevention and Reconstruction Team), a Post-Conflict Fund, and a conflict research program, the World Bank has taken the plunge. Adoption of a more proactive Bank role with respect to prevention in the twenty-first century would go a long way toward establishing this objective with the gravity it deserves.

A more proactive posture would also reinforce the World Bank's coordination with that whole group of bilateral aid agencies, which have already moved to strengthen their capabilities and cooperation on the problems of conflict. Under the aegis of the Development Assistance Committee of the Organization for Economic Cooperation and Development (OECD), the twenty-two member countries and the European Commission have formed task forces, issued guidelines, and undertaken evaluations of their conflict-response experience. Some of the aid agencies have created special units to focus on crisis prevention and response (e.g., the Peacebuilding Unit of the Canadian International Development Agency). Coordination could also be strengthened with agencies in the U.N. system that have been moving in the same direction. For example, the U.N. Development Programme recently elevated its Emergency Response Division, created in 1996, to the status of a bureau, renaming the unit the Bureau for Crisis Prevention and Recovery. The resources ostensibly devoted to conflict prevention have been growing under these evolving policies and institutional initiatives.

The relevance and efficacy of development aid as an instrument for change in developing countries has long been clear. The questions of interest to us, which I examine next in Chapter 2, have to do with aid's relevance to conflict, whether deliberate or unintended, positive or negative.

Notes

1. Carnegie Commission, 1997, p. 11.

2. Stremlau and Sagasti, 1998, p. 13.

3. Samuel P. Huntington, "The Clash of Civilizations," in *Foreign Affairs* 72, no. 3 (1993): pp. 22–49.

4. "Chechnya's President, Asian Maskhadov . . . appealed to Pope John Paul II to intercede, saying that Islamic nations had failed to help Chechnya. 'In your name, we are asking the entire Christian world to save the Chechen people from another genocide. . . . We are sending this appeal to you only after we have become convinced that the Islamic world has remained indifferent to our appeals,'" *New York Times*, October 29, 1999, p. A13.

5. Paragraph drawn from Martin O. Heisler, "Ethnicity and Ethnic Relations in the Modern West," in Montville, 1991, pp. 21–25.

6. Peter Wallensteen and Margareta Sollenberg, "Armed Conflicts, Conflict Termination, and Peace Agreements, 1989–96," in *Journal of Peace Research* 34, no. 3 (1997), cited in Tellis, 1997.

7. European Platform, 1998. Details on numbers of fatalities, refugees, and displaced persons are published in the annual *World Disasters Report* by the International Federation of Red Cross and Red Crescent Societies, issued by Oxford University Press. Additional information on refugees and internally displaced persons, country by country, is published annually in the *World Refugee Survey*, by the U.S. Committee for Refugees.

8. In *Children on the Frontline: The Impact of Apartheid, Destabilization and Warfare on Children in Southern and South Africa*. New York: UNICEF, 1989.

9. For one review of the types of economic effects of violent conflict in Africa, see Nicole Ball, *The Effect of Conflict on the Economies of Third World Countries*, in Deng and Zartman, 1991. For a brief survey of estimates of direct and indirect civilian war deaths since 1945, and of analytic approaches to estimating economic costs of warfare, see Geoff Harris, "Estimates of the Economic Cost of Armed Conflict: The Iran-Iraq War and the Sri Lankan Civil War," in Jurgen Brauerand and William G.

Gissy, eds., *Economics of Conflict and Peace*. Aldershot, UK: Avebury, 1997, pp. 269–290.

10. Lisa Morris Grobar and Shiranthi Gnanaselvam, "The Economic Effects of the Sri Lankan Civil War," in *Economic Development and Cultural Change* 41, no. 2 (January 1993): 395–405.

11. World Bank, 1998, Synthesis, p. 19. The report notes that these estimates should be taken as indications of unprecedented economic decline, but probably overstate the drop in activity by omitting unrecorded activity.

12. Messer et al., 1998, citing R.H. Green and M. Mavie, "From Survival to Livelihood in Mozambique," in *IDS Bulletin* 25, no. 4: 77–84.

13. Amartya Sen, "Economic Regress: Concepts and Features," in *Proceedings of the World Bank Annual Conference on Development Economics*, 1993, pp. 330–331.

14. Messer et al., 1998, p. 4.

15. Cambodia is often cited as a country socialized to political and interpersonal violence as a consequence of its recent history. For example, commenting on several brazen assaults on young women (apparently followed by desultory police investigation), one prominent Cambodia watcher observed that "Most Cambodians are deeply concerned about the level of savagery in this society." Bill Herod, in *The Cambodia Daily*, January 24, 2000. El Salvador is another example. "Among perhaps the most disturbing social phenomena of contemporary El Salvador that the Peace Accords implementation did *not* resolve is that of the serious and growing problem of violent crime. This problem of the *microinsecurity* of individuals and enterprises (rather than the *macroinsecurity* of the state) is in part a legacy of the conflict." World Bank, 1998, Vol. III, p. 10.

16. German Foundation, 1996, p. 8.

17. See, for example, Jennifer Leaning, S. Briggs, and L. Chen, eds., *Humanitarian Crises*. Cambridge, MA: Harvard University Press, 1999; K. Cahill, ed., *A Framework for Survival: Health, Human Rights and Humanitarian Assistance*. New York: Routledge, 1999; B. Levy and V. Sidel, *War and Public Health*. New York: Oxford University Press, 1997.

18. Examples of programs offered in 2000 include master's degrees in complex humanitarian emergency management at Columbia, Tulane, Tufts, and Johns Hopkins universities, with specializations in such areas as disaster management, and forced migration and health; short courses on emergencies and public health (disease, psychosocial trauma, etc.) in developing countries, sponsored by the U.S. Office of Foreign Disaster Assistance; a course in policy, health, and conflict given by the London School of Hygiene and Tropical Medicine; a training course on children and families in humanitarian emergencies, by Case Western University; a short course on public health and humanitarian aid at the Center for Research on the Epidemiology of Disasters, in Brussels; and a summer program in forced migration by the Oxford University Refugee Studies Program. The U.N.-related training programs are described on http://www.reliefweb.int/training.

19. For one evaluation of the continuum proposition in four postconflict cases, see Donald G. McClelland, *"Complex Humanitarian Emergencies and USAID's Humanitarian Response."* Washington, DC: USAID, 2000.

20. Dani Rodrik, "Where Did All the Growth Go? External Shocks, Social Conflict, and Growth Collapses" (mimeo). Cambridge, MA: Harvard University, 1998, p. 28.

21. Examples drawn from Henri Pirenne, *Economic and Social History of Medieval Europe*. New York: Harcourt Brace Jovanovich, 1927, pp. 3–33, 67, 142–148, 196.

22. "The new charter adopted by the meeting reflected the lessons of Kosovo and other internal conflicts that have erupted since the collapse of Communism. It envisioned a new role for the Organization for Security and Cooperation in easing tensions before they explode into war, including the possibility of intervening not just in conflicts between states, but within states. 'We have witnessed atrocities of a kind we had thought were relegated to the past,' the charter declared. 'In this decade, it has become clear that all such conflicts can represent a threat to the security of all O.S.C.E. participating states. Participating states are accountable to their citizens and responsible to each other for their implementation of their O.S.C.E. commitments,' it said. 'We regard these commitments as our common achievement and therefore consider them to be matters of immediate and legitimate concern to all participating states.' The document envisions rapid-response teams that could be deployed quickly to manage crises." *New York Times*, November 20, 1999, p. A5.

23. For a review of the evolution and status of international law respecting civil wars, humanitarian assistance during armed conflicts, treatment of refugees, peacekeeping, and international organization coercion, see Hilaire McCoubrey and Nigel D. White, *International Organizations and Civil Wars.* Brookfield, VT: Dartmouth, 1995.

24. David Rieff, "Wars Without End?," *New York Times*, September 23, 1999, p. A27.

25. *National Intelligence Council*, 1999.

26. Romeo A. Dallaire, in Feil, 1998, pp. v–vi.

27. Carnegie Commission, 1997.

28. For a brief review of findings on economic sanction effects and of the issues raised by the sanctions experience during the 1990s, see Kimberly Ann Elliott and Gary Hufbauer, "Ineffectiveness of Economic Sanctions: Same Song, Same Refrain? Economic Sanctions in the 1990's," in *American Economic Review, Papers and Proceedings* (May 1999): 403–407.

29. Avruch, 1998, p. 102.

30. Ibid., pp. 101–102. Italics in original.

31. Ibid., p. 103. Italics in original.

32. For a detailed analysis of the peace accord provisions and their flawed implementation, see International Crisis Group, *Is Dayton Failing? Bosnia Four Years After the Peace Agreement.* Brussels: International Crisis Group, 1999.

33. Jean-Louis Sarbib et al., "Fighting Poverty Remains a Global Imperative," *International Herald Tribune*, November 17, 2001.

34. Jentleson, 2000a, p. 10.

35. Jentleson, 2000b, p. 23.

36. Ibid., pp. 11–12. The Great Lakes region of Africa provides a recent example of conflict escalation involving several countries.

37. J. Brian Atwood, "Suddenly, Chaos," *Washington Post*, July 31, 1994, p. 9.

38. *Testimony of Andrew Natsios, Administrator, USAID, before the Senate Appropriations Committee,* May 8, 2001, www.usaid,gov/press/spe_test/testimony/2001/ty010508.html, p. 4.

39. Ted Morse, "How Do We Change the Way We Use Foreign Assistance to Help Prevent Deadly Conflicts?" in USAID, 2001, pp. 86–87.

40. Jentleson, 2000b, p. 36.

41. Aid figures from World Bank, *World Development Report*, various years.

42. World Bank press release, October 19, 1999. World Bank Web site.

43. World Bank, *The Economic Development of Malaya*; *A report of a mission organized by the International Bank for Reconstruction and Development at the request of the Governments of the Federation of Malaya, the Crown Colony of Singapore and the United Kingdom*. Baltimore, MD: Johns Hopkins University Press, 1955.

44. World Bank, *The Economic Development of Ceylon*; *A report of a mission organized by the International Bank for Reconstruction and Development at the request of the Government of Ceylon*. Baltimore, MD: Johns Hopkins University Press, 1953.

45. Cited in Klitgaard, 1991, pp. 199–200.

46. Ibid., p. 200.

47. An early example is by Hla Myint, "An Interpretation of Economic Backwardness," in *Oxford Economic Papers*. Oxford, UK: Oxford University Press, 1954. Although Myint stresses the ethnically dualistic character of colonial economies, he treats the "indigenous" populations (erroneously) as homogeneous opposite the colonials and their imported immigrant workforces.

48. See Richard Wade, "Greening the Bank: The Struggle over the Environment, 1970–1995," in Kapur et al., 1997.

49. World Bank, 1994, p. vii.

50. Cassen, 1986, p. 13. Italics in original.

51. Ibid., p. 11.

52. Ibid., p. 12.

53. Glenn P. Jenkins, "Project Analysis and the World Bank," in *American Economic Review, Papers and Proceedings* (May 1997): p. 41.

54. Shantayanan Devarajan, David Dollar, and Torgny Holmgren, *Aid and Reform in Africa*. Washington, DC: World Bank, 2001.

55. Michael Gavin and Dani Rodrik, "The World Bank in Historical Perspective," in *American Economic Review, Papers and Proceedings* (May 1995): 332.

56. Ibid., pp. 332–333.

2. Conflicts Fought, Conflicts Avoided
Nine Cases

Examples of factors that have been associated with internal developing country conflict, both positively and negatively, are scattered throughout this book. In this chapter I review the conflict experiences of nine countries. Five fell into violent conflict. Four took steps that prevented social conflict, or low-level violence, from escalating into general violent conflict. In at least seven of these cases, the international development agencies (in one case the IMF) has played (or is now playing) a significant role with respect to some of the root causes of the actual or potential conflicts. The cases illustrate (among other things) how these agencies can be relevant, either through (a) their influence on government conflict-relevant policies, (b) their financial support, strengthening government capabilities to carry out such policies, or (c) through specific development projects (in agriculture, education, transportation, etc.). The cases include examples of agency activities that ameliorated tensions and contributed to conflict avoidance; that missed amelioration opportunities; or that made things worse. In two cases (Pakistan and Sri Lanka), lacking an explicit amelioration concept or program framework, the donors worked at cross-purposes, simultaneously exacerbating and ameliorating with various policies and projects.

For the cases that fell into conflict, we sketch a few counterfactual ("what-if") scenarios: how different agency actions might plausibly have produced a better, conflict-avoiding, outcome. The cases also suggest lessons for future conflict mitigation or prevention, which will be drawn together in the final chapters. The accounts of Mauritius and Bhutan are included mainly as brief additional examples of successful conflict prevention and management based on policies of the types that development agencies commonly encounter.

It is insufficient and sometimes misleading merely to draw connections between economic growth and political stability, and then conclude that the development agencies can rest on the assumption that growth-promotion translates into conflict-prevention. If that assumption were the whole story, the responsibility to help prevent conflict would be fully met by the agencies' continuous work on strengthening their contributions to development. Because that assumption is not the full story, it is regrettable that there have not been many case-study examinations of the conflict relevance of development (as contrasted with humanitarian) aid. The country experiences brought together in this chapter illustrate how such research could yield lessons about the conflict-ameliorating potentialities of the development agencies through both policies and projects. I believe the importance of such lessons is indisputable, especially those drawn from the experience of conflicts successfully contained or prevented. At the same time, the reader should bear in mind that the policy histories here are reviewed mainly from a conflict perspective. In retrospect, successful internal "peace promoting" policy packages may also be judged to have been deficient from other perspectives (e.g., environmental impact, rich-poor income gaps, or financial sector development). We make no attempt to view our cases from these other, much-studied, angles.

Conflicts Fought: Aid Complicity

Pakistan: Complicity of Donor Advice

The role the donors played in Pakistan in the 1950s and 1960s is especially interesting because of its relatively unambiguous character, and the authoritative account provided by one of the important actors. Edward Mason, co-author (with Robert E. Asher) in 1973 of the first history of the World Bank, had been head of the foreign economic team advising the Pakistan planning commission. In the World Bank history, Mason and Asher describe the relationship of the donors (mainly the bank, which was convener and intellectual leader of the aid consortium group) with the government of Pakistan, and they lay out the economic disparities and policies that were among the major reasons for East Pakistan's secession and the civil war. Before turning to their account, it will be helpful to recall the essential events.

Pakistan was born in the partition of India in 1947. While the Congress Party of Gandhi and Nehru wanted a united India, the British had to cede to the preference of Mohammed Ali Jinnah's Muslim League for a separate state comprising two regions in which the majority of the population was Muslim. Although partition led to vast population movements (and 800,000 fatalities) as Hindus and Muslims moved out of the jurisdictions where they would have ended up minorities, a sizable population of Muslims remained in India. The two wings of independent Pakistan were separated by 1,000 miles of Indian territory. The West wing economy was moderately more advanced than that of the East and grew more rapidly in the years after independence. The widening of this gap was a deliberate result of central government policies to give priority to the economic development of the West. E. Wayne Nafziger summarized these policies as follows:

> The Pakistan government redistributed income from export and subsistence agriculture to industry and domestically oriented commercial agri-

culture through policies of an overvalued rupee (which favored imported inputs for industry and large-scale agriculture relative to jute, tea, and other primary-product exports), a compulsory government procurement of foodgrains at low prices for urban areas, generous tax concessions to industry, and the lack of these to peasant agriculture. These policies transferred savings from agriculture to industry, primarily a transfer from Eastern small farming to Western industry. Conservative estimates, based on world prices, indicate that over 24 percent of gross product originating in the agriculture sector—or about 70 percent of its savings—was transferred to the nonagricultural sector in 1964–65. As Eastern peasants and small farmers became increasingly conscious of the way in which much of economic policy was being used largely on behalf of a Western industrial and commercial ruling elite, discontent with the political leadership intensified, contributing to the humanitarian disaster of 1971.[1]

The economic gap was also manifest in substantial underrepresentation of Bengalis in the senior ranks of the professions and the bureaucracy.

Although the two wings shared Islam, the Bengali population of the East was traditionally more tolerant of diversity and less drawn to orthodox fervor. The two wings also differed in language and other cultural characteristics. Early on, Jinnah decreed that Urdu, the dominant, but not only, language of the West, would be the sole official language of Pakistan as a whole. This was deeply divisive even within the East wing where an Urdu-speaking minority, Biharis, were favored over the majority Bengalis for government jobs requiring use of Urdu. A mere five years after independence, the language issue "crystallized" a Bengali nationalism that was being fired up by a combination of economic, cultural, and political grievances.[2]

Pakistan was unable to establish a stable, democratic system. Military dictatorships recurrently interrupted periods of unstable and corrupt parliamentary governments. In addition, the country had fought and lost two wars with India prior to the East Pakistan crisis in 1971. In late 1970, after a year of rising unrest in both wings, the general in power, Yahya Khan, called for the first direct general elections since independence. The population of East Pakistan then numbered 53 percent of the country's total. Consequently, the East wing representation in the national parliament was slightly larger than that of the West. In the election campaign, the long-standing Bengali complaints over the range of policies seen as discriminatory were reflected in the platform of the Bengali party (the Awami League, headed by Sheikh Mujib Rahman). The platform called for a new political structure under which all federal government powers except defense and foreign policy would be devolved to the provinces. East Pakistan would have its own independent taxing policies, monetary, fiscal and trading authority, and foreign exchange control. Sentiment against the West had hardened the previous year, when the East had received little help from the central government in the wake of a disastrous cyclone and tidal wave that had killed an astonishing half million East Pakistanis.

The Awami League went on to capture almost all the East wing seats, thereby winning an absolute majority in the national parliament. Civil war was precipitated after Yahya Khan and the main political party of the West refused to permit Sheikh Mujib to form the national government. Instead, Yahya Khan arrested Mujib and in March 1971 launched a military repression and rampage that killed at least 300,000 Bengalis. In the end, between the logistical difficulties of Pakistan's split geography, and the intervention of the Indian army in late 1971, Pakistan was forced to concede the independence of the East wing (i.e., Bangladesh).

I turn now to the Mason–Asher account. It focuses on the economic disparities that contributed so importantly to Bengali disaffection, overwhelming the founding national sentiment of religious community.

> The breakup in late 1971 of the uneasy amalgamation that had for twenty-four years been known as Pakistan raises acutely embarrassing questions for the [World] Bank and other would-be developers. . . . How relevant and how timely was the Bank's advice on economic policy. . . . When the fall from grace began [in the late 1960s, after Pakistan had earlier been a model of good macroeconomic behavior], how hard should the Bank or the members of the Bank-chaired consortium have pressed Pakistan to carry out policies to which some of the outsiders attached importance and to which the government paid lip-service?[3]
>
> In Pakistan, between 1960 and 1965, GNP increased at an average annual rate of 5.5 percent, agricultural output at 3.5 percent, export earnings at 7 percent, and large-scale industrial output at 13 percent. Pakistan was on the way to becoming a success story. Or was it? Influential circles in East Pakistan felt exploited and expressed grievances, which were not withheld from the World Bank. . . . David L. Gordon, resident representative of the Bank and confidential adviser to the minister of finance, prepared a long memorandum in 1961 on economic relations between East and West Pakistan . . . [analyzing] the deeply held feeling of east wing intellectuals that their region was being exploited.[4]

Gordon's memorandum, given to Pakistan cabinet members and sent to bank headquarters in Washington, listed the East's arguments: the East's share of public expenditures should be sharply increased to reverse the widening of the income gap between the two wings, to promote a faster rate of development in the East over that of the West, and to end the discriminatory policies under which there had been net financial transfers from East to West, higher government spending and investment in the West, the use of the East's foreign exchange surpluses to finance the West's imports, and high protected prices for Western industrial products sold in the East. (In a Catch-22 argument that appeared to demonstrate central government discrimination against the East, the financial authorities regularly blocked release of budget funds formally allocated to East Pakistan on the grounds that previous releases had been underspent.) In addition, the overvalued exchange rate worked to the disadvantage of the East.

The Bank had close relations with the Pakistan authorities. "Bank experts have collaborated intimately with their Pakistani colleagues. . . . The Bank also helped to finance continuing assistance by the Development Advisory Service of Harvard University to Pakistan's Planning Commission and the Provincial Planning Departments."[5] Because the East's grievances were largely economic up until the West's refusal to accept the election result created the overriding issue of power at the center of the state, the question arises: Given the policy and financial importance of the donors, could the civil war have been avoided if the aid-providers had acted earlier and stronger? Could the donors have effected a reversal of the economic trends and policies sufficient to put the relations between the wings on a different course? In their account, Mason and Asher made it clear that the donors understood the basic political economy problem of Pakistan at least a decade before the breakup. Unfortunately, neither in their technical policy assistance nor in their allocation of their own aid resources did the donors move early enough, or with enough resources, to initiate an adjustment of the economic relations between the wings.

> The Bank favored the kinds of projects it was best at, and these were generally large, engineering-type undertakings. It usually selected those promising the highest rates of return, and they tended to be in West Pakistan. In evaluating an ongoing activity such as the PICIC (Pakistan Industrial Credit and Investment Corporation), the Bank concerned itself more with the efficiency of the management and with the rate of return in PICIC investments than with the geographic concentration of those investments. . . . Its advice on liberalizing the network of import controls and giving the price system a chance to work [advice favorable to the East] was good. It often took sympathetic note of objectives such as rural development and regional balance, but until the late 1960s it was far from vigorous in their pursuit. It did not actively support the Comilla approach to rural development [an innovative program in the East] when the potentialities of that approach were first being demonstrated. Nor at the June 1965 meeting of the [aid] consortium . . . did it support or encourage the drive for social justice envisaged by the planners in their [draft five-year plan] chapter on "Economic Problems and Policies."[6]

Although the planning technocrats were coming around in the late 1960s to recognize the need for addressing the regional imbalance, they were not in control. "Despite the fine words in the plan, the more meaningful cue—the 1970–71 budget—reconfirmed the old bias toward West Pakistan. By mid-1970, the Bank's team produced an action report for East Pakistan, which was of immense promise and included a major rural development program. . . . In retrospect, it is unfortunate that the strategy of development that the Bank had arrived at by mid-1970 did not dominate its thinking five years earlier."[7]

Mason and Asher's conclusions respecting the role of the World Bank apply equally to the donors as a group. Expenditure allocation and net transfers between the two wings did not arise as a subject for discussion at the donors' consortium meetings. The consensus view was that the central government was carrying out good economic policies overall and that it made economic sense to focus investment in the West where long-term development prospects were better. The American officials responsible for U.S.–Pakistan aid relations were also responsible for U.S.–India aid relations (as was probably the case for the other donors); Pakistani officials were seen in a relatively favorable light as more responsive to donor advice than were the Indian officials. The "green revolution" was starting to yield substantial crop production increases in both India and West Pakistan; agricultural policy, fertilizer pricing policy, and the excitement over irrigation well expansion were the principal development preoccupations. By contrast, the green revolution innovations, highly dependent in the case of rice on controlled water applications, did not seem suitable to East Pakistan. At risk to the region's frequent and heavy flooding, the East's farmers, quite rationally, relied on rice varieties that, while low-yielding, would grow rapidly when water levels surged. The East was viewed as lacking development potential, an essentially humanitarian problem, and was considered one of the world's major backward regions needing large-scale food aid for the foreseeable future. (The "backward-region" problem, especially where its population is potentially mobilizable, presents special difficulties we return to below.)

The dominant view within USAID agreed that investment and aid should favor the region with the presumed better economic prospects. As was the case with World Bank staff, the USAID and U.S. embassy personnel stationed in the East were early critics of the aid-allocation pattern. More sensitive to the disaffection of the Bengali elite, and seeing development opportunities earlier than their colleagues stationed in the West, the Embassy and USAID staffs in Dhaka, East Pakistan, pressed Islamabad, and Washington directly, for allocation of more aid resources to the East wing. While the USAID leadership, located in Islamabad, appears to have been ahead of the World Bank in the search for investment possibilities in the East (an example was the scope for local manufacture of low-lift irrigation pumps), they were unable to make headway against the central government's opposition to any (nonhumanitarian) aid allocation shift until 1969, too late for any significant implementation.[8]

There can be little doubt that forging a unified state out of a newly carved-out country, one divided in two and separated by a thousand miles of another state with which relations are hostile, would face formidable difficulties even if other conditions were more favorable. Nevertheless, it is plausible to argue (as Edward Mason implies) that Pakistan could have avoided the violent breakup if the policy changes the Planning Commission and the donors had come to by the late 1960s had been initiated several years earlier. By the end of the decade the results of such a change would have been very visible in the East—in terms of the prices for the West's industrial goods, the water control systems and other infrastructure that would have dotted the East's landscape (and that have been aid-financed since Bangladesh's independence), the employment these public works would have generated in the East, the spread of the Comilla project's social engineering and its palpable impact of small incremental improvements in peasant living standards, and the opportunities and benefits such programs would have created for the Bengali elite. Perhaps, as Mason suggested, five years would have been sufficient; although visible fruits would have been limited, five years, above all, would have demonstrated credible intent in West Pakistan to reduce the disparities and reverse the direction of transfers.

Under such circumstances, an electoral platform calling for stripping the central government of all powers except defense and foreign policy would have had little economic rationale for the East, and might not have been put forth by the Awami League. A League victory in the 1970 elections would then not have posed to the West, and to the army, a fundamental challenge to the role and nature of the state. One might well object to this scenario that the industrial elite families of the West would not likely have agreed to such policy changes in the early 1960s. But even a modest shift could have supported an apparent long-term equalizing intent, and could have been made credible had the consortium members made regional distribution a major subject of the aid dialogue and had shifted the regional balance of their own projects a few years earlier, rather than waiting until it was too late.

In sum, the policy views, the technical planning assistance, and the resource allocations of the donors were highly relevant to the central issues between East and West Pakistan. The donors recognized the depth of resentment in the East, but they acted to address this resentment too late and with too little determination. Donor influence on economic matters in West Pakistan was substantial. The relationship between the government and the donors was cordial. Because the rebuff USAID received was not followed by a joint second try, one can only speculate: could unified donor pressure have elicited government agreement to a regional shift in the government's budget expenditures, or even just in the allocation of aid funds? The record does show that donor resources, when focused on some specific policies, were important enough to move those policies in directions the authorities were reluctant to take otherwise. Evaluation of the policy-change effectiveness of American balance of payments assistance, the so-called program loans that provided general, or nonproject, financial aid, found a close relationship between aid availability and government policy changes.

> The most immediate test of program loan leverage ought to be GOP [Government of Pakistan] performance in import liberalization (and industrial decontrol)—the policy area of highest U.S. priority. Here performance has been spotty. Considerable progress before the [India–Pakistan] war was wiped out by renewed restrictions in the year following it (1966). This ground was regained, however, and there has been a further move toward relaxation in FY [fiscal year] 1968. To a large extent, however, the variable behavior reflected the GOP's expectations of the availability of foreign exchange, an indication that both progress and retrogression were as much the result of A.I.D.'s willingness to finance import liberalization as it was of leverage.[9]

Though my what-if scenario leading to conflict avoidance can be only speculative in retrospect, taking the geographic and other factors of Pakistan into account, it is noteworthy that the formal World Bank history, and one of the principal architects of the advisory role, sums up the experience as a regrettable lost opportunity. Between advice, donor pressure, and aid reallocation, different donor actions might plausibly have resulted in a different, and better, outcome.

Rwanda: Donor Culpability

There is little doubt that the "international community," that is, mainly the United Nations, Belgium, France, and the United States, could have prevented the genocide in Rwanda in April–June of 1994. The U.N. peacekeeping force had hard and unequivocal evidence that a massacre was about to take place. In the critical days when additional modest forces, authorized to take the necessary actions, would have been sufficient to prevent the bloodshed, the appeal of the force's commander for such an increase was rejected by the U.N. Security Council. The public record on this eleventh-hour failure is voluminous.[10] President Bill Clinton later conceded that American failure to act was a grievous error. Out of a population of 7.5 million, about 800,000 Rwandans were slaughtered. Some 85 percent of the Rwandan Tutsi population were murdered, a clear case of genocide. Over 2 million Rwandans fled to neighboring countries.

The massacre of the Tutsi minority, along with a relatively small number of Hutu who were supporting the policy of accommodation being negotiated under international auspices, appeared to erupt very suddenly. The World Bank noted in 1998: "Although there were 'warning signs' from 1992 to early 1994 that extremist elements were intensifying hate propaganda and laying plans for genocidal attacks, the calamity of April to July caught the international community by surprise."[11] In the first weeks of the genocide the U.N. Security Council actually reduced the size of the peacekeeping force to a nominal 270 members. The Security Council reversed itself in mid-May 1994, but by the time (end of July) full agreement had been reached to expand the force (by 5,500) the genocide was already accomplished, halted by the assumption of power by the Tutsi exile force that had invaded from Uganda beginning in 1990.

The underlying causes and potentialities were evident for many years even before the appearance of the "warning signs." In the last few years of Belgian rule prior to independence in 1962, a Hutu movement had risen against the colonial power and against the traditional Tutsi kingship through which Belgium had ruled. Tens of thousands of Tutsi were killed and fled as a Hutu-based party took power. The next year a second wave of refugees fled when more Tutsi were killed in response to attacks by Tutsi exiles. In 1972–1973, to deflect discontent with the current regime, the government strictly implemented quota policies that had been on the books, throwing thousands of Tutsi students out of schools and adults out of jobs.

As is the case with all calamities of this scope, "There are no simple answers. The truth is that the present can be explained only as a product of a long and conflict-ridden process, in which many factors contribute to the total picture."[12] The widespread participation of the Hutu population in the successive slaughters has been seen by many observers as reflecting the prejudicial and racist character of the conceptions both groups had of each other, dating back to earlier Tutsi conquest and colonial Belgium's exaggeration and manipulation of Tutsi/Hutu ethnic difference.[13] While elite manipulation of ethnic hatred was undeniably significant in preparing the ground for the waves of violence, the elites "were harnessing real social forces, embedded in the structure of the society, and in the perceptions of many of its members."[14]

Unfavorable economic factors are also credited with having contributed to the potentialities for violent conflict. The World Bank's evaluation of its experience in Rwanda noted the estimates of one economist that related long-term population pressure on the land, declining yields, and drought and conflict-related displacement, to severe undernourishment of nearly half the population in 1994. "[Jef] Maton suggests that large numbers of the rural population were susceptible to hate propaganda under the duress they were facing in 1993 and 1994. [Gerhard] Prunier, while giving some credence to population pressures, does not give this factor dominant weight."

> Grim as it may seem, the genocidal violence of the spring of 1994 can be partly attributed to that population density. The decision to kill was of course made by the politicians, for political reasons. But at least part of the reason it was carried out so thoroughly by the rank-and-file peasants . . . was the feeling that there were too many people on too little land, and that with a few less there would be more for the survivors.
>
> But greed was not the main motivation. It was belief and obedience—belief in a deeply imbibed ideology which justified in advance what you were about to do, and obedience both to the political authority of the state and to the social authority of the group. Mass-killers tend to be men of the herd, and Rwanda was no exception.[15]

What was the relationship between Rwanda and the World Bank and other donors during the three decades of independence preceding the genocide? The donors provided substantial economic and technical assistance; how did this aid affect the predispositions of the elites, and the underlying problems that prepared the ground for the genocide? Given the importance of the Rwandan tragedy, and the illustrations it provides of interactions between aid activities and conflict-relevant economic and social problems, it is worth drawing at length on the World Bank itself, specifically the above-cited critical evaluation.

It is clear that the donors had ample opportunity to learn the facts. Quite apart from the ordinary reporting that the various embassies in Rwanda must have been sending back to their governments, the World Bank began sending missions and issuing economic reports six years before Rwandan independence. Starting with a highway project in 1970, the World Bank undertook forty-eight operations prior to the genocide. These operations covered a wide range of Rwandan economic and social activity including physical infrastructure, agriculture and rural development, education, health, family planning, urban institutions, public enterprise reform, private-sector development, and general financial support for structural adjustment.[16] Although the full-scale war began in 1990 with the Tutsi exile invasion, the World Bank (along with the other donors) continued with an "active portfolio" up to the beginning of the genocide.

In fact, the portfolio was expanded by eight investment operations and an adjustment operation between November 1990 and November 1993. The most significant of these operations was the Structural Adjustment Credit (SAC) for US$90 million, approved in June 1991.... In response to mounting pressures on both the trade account and fiscal budget, caused in part by the collapse of coffee prices, the GOR [Government of Rwanda] had initiated discussions with the Bank and the Fund in 1990 that led to the SAC as well as access to a IMF Structural Adjustment Facility (SAF). The Structural Adjustment Program, of which the SAC was a component, called for a wide range of policy reforms under three headings: macroeconomic stabilization and improved international competitiveness; reduction of the role of the state in the economy; and protection of the vulnerable with a social safety net. Civil service reform was also a condition.[17]

In the event, the SAC was suspended following the first tranche (partial release of funds) after the government failed to meet the budget, civil service, and price subsidy conditions. Most donors, including the World Bank, terminated their programs after the genocide began.

The donors' continued support of the Rwandan economy and its development programs can be criticized on several counts. First, in the face of a long history of Hutu–Tutsi animosity, and despite the unabashed Hutu agenda of hegemonic reversal, civil war, and pogroms, the donors undertook to support Rwandan economic development in a vacuum, so to speak. Their support was not made conditional on any changes respecting internal "political" issues. They acted, in effect, as if the aid projects were ethnically neutral, existing within a separate developmental sphere. By applying criteria pertaining only to this separate sphere, the donors were able to judge Rwanda's performance as outstanding.

Substantial support from the multilateral and bilateral donor community contributed to, and was attracted by, Rwanda's progress and policies. The country drew international attention owing to its low rural-to-urban migration rate, its sound macroeconomic policies, and the active involvement of government and civil society in antierosion and reforestation activities and health and education services. Official development assistance (ODA) to Rwanda grew rapidly, from an annual level of $35 million between 1971 and 1974 to $343 million between 1990 and 1993, the latter figure representing about $50 per capita and almost 25 percent of GNP, and exceeding the sub-Saharan Africa averages of $35.7 ... and 11.5 percent, respectively.[18]

The fact that the low urban migration was viewed favorably is striking under today's international human rights sensitivities. The evaluation notes that the low rate was "in part the result of heavy restrictions on mobility and strict enforcement made possible by complex and highly organized governmental administrative structures right down to small local 'hill' units." There are further ironies in this observation. The World Bank was so impressed with the local administrative system and the lessons it might hold for other countries in Africa that it commissioned a detailed field study. Not only did the authors of the study avoid any mention of Hutu or Tutsi, feeling constrained by Bank practice to eschew (published) comment on client country politics, but this very administrative structure played an important role in the orchestration of the 1994 massacres.

The World Bank's silence on the government's regressive policies apparently extended to all its formal documentation. If informal internal reports did cover these policies, there is little evidence they had any effect on the Bank's programs.

> The first and most sweeping criticism leveled at the Bank and other donors is that they ignored the signs of growing ethnic tensions and unraveling of the political framework in the 1980s. If they were aware of growing problems, their documents showed no indication of such awareness, and in any event, no consequent actions were taken in policy dialogue with the government or with regard to their portfolios. The most explicit critic in this respect is Peter Uvin. . . . Citing nine Bank documents . . . , Uvin finds frequent references to Rwanda's putative "prudent, sound management, concern for its rural population, political stability," and even "the cultural and social cohesion of its people" and "the ethnic and socioeconomic homogeneity of the country." But he finds no references to such issues as "state-sponsored racism; authoritarian government and condescending extension; a festering refugee problem; and social, ethnic and regional inequality."[19]

The evaluation itself reviewed a further twenty Bank documents (such as project appraisal and completion reports, and economic reviews) and found similar anomalies. A poverty assessment made no mention of "ethnic fissures or related exclusionary and predatory policies and practices." This anodyne treatment was not limited to the World Bank. According to Uvin, "no aid agency ever denounced the official racism or the quota system or the ethnic IDs—not even in the 1990s, when it was clear they were being used to prepare for mass killings."[20]

Second, by ignoring divisive aspects of aid-supported activities, or giving them insufficient weight, donors (perhaps, if given the benefit of the doubt, inadvertently) could actually finance the execution of inequities, thereby exacerbating ethnic relationships. The experience of one project shows how the conservative interpretation (by its legal counsel and its governing board) of the World Bank's governing Articles of Agreement, stipulating political noninterference, could lead the institution to ignore ethnic inequities and to continue to support activities that were contributing to the overall pattern of discrimination. In one agricultural development project,

> despite evidence that Tutsi and Hima pastoralists were being discriminated against in favor of Hutus, and in spite of opportunistic behavior resulting in the "hijacking" of project resources by project managers and staff, the Bank favored the effort with a *second* project. Looking back, it is hard to justify the Bank's going ahead with a "repeater project." The rationale given at the time was that the first project had "established a dialogue between the Bank and the Government." Instead, the second *Mutara* project rewarded a pattern of opportunistic behavior and discriminatory practices that by the early 1990s had become much more pervasive, a pattern that by that time, several Bank staff interviewed for this study indicated they were well aware of.[21]

Third, the aid flows provided a major increase in the total resources available to the Rwandan government for pursuing its overall agenda, including the programs that were affecting the relative positions of the Hutu and Tutsi as a whole. The donors ignored the fact that, almost invariably, aid to and through a government aids the incumbent group. Admittedly, establishing direct connections between politicized allocation and the resources provided in the general, financial form of budget or balance of payments support, under structural adjustment credits, is inherently more difficult than in the case of specific projects like the Mutara. (We will return to the subject of structural adjustment and conflict below.) The search by some critics for a SAC (Structural Adjustment Credit) smoking gun, besides being questionable in some of its allegations,[22] missed the point that sheer finance, as provided under general support loans, is the most fungible form of development assistance. (That is, budget support provided for general administration, or even preapproved essential expenditures, frees up an equivalent amount of other government revenues not bound with the same restrictions as SAC funds.) In the Rwandan case, the impact of the SAC is unclear. Some of the economic policy changes it called for that might have increased political instability were never carried out, and the credit was cancelled in 1992 after only partial disbursement.

The larger question is this: If the donors had adopted an early tough stand against the discriminatory and divisive policies, could the outcome have been substantially better? Could the genocide have been avoided by deflecting the whole course of root-cause events? Or to put the question in its most invidious form: Did the totality of the long flow of donor resources enhance the ability of the Hutu extremist elite to call forth the genocide?

By 1993, economic aid no longer had prevention leverage. In fact, the focus was on diplomatic pressures that appeared to be bearing fruit. Rwanda had signed on to the Arusha Accords that called for power-sharing between the government and the Tutsi party. The World Bank even convened a meeting with both sides "to discuss an economic framework. This meeting was viewed as positive on all sides and Bank staff concluded the meeting with a sense of optimism." In any event, nothing came of these discussions, as the situation deteriorated rapidly in early 1994. In response to the question of the possible efficacy of much earlier leverage, the Bank's evaluation makes interesting observations but does not attempt to lay out any alternative scenarios.

> When might a "lesser option," such as a coordinated withdrawal of economic assistance, have had an impact? This may have been as much as a decade or two earlier, before Hutu extremism became entrenched. This poses a dilemma: while the leverage of the donor community is likely to be greater some time before the cusp of disaster is reached, the evidence of predation and extremism will also likely be weaker and therefore, international support for interventionist approaches less. There is also the risk that a coordinated withdrawal of aid could *increase* state-imposed repression and violence against its citizens. While such a risk cannot be ignored, the fact that donors in very low-income countries, such as Rwanda, typically provide resources equivalent to a major share of the government's budget means they do (or could) exercise considerable leverage.[23]

Aid cancellation is a drastic action that we return to in the final chapter. While there might be cases where one could argue that donor withdrawal would have a perverse effect, Rwanda seems an unlikely candidate. Despite the presence of a substantial aid program over a long period, Rwanda plunged into a paroxysm of state-imposed violence of the most extreme form conceivable. If aid had been cancelled as a form of preconflict pressure, the effects on the population's welfare could hardly have been worse than what actually occurred. Many donors have taken a different approach in countries with governments that are indifferent to, or ineffective in, attacking poverty, but not so egregious in their behavior as to prompt donor sanctions. Instead, donors will bypass government, channeling their aid to local civil society (i.e., nongovernmental organizations). Unfortunately, as Rwanda illustrated, civil society may be co-opted by the same authorities the donors are trying to avoid.[24]

Peter Uvin, whose study (1998) of aid and the Rwandan genocide is the most closely argued yet published to my knowledge, judges the effects of the sustained aid more harshly than does the World Bank evaluation. Uvin describes at length the inequalities, injustices, and deprivations the people of

Rwanda had suffered throughout their modern history. To capture the fact that these ills were imbedded in the social system and political cultures, and were unremitting, he adopts the term "structural violence." He sees structural violence, experienced by the Hutu majority, as an explanation of the response of ordinary adolescents, farmers, and women to the extremists' calls for mass physical violence.

> For the large mass of poor Rwandans, life was characterized by a constant reduction of life chances and increase of socioeconomic vulnerability; the absence of opportunities to acquire information and education; oppressive, authoritarian, and condescending treatment by the development system; growing social, ethnic, and regional inequality; and a history of impunity, corruption, and abuse of power by local and national elites, often committed in the name of development. . . . I identify this condition as one of "structural violence," thus drawing attention to the fact that such structures and processes are violent because they needlessly and brutally limit people's physical and psychological capacities. . . . [Structural violence] creates anger, resentment, and frustration, which contribute to the erosion of social capital and norms in society. A population that is cynical, angry, and frustrated is predisposed to scapegoating and projection, vulnerable to manipulation, deeply afraid of the future, and desperate for change. It is this population that bought into racist prejudice in the 1990s and was willing to kill out of fear, anger, resentment, and greed.[25]

Uvin poses the same four questions that underlie this book. Did aid seek to halt the structural violence processes? Did aid affect these processes unintentionally? Should aid have done differently? Could it have? To the first question, Uvin answers no, which the record appears to bear out. In response to the second question, which relates to the broad issue of the overall impact of a sustained aid effort, Uvin argues that a continuation of aid in the face of abuses is tantamount to an international license, even complicity, since

> the military and diplomatic support to the regime by some countries, as well as the general passivity toward the rights abuses, racism, and militarization inside the country by the entire international community, undoubtedly facilitated if not encouraged the forces of genocide to reach their final conclusion. The fact that the development business continued as usual while government-sponsored human rights violations were on the rise sent a clear signal that the international community did not care too much about the racially motivated and publicly organized slaughter of citizens.[26]

In response to the third question, should donors have acted differently, he concedes that the international community may have (mistakenly) viewed its diplomatic efforts alone as sufficient to promote democratization and tolerance.

Finally, could aid have changed Rwanda's course? Uvin agrees with the World Bank evaluation that exercising leverage might have been fruitless. Even if the Rwandan president had acceded to pressure to reverse the anti-Tutsi policies, the extremist clique was probably beyond his control. More important from our perspective was the failure, as cited by Uvin, to use aid to attempt earlier to ameliorate the root causes.

> [B]esides the use of negative conditionality, the international community can employ other instruments to influence social processes in recipient countries. The development aid agencies could have continued to assist the Rwandan population toward development but adapted their goals, strategies, and allocations to the new realities and challenges the country faced. In the 1990s, it seems, these challenges were rapidly becoming those of violence, hatred, manipulation, conflict, human rights abuses, and militarization. New projects could have been started to intervene in these factors, or existing projects could have been reoriented to take more account of them. This is not necessarily easy to do—indeed, there are no clear-cut, pre-packaged solutions to these challenges—but it was imperative to try. Faced with the disintegration of Rwandese society, the development community should have tried to rethink its mission and reorient its actions. It did not do so.[27]

Uvin himself did not attempt (at least in the book I am citing) to translate his retrospective challenge into specifics. He believes punitive conditionality should have been tried despite its uncertainties, especially since business-as-usual signals indifference. His suggestion, namely that aid agencies should have sought out, and through their projects, supported the "many people" in Rwanda who "preferred harmony over hatred," has merit, and should be taken into account by aid programs in all deeply divided societies. But by Uvin's own account, it would be difficult to construct a persuasive and credible what-if scenario that could have prevented Rwanda's conflicts. Nevertheless, if greater pressure combined with aid activities that awarded only moderates and moderation could have constrained the extremists to merely (!) maintaining a society of structural violence, short of genocide, that would have been a massive accomplishment—although unknowable, of course, since genocide was viewed as "unthinkable" until the very last moment and would have been viewed as a low-probability scenario had it not occurred.

Sri Lanka: Opportunities Taken, and Missed

The relationships among domestic policy, development aid, and conflict in Sri Lanka are instructive on several accounts and worth covering in some detail. In common with many ethnic conflicts, there were multiple causes for Sri Lanka's civil war. While the Sinhala-dominated government was ready to suppress an insurgency in 1971 of unemployed Sinhalese youth, the major conflict has pitted the government against Tamil insurgents fighting for secession. The Sri Lankan conflict is a clear case where ethnic-mobilization rhetoric gradually crystallized a deep polarization that did not rest on historic "primordial" grounds.

> This [civil war] outcome is puzzling because of the absence of sustained ethnic conflict prior to the late 1970s and the remarkable developmental record of Sri Lanka as a model for provision of "basic human needs" within the context of a well institutionalized democratic political system that allowed significant opportunities for participation and mediation. . . . Many on both sides abhorred the political projects of those who employed appeals to ethnicity or "race" as grounds for mobilization and victimization. There were islands of peace and cooperation even in strife-torn areas. . . . As in most "ethnic" conflicts, the stakes were multidimensional: material advantage, territoriality, cultural validation, and political power. Nevertheless, the conflagration did bring into play reciprocal stereotypes and political language of the sort we commonly associate with ethnicity.[28]

Although the insurgency began with young Tamils in the Jaffna region, the conflict had roots in long-standing stereotypical perceptions and fears about relative economic roles, historic ethnic territorial "rights," and cultural assertions and threats. According to Donald Horowitz (1985), the Sri Lankan polity failed to cope with these problems through the workings of its parliamentary institutions because of its political party and electoral configurations: the parties were ethnically based and the process was not conducive to interethnic coalitions. Thus, the establishment in the 1972 constitution of Sinhala as the sole official national language (it had been the sole language of administration since 1961), and the introduction of a university quota system designed to reduce Tamil representation (which had been disproportionately high) in higher education and in the civil service, had emerged out of the competition between Sinhalese parties vying for the Sinhalese vote. By the early 1970s, these and other measures were already creating a sense of injustice in the Tamil community, especially in the Jaffna area inhabited by the centuries-old Ceylon Tamil community (the inhabitants in the other, eastern, area of Tamil concentration were the so-called Indian Tamils, of more recent colonial immigration as labor for the tea plantations), and especially among the Jaffna Tamil youth, who reacted with militancy.[29] In this context, the flood of foreign aid after 1977 sanctioned, or at least tolerated, the state's programs, and provided the financial means for the government to conduct policies that deepened the society's divisions. These policies had several dimensions: investment location, beneficiary selection, exposure of previously protected producers to freed-up prices and liberalized imports, and ethnonationalist symbolism.

According to Ronald Herring, the enabling role of donor finance played out as follows. Development strategy was the key issue in the Sri Lankan elections of 1977. The victory of the United National Party (UNP) launched a reversal, from the previous highly regulated, welfarist, inward-looking strategy to a market-oriented, liberalizing, trade-enhancing strategy that also promised more evenhanded, less corrupt governance. Armed with the blessing of the IMF for its economic reform program, the UNP obtained donor endorsement and a sharp increase in external assistance to help finance an expanded program of public-sector investment. Aid enabled the government to embark on a massive public works program to (among other things) generate employment, financing about 70 percent of the net government budget deficit by 1980. Major pieces of the investment program were implemented in a manner that discriminated against the Tamil minority (about 18 percent of the population) and blatantly celebrated Sinhala ethnonationalism. In addition, some Sinhala intellectuals and politicians interpreted the effects of the macroeconomic liberalization measures as heavily weighted against Sinhala economic interests, which were already, according to this view, subordinated to Tamil domination in several sectors—a view that justified a call for ethnically based corrective policies, and that comprised one explanation for the anti-Tamil riots of 1983 in Colombo, Sri Lanka's capital.

Herring argues that the liberalization program exacerbated interethnic hostilities. (While this should stand to sensitize donors to the need for assessing the conflict implications of liberalization programs—we return to such implications of liberalization and structural adjustment programs below—his argument is subtle and appears to lack the concreteness of the project-level effects in Sri Lanka that I will describe momentarily.) Although there were common perceptions among the Sinhalese that Tamils dominated public-sector employment, bank credit, real estate, and the private sector generally, the realities of ethnic representation in economic areas were apparently unclear. There were comparable perceptions that the liberalization policies caused more dislocation to Sinhalese workers and business. There was also a group of monks who saw liberalization as "a westernizing project which threatened the cultural identity of the Sinhalese Buddhist community."[30] The tax and food ration and subsidy reforms increased income inequality and seriously affected the income and nutritional status of the very poor. The absence of any street response, any "IMF riot," was only partially explained by the offsetting expansion of the economy, leading to a theory that the reaction had been displaced into ethnic resentment.

According to Herring, Sinhala frustration over real wage cuts was diverted into ethnic hostility sufficient to cause terror among the Tamil and to make ethnic compromise untenable. "The 'open' economy provided both symbolic materials and exacerbation of real cleavages to facilitate scapegoating," Herring noted. Ethnic lines hardened, overcoming the earlier intraethnic divisions between hawks and doves. Herring points out that the liberalization program clearly hurt Tamil agriculture in the Jaffna region, yet no coalition of Tamils and Sinhalese injured by liberalization was possible given the Tamil conviction that the Sinhalese were capturing all the benefits of development projects.

At the heart of the argument is the distinction between necessary and sufficient causes. The aid flows are seen to have been enabling, not co-conspiratorial or aligned by intent with the political program of the government.

> Political escalation of ethnic conflict was not caused by foreign aid or structural adjustment. Indeed, official repression was criticized by the development community. But criticism did not preclude continued international support for the government. Given the dependence of the government and its economic miracle on foreign resource flows, external demands for reconciliation must certainly have had more potential purchase than was realized; it is doubtful that the regime could have continued had it been abandoned by the development community. But collective action among donor nations was impeded by intra-governmental conflict over aid objectives, commercial interests of donors and coordination problems. Moreover, the target economy was growing.[31]

The debate within the Canadian government between those critical of Sri Lanka's human rights violations and the UNP government's unwillingness to moderate, and those calling for separating development aid from foreign policy (and not wanting to disturb Canadian business interests with large aid-funded contracts in Sri Lanka), finally resulted in Canada's withdrawal from the massive Mahaweli River irrigation project. By the time of the withdrawal, however, the large reservoir component that Canada had been financing was virtually completed. The United States attempted to offset its continuing participation in Mahaweli (from which a Jaffna component canal had been dropped by the government) by funding an urban water and sewer project in the Jaffna area.[32]

The national aid-assisted housing program is worth citing as a clear case of ethnic exclusion and resentment. The program had met with divided donor response. The World Bank and International Monetary Fund opposed the scheme as a low-priority diversion of investment funds, a common view of housing in the development community. USAID favored the project, however, and provided substantial funding indirectly through its housing guarantee facility, an authority under which USAID facilitates the flow of private money from American savings and loan institutions. One village study showed how the program's rhetoric celebrated Sinhala nationalism and how the allocation of new houses rewarded UNP supporters.[33] The USAID office in Colombo was aware of the program's politicization at the village level. The USAID housing office in Washington saw U.S. involvement as an opportunity to improve a large Sri Lankan program, both technically and by reducing the size of the interest subsidy. In any event, USAID/Colombo's reservations did not reduce U.S. support to the housing program.

I turn now to the history of two irrigation projects in Sri Lanka, which provide striking examples of aid agency relevance to the course of ethnic conflict. One project improved the relationships between Sinhalese and Tamil farmers living in one irrigation system area, turning hostility, separation, and interest conflict into friendship and voluntary promotion of mutual interest. The second was a much vaster project in which the aid agencies missed an opportunity (or, more precisely, failed to persist in an attempt) to pressure the authorities to include rather than (deliberately!) exclude Tamil farmers. The two examples illustrate aid agency relevance operating through the interaction of project- or local-level activities with national-level policy and conflict.

In the first, USAID supported a project beginning in 1980 to rehabilitate the Gal Oya river irrigation system in the southeastern part of the country. Gal Oya had been built between 1948 and 1952, financed entirely by the Sri Lankan government without any foreign aid participation. It served roughly 12,500 farmers cultivating 40,000 hectares.[34] The project had deteriorated over the years. The population in the project area had risen, channels were silted up, 80 percent of the outlet gates and other structures were inoperable, and the system's management was haphazard and characterized by hostile relations with the farmers. Most telling, the system delivered insufficient water for dry-season cultivation. The lower third of the system—the "tail-end" farmers—seldom received irrigation water and had to rely entirely on rainfall. The scarcity of water caused conflicts among farmers. The upstream areas had been settled by Sinhalese farmers, while the tail-end allotments had been given to Tamil settlers. "When water did not reach the tail, Tamils could attribute this to maliciousness of Sinhalese settlers upstream rather than to geographic factors. The minority's sense of grievance was not allayed by the fact that a majority of Irrigation Department engineers were Tamil."[35]

The institution-building part of the Gal Oya project covered the left bank of the system, and is unusually interesting on several counts. It was an outstanding case of a foreign aid success. While the implementation of the project was complex, and had its ups and downs, it turned an irrigation scheme that had been an economic and social disaster into a productive and harmonious agricultural complex. In Norman Uphoff's account, substantial credit goes to the farmers themselves who responded to the "social engineering" and organizing activities designed, and continually adapted, by the external technical assistance professionals and their dedicated local implementers. The Gal Oya experience is well known for its "participatory" character and techniques. It also had a striking positive impact on ethnic relations.

When the Gal Oya rehabilitation project began, interethnic conflict in Sri Lanka was still at a low level of intensity. It had been developing ever since the mid-1950s in response to ethnonationalist language, employment, and other policies introduced by Sinhalese dominated governments. Violent protest tactics were employed both by Tamil and Sinhalese extremists, the latter objecting during the periods when government policy, in their view, was too accommodative. Widespread riots in 1983 escalated the conflict to an outright civil war that has killed over 50,000 Sri Lankans.

The Tamil minority comprises about 18 percent of Sri Lanka's population. In the left bank project area the Tamils were 30 to 40 percent. Soon after the project got under way, the social engineering designed with the assistance of Cornell University advisors changed the farmers' behavior from a pattern of noncooperation and (often hostile) competition over the critical component of any irrigation project—distribution of the available water—to one of cooperation. One pre-project survey had found farmer behavior the main weakness of Gal Oya; there were instances of "water theft, lack of field channel maintenance, staggered planting [instead of simultaneous, to make best use of water provided to specific areas of the system at specific times], breaking [water control] gates, cutting bunds to get water directly from larger channels."[36] (There were also serious weaknesses in the Irrigation Department's management of the system.) Within a few weeks into project implementation, these uncooperative and contentious farmers were cleaning their irrigation channels and rotating water deliveries so that all would get a fair share of that scarce resource, with some groups even saving water to send to downstream farmers.[37]

Most surprising, and the most interesting feature of the project from the perspective of conflict prevention, was the willingness of head-end Sinhalese farmers to voluntarily reduce their water offtake in order to send more water to Tamil farmers at the tail end. The Sinhalese farmers' satisfaction with the rehabilitation project and the cooperative relationships developed to improve system self-governance by the farmers at the bottom, so to speak, were sustained when the general interethnic conflict erupted in the region where the project was located. Sinhalese farmers protected Tamil project staff and farmers who would have been at risk otherwise from attacks of extremists.[38] This was a remarkable outcome, considering that the area had seen violent ethnic conflict in 1957, 1977, and 1981, during which Tamil homes were burned, whereas the groups were now engaged in cooperative water distribution and channel cleaning.

Norman Uphoff attributes the change in Sinhalese farmers' behavior to a combination of self-interest and altruism. One aspect of self-interest concerned reputation: in meetings with large numbers of neighbors, a head-end farmer could not afford to appear selfish by refusing to participate in a more equitable distribution of water to tail-enders. Uphoff ascribes the power of the project to bring about such changes to the interpersonal organizational arrangements (carried out by young fieldworkers called institutional organizers) that created new "behavioral settings."

Uphoff notes: "When institutional organizers entered Gal Oya communities, they were proponents of cooperative action, suggesting that groups get together to tackle whatever problems they could not resolve by individual effort, and particularly endorsing . . . campaigns of voluntary collective labor. They also encouraged sharing water equitably to help tail-enders who would otherwise not be able to cultivate a crop and maintain themselves. The result was to shift farmer behavior from selfish individualism to other-regarding cooperation in a matter of weeks."[39]

Years after the formal end of Cornell University's involvement, the organizing and motivating institutional arrangements are still functioning. During the severe dry season of 1997, water supplies were sufficient, if distributed at normal coverage volumes, to irrigate only a small percentage of the left bank area. Nevertheless, farmers continued to share the available water, and improved cultivation methods enabled them to cultivate a good crop despite using minimal quantities of water. By 1997 the Tamil Tiger militants' control had penetrated to an area inside the Gal Oya project area. Despite efforts by the militants to intimidate the Tamil farmers into withdrawing, the cooperation arrangements between the Sinhalese and Tamil farmers remained strong.[40]

I need not repeat here in any detail the extensive treatment Uphoff gives to the questions of motivation and social change. Some of what worked in Gal Oya may have been specific to Sri Lankan conditions. (The system was not unique to Gal Oya conditions; it was replicated in some other areas in Sri

Lanka, but not in the Mahaweli project I turn to next.) However, the emergence of cooperant (economically relevant) behavior, not undermined by any significant "free riding" selfishness (contrary to what the "collective action" literature would expect), has been observed in other countries as well.[41] In any case, in the context of conflict prevention, the experience suggests some important lessons.

First, it demonstrated the feasibility of inducing a change from hostile and noninteractive relations to altruistic and cooperative relations between sets of people of different ethnicity, who live or work within a potentially integrated context, even in a country where violence generally already marks the overall relationship between these ethnic groups.

Second, it shows that economic interests, combined with deliberate efforts to promote harmony and strengthen altruistic potentialities at the individual and community levels, can develop salience strong enough to override appeals, perhaps even pressures, for a reversion to ethnicity-based hostility and noncooperation.

Third, the essence of that economic interest was reduction in disparity, between farmers who had water and those who had been excluded.

Fourth, there was no trade-off between (interethnic) equity and efficiency: the less intensive water use by the head-end Sinhalese farmers was agronomically superior to their precooperation water monopolization. It is worth noting that the technical assistance that produced these results cost only 3 percent of the total USAID investment in Gal Oya.

One must also draw the realistic conclusion that isolated cases of conflict avoidance and ethnic harmony promotion, even if robust enough to withstand pressures from surrounding antagonists aimed at disrupting such oases, are not likely to be sufficient in themselves to induce the antagonists operating on the large outside stage of the nation as a whole to move toward accommodation and resolution. Scale is important. Can development assistance programs in a conflicted country undertake enough projects, enough activities as a whole, involving sufficient numbers of people and potentially cooperative activities, and perhaps complementing diplomatic and nonofficial (so-called track two) mediation efforts, to turn the scales?

Sri Lanka also provides an example of a missed opportunity that might have been of such a critical scale. The example is a second irrigation scheme, the Mahaweli. Planning for this large-scale irrigation and hydropower project on the Mahaweli River began in 1958. In the mid-1960s, a master plan was drawn up with assistance from the U.N. Development Programme (UNDP) and Food and Agriculture Organization (FAO). The World Bank provided the first donor funding for construction, starting in 1970.[42] Mahaweli is a massive project compared with Gal Oya. It was to be developed over 30 years, and was to include 15 reservoirs, 500 megawatts of hydrostation capacity, and irrigation for 365,000 hectares, nine times the cultivated area of Gal Oya. The costs of the scheme amounted to a significant fraction of all public-sector investment and recurrent cost expenditures, contributing importantly to Sri Lanka's lengthy inflation.

In 1977 the Jayawardene government launched the Accelerated Mahaweli Development Program (AMDP) designed to speed up the project and to mobilize donor support, which was then forthcoming to support a government apparently bent on economic reform and ethnic accommodation. As described by a World Bank evaluation in 1998, the program had "major implications" for Sri Lankan ethnic politics. There were two issues—which geographic areas were to receive irrigation, and who would be settled in these areas. Tamil leadership complained that the Tamil areas of the north had been dropped from the original scheme. As the new configuration was being debated in the early 1980s, the USAID mission urged the inclusion of distribution to the northern Tamil region. The government held its ground. It cited cost and geographic factors to explain the change; a proposal put forward by the Permanent Secretary of Agriculture in the Jayawardene government for an alternative method of moving Mahaweli water to the north was not adopted.

The question of who would be settled in the new areas that were to be irrigated arose because the largest of these areas was contiguous with a region that had been long settled by Tamils. The Tamil leadership proposed settlement in proportion to each ethnic group's percentage of the country's population. Under pressure from unemployed Sinhalese, the government rejected this proposal, making concessions to Tamil settlement only later, in 1986, three years after the outbreak of high-intensity conflict. In effect, the project transferred Sinhalese settlers into areas the Tamils had long considered as their own. The Tamils viewed the policy in ethnic terms as designed to establish a strong Sinhalese presence in traditionally Tamil areas. The policy served to "undermine a rightful sense of political and economic security on the part of the Tamils and thus further alienate the Tamils from the Sri Lankan government."[43] The policy clearly contravened the pacts that had been made by the Sinhalese and Tamil leadership in 1957 and 1965 to protect Tamil interests with respect to colonization. As the World Bank noted, these virtually exclusionary policies "reinforced Tamil perceptions that the [government] was exclusively interested in the development of Sinhalese majority areas."[44]

The perception that Mahaweli was a major demonstration of Sinhalese hegemonic intentions was reinforced by the ethnonationalist rhetoric the Jayawardene administration employed when referring to the project. David

Little stated that "it is hard to deny that the Jayawardene administration itself did make something of the 'golden threads' that were supposed to connect contemporary irrigation and colonization projects with those of ancient Sinhala kings. . . . In justifying its irrigation policies, it is likely the government could have contributed to improved ethnic relations by concentrating on economic development and by disregarding altogether inflammatory references to past Sinhala glory."[45]

Considering what Gal Oya was able to accomplish, and the symbolic and economic importance of Mahaweli, it seems obvious that the latter might have made a significant contribution to interethnic harmony and to allaying Tamil fears had the authorities applied an approach similar to that used in the former project. As a counterfactual assumption, of course, such a potential effect on Sri Lankan politics can only be conjectural. At the time, however, the donors did recognize this potentiality and proposed to the Mahaweli authority that it adopt the lessons of Gal Oya. The authority rejected the donors' recommendation. Rather than applying more severe pressure, or using a threat to withdraw their financing, without which Mahaweli would have collapsed, the donors proceeded to support the program anyway.

Much later, the World Bank evaluation concluded that the decision to proceed represented a potentially significant missed opportunity for promoting conflict avoidance:

> If the Bank, along with other donors, had *forcefully* raised concerns about regional and ethnic balance and had convinced the [Sri Lankan government] to appropriately modify the "Accelerated Mahaweli Development Program," it is by no means certain that this alone would have prevented the full-scale conflict that erupted in 1983. However, this is not to say that such concerns should not have been raised and *been made part of conditionality.*[46]

The suggestion that Tamil inclusion should have been made a condition for World Bank and other donor support of Mahaweli is the most important conclusion from this story. As in the East–West Pakistan case, the possibility that the tensions might have been mitigated, perhaps rendered more amenable to negotiation and nonviolent resolution, remains an untestable hypothesis. Actually, the hypothesis takes different forms for the two cases. Mahaweli would have been an example of the multilevel approach, or a component of what Kevin Avruch (1998) terms the "restricted" concept of dispute resolution, the concept that resolution requires settlement of fundamental issues pervading the society. Mahaweli's contribution could have been to create cooperant, interest-based relations among large numbers of nonelite Sinhalese and Tamil farm families, and to serve as a primary national symbol of minority inclusion. As a significant offset to factors working in the opposite direction, Mahaweli might have changed Tamil perceptions that the Sinhalese were unambiguously bent on hegemony and exclusion, reciprocally strengthening Sinhalese willingness to moderate the language and other policies driving Tamil extremism. Or, more precisely, a shared-interest Mahaweli could have increased the numbers of moderates on both sides and reduced the polarizing leverage of the extremists.

In contrast, in the Pakistan case the negotiation game, or "realist" chess model, could have applied. Artful third-party mediators could have facilitated a bargaining process that focused on material interests. The driving grievances were those of the Bengali elite. Negotiations between a small number of elite leaders in both wings, involving "stroke of the pen" economic issues (budget allocation, exchange rate, protective tariffs), might have satisfied the East wing and created relations of trust, which, in turn, might have kept Pakistan whole. If the civil war had not occurred, the Indian military intervention would not have occurred; thus, two-wing viability also would have avoided one of the major armed conflicts between India and Pakistan.

We cannot be confident, of course, that the donors would have succeeded had they chosen to press harder in the case of Mahaweli, or to shift their geographic allocation earlier in the case of Pakistan along with strong efforts to secure other allocative policy changes. Realizing the potentialities of external influence can be a complex process, varying substantially from one country to another and from one point in time to another, and depending on the political sensitivity of the issues in question. To put the Sri Lanka case in its proper context, it is important to note that the World Bank's efforts to impose much less socially intrusive conditions in the 1960s caused a storm from the parliamentary opposition. The conditions concerned certain provisions of a Bank loan for Mahaweli, requiring, for example, that consultants to be employed had to be acceptable to the Bank, and that the Sri Lankan government would raise irrigation water fees. Such conditions are standard for World Bank projects.

According to Mason and Asher, the problem arose because the World Bank had had years of good relations with, and had become identified with, one political party (which had adopted economic policies of which the World Bank approved), while having unfavorable relations with the other.[47] As a result, the Bank had swung between years of active lending and years of little activity, depending on which party was in power. The opposition party at this particular time would probably have opposed World Bank loans on any grounds that could be exploited.

The lesson that should be drawn from this experience is that the acceptability of loan conditions depends on the political circumstances at the time and on the nature of World Bank communications and relations with groups inside and outside government. The absence of Bank relations with political figures outside government, and with political figures who opposed basic tenets of the Bank's development philosophy, was not confined to Sri Lanka, nor was this self-limitation confined to the World Bank among donor agencies. In this kind of isolation the Bank would have had little influence for conflict prevention even if it had been alert to such dimensions of its activities. Conditions in Sri Lanka after the UNP election victory in 1977, however, were more favorable. A more assertive role on Mahaweli, especially as part of a unified donor position on the ethnic problem as a whole, as suggested by Ronald Herring, might have helped ameliorate rather than exacerbate Sri Lanka's core political problem.

There is an important qualification to the Mahaweli story. In retrospect, the Mahaweli scheme was not an economically sound investment. Given the size of domestic and foreign aid resources Mahaweli absorbed, and the very low returns the project has realized, an ethnic harmony objective—had it been incorporated, as in our what-if scenario—would not have been sufficient itself to justify undertaking the program. However, if any Sri Lankan government could have been persuaded by a more forceful donor effort to adopt such an objective for this overwhelmingly large project, it would by presumption have been open to persuasion to adopt a more accommodating general policy toward the Tamil minority, including more accommodating orientation toward any sets of alternative projects with stronger economic justification.

Yugoslavia: Economic Rights and IMF Responsibility

Given the complexity of Yugoslavia's modern history, and the interlinked warfare among Balkan nationalities, different scholars, over time, are likely to weigh differently the causes, decisions, and events that led to the demise of the Yugoslav state and to the ensuing wars. This is an important case from our perspective because it is one where serious scholarship has laid some degree of responsibility (for conflict beyond a passing riot) on the doorstep of the International Monetary Fund (IMF). To greatly oversimplify, Susan L. Woodward's account (1995) cites the loss of certain economic rights the "republics" had held under the highly decentralized Yugoslav system as one of the significant motivations behind the secessions of the Croatian and Slovenian republics, which Serb military action then attempted to reverse (along with the subsequent secession of Bosnia).[48] These rights had been recentralized to federal control in accordance with a stabilization program designed and negotiated under IMF leadership. It is worth taking a few extracts from Woodward's account to get a sense of the conflict potentialities that were inherent in Yugoslavia, and of the destabilizing power of reformist changes in economic rights.

Woodward describes the evolution of Yugoslavia as a multiethnic state ("a patchwork quilt of ethnicity") with a highly decentralized structure, a system designed to contain its inherent centrifugal forces by devolving to the republic and local levels a large fraction of the rights and authorities more commonly found at the level of central government. While each of the Yugoslav republics lay within internal borders that had much longer histori- cal continuity than, say, the borders of most African countries today, and had its own concentrated ethnic majority, each republic was also ethnically het- erogeneous, containing minorities that in some cases shared ethnicity with the majority in some other republic. In many ways, the measures Yugoslavia took to reduce economic disparities and to accommodate to its multiethnic composition went beyond those of Malaysia (our next case country). These measures included, among others, education in native languages; state fund- ing of separate cultural expression; promotion of a nonascriptive Yugoslav identity as an alternative to the traditional Croat, Serb, and other national- isms, especially attractive to the 14 percent of the (1980) population that were in (or the children of) ethnically mixed marriages; official recognition of a religious group, the Muslims, as a "nation," politically equivalent to the traditional (Slovene, Serb, etc.) "nations"; and an unusual system for dem- onstrating judicial evenhandedness, under which the authorities "often went out of their way to balance a particular prosecution with charges against persons from other ethnic groups in the area."[49] The fiscal system included transfers from the richer to the poorer republics and provinces. "Decentrali- zation by the early 1970s had led to so much *de facto* independence that political life was primarily centered in the republics."[50] Perhaps because of this system, elaborately sensitive to the need to offset divisive forces, the conflicts took on a religio-ethnic character only after the disintegration had gone quite far.

> Tensions along ethnic, racial, or historical fault lines can lead to civil vio- lence, but to explain the Yugoslav crisis as a result of ethnic hatred is to turn the story upside down and begin at its end.[51]
>
> The real origin of the Yugoslav conflict is the disintegration of govern- mental authority and the breakdown of a political and civil order. This process occurred over a prolonged period . . . , the result of the politics of transforming a socialist society to a market economy and democracy. A critical element of this failure was economic decline, caused largely by a program intended to resolve a foreign debt crisis. . . . Normal political conflicts over economic resources between central and regional govern- ments and over the political and economic reforms of the debt-repayment

package became constitutional conflicts and then a crisis of the state itself among politicians who were unwilling to compromise. . . . [T]he contestants were government leaders fighting to retain or enhance their political jurisdictions and public property rights over economic resources within their territories.[52]

Despite substantial warning of the consequences, Western governments did not intervene to alter the roles and perceptions that were feeding the escalating cycles of disintegration and violence; instead, they contributed substantially to the drama.[53]

The oil price shocks of the 1970s and the skyrocketing interest rates for foreign borrowing created a severe liquidity and debt crisis for Yugoslavia. The inability of the country's political institutions to manage a coherent response turned the economic crisis into a crisis of governance. Economists, both Yugoslav and foreign, argued that the crisis was essentially political.

Successive Yugoslav governments during the 1990s had failed to adjust to the changing terms of foreign trade because of too much government regulation, political interference in investment decisions, an overvalued exchange rate that protected domestic manufacturers, and especially the political reversal to the market-oriented reforms of the 1960s. . . . No effective reform [in the economists' view] would occur without accompanying political change. By 1983 the leadership . . . concurred and appointed a party commission to discuss the political system. The commission's preliminary proposals for amendments to the 1974 Constitution entered public debate in 1985. So the entire constitution of the state was open for criticism and revision at the same time as the systematic shocks of drastic austerity and proposals to curtail the economic powers and resources of governments. . . .

The problem . . . led to major political quarrels between the republics and the federal government over the federal budget, taxation, and jurisdiction over foreign trade and investment. Expectations of greater economic integration were not realized. Instead, the result by the end of the decade was a breakdown in all elements of the domestic order, political disintegration, and rising nationalism.[54]

Into this maelstrom stepped the IMF and its associated consortium of foreign banks holding Yugoslav debt. Amidst a general social and political deterioration, the obvious solution was for the central Yugoslav economic authorities to recapture the requisite financial controls.

While signs of social dislocation and anomie were growing at the mass level, the restrictive monetary, fiscal, and foreign trade policies also required a fundamental change in political authority over economic assets—specifically, over the social property rights of governments. In contrast to the extreme territorial decentralization of the 1970s, these emergency policies required federal assertion of economic authority over the republics, leaving little room for negotiation. . . . And, perhaps most significant, control over foreign exchange operations and allocation was returned to the National Bank in Belgrade; only five years earlier, as part of decentralization, the assets and debits of the balance of payments of this same bank had been distributed among republican governments, and they had been granted corresponding authority for foreign economic relations.[55]

It would take us too far afield to draw out the complexities of the disintegration process, the differing interests of each of the republics, the compounding nature of the struggle over Kosovo's status, or the pulling and hauling among various groups in each republic holding different views on the directions policy should take regarding centralization, economic liberalization, and pursuit of the IMF reform package. In the event, however, regardless of how historians may reinterpret this period, it is clear that the policy package the IMF/bank consortium (supported by many Yugoslav economists) required for helping Yugoslavia cope with its financial crisis was one of the central factors in the secession of Croatia and Slovenia and in the dynamics of the country's disintegration. "The primary problem . . . lay in the lack of recognition and accommodation for the socially polarizing and politically disintegrating consequences of this IMF-conditionality program. . . . The architects of the programs of macroeconomic stabilization and economic austerity ignored the necessity of creating not only social safety nets but even more important a political capacity to recognize and manage these conflicts."[56]

In Woodward's analysis, economic reform in socialist transition entails changes that "fundamentally alter the existing distribution of rights and power." In Yugoslavia, the program, *inter alia*, recentralized monetary policy, stripped exporters of their nonmarket allocation rights over foreign exchange, made the central bank independent of political influence, and increased the effectiveness of the federal government over economic matters. "Technocratic" assumptions led to "a fateful confrontation over the nature of the state." In fact, the economic program and its legitimating rhetoric of free enterprise and property rights encouraged autonomous demands by regional or local governments and by politicians who could exploit the exclusionary language of nationalism and its narrowing definition of those entitled to rights in a time of cuts.[57]

The Yugoslav case was not typical of the countries we are concerned with here. The former Yugoslavia was much more advanced economically. Both its economic organization and its political structure were unique, even among the socialist states. Few if any developing nations, even among the large federally structured countries, approach its degree of decentralization. Thus, for a state failure and a civil war that can be attributed in significant part to an economic reform process, Yugoslavia stands out as an exceptional, probably unique, case. Nevertheless, it is a powerful illustration of the dangers of approaching economic reform in a deeply divided society as a technocratic problem, and of the importance of understanding the intricate connections between even single strands of reform and the distribution of rights among competing groups. It shows how orthodox or mainstream stabilization measures, in the guise of institutional changes, can exacerbate a conflict situation, especially where the lines that demarcate the assignment of economic rights coincide with ethnogeographic fault lines. The fact that the disintegration unfolded over more than a decade, and was the result of the interaction of many factors, among which the economic were salient, suggests that early decisions and interventions by the international players different from those actually taken, and more carefully calibrated to take account of Yugoslavia's particular conflict potentialities, might have produced a happier outcome by having more benign effects on the noneconomic factors at play.

Yugoslavia remained viable as long as its "delicate balancing act in the international arena" and its system that "provided government protections of social and economic equality and of shared sovereignty among its many nations" held together. "[T]he cracks in the system were not the fault lines between civilizations that came together in the Balkans, but those that defined the country's domestic order and international position during the socialist period. The country's institutions of civil order and common purpose were the object of erosion and attack, and division occurred according to the system of national defense, the concurrent rights and jurisdictions of the political and economic system, and social strata."[58] The viability of other multiethnic countries with relatively short independent histories in their present configurations may also depend on delicate balancing acts and domestic systems of allocation of rights, including economic rights, that are often affected by aid projects and by aid conditionality and the intellectual influence of the international agencies.

Conflicts Contained, Conflicts Avoided: Some Aid Assists

Malaysia: Conflict Prevention as the Political–Economic Core

Malaysia is often cited, and much studied, as perhaps the world's outstanding case of successful management of interethnic relations, a country where ethnicity was long at the core of national politics. At independence in 1957,

Malaya, as it was first known, comprised only the former peninsular Malay States; in 1963, with the addition of Sarawak and Sabah (and for a brief period Singapore), the name Malaysia was adopted. A Communist insurgency the British had been fighting since 1948 had been marginalized by the time of independence, the remaining few hundred combatants having fled to refuge in the jungles of southern Thailand. As an anticolonial struggle, this first internal conflict is of interest to us only for an ironic unintended consequence. Although virtually all the insurgents were ethnic Chinese, their efforts to appeal to the Chinese plantation and mine workers (to operate as "fish" in a "sea" of sympathetic discontents, following Mao Zedong's famous dictum for guerrilla warfare) had an opposite effect. The British gathered the Chinese workers into new villages to secure them from insurgent contact. By giving them tenant rights and proof of residence and citizenship, the village settlement strategy amounted to a program for inclusion, turning large numbers of potentially disaffected ethnic Chinese into stakeholders in the new country's success.

The Malayan constitutional structure was based on a "bargain" between the Malay and Chinese elites, brokered with good offices of Great Britain as the decolonizing power. Under the bargain, the Chinese acceded to Malay predominance in the armed forces, politics, and the civil service. In return, the Chinese were granted citizenship, civil and political rights, and a guarantee against economic confiscation. As in Thailand and elsewhere in Southeast Asia, the ethnic Chinese minority was generally wealthier and more urbanized than the majority ethnicity, and was predominant (along with expatriate enterprises) in the country's commerce. Except for the Singapore city-state where the Chinese formed a large majority, Malaysia was unique in the region in that its ethnic Chinese minority comprised a relatively substantial fraction, roughly one-third of the total population, while the "indigenous" Malays numbered a bare majority. Many Chinese families in fact had a longer history of local residence than many Malays, whose forebears were more recent arrivals from Sumatra. Nevertheless, the Chinese based their claim to equal citizenship rights on their residence and economic contribution, without contesting the Malay self-definition as the native "sons of the soil." Rather than asserting rival claims to a mutually exclusive national identity, the two communities (and the much smaller ethnic Tamil community) adopted an overarching pluralist national identity. Affirmative action, initially not very extensive, was to be employed to improve the relative economic position of the Malays. Malay was to become the sole official language over ten years, but Parliament might then extend the use of English as an official language. This was a bargain "steeped in the ethnic division of labor and in the use of time to allay insecurities on both sides."[59]

The political viability of this bargain was ensured by the inclusive and consociational relationship among the three ethnic elites. Unlike in many other deeply divided polities (including Sri Lanka), the principal ethnicity-based political parties formed an electoral Alliance. This arrangement avoided the polarization that would have resulted from a system that offered rival single-ethnicity alternatives in winner-take-all constituencies. While the Alliance has lost control of some important subnational jurisdictions with religiously conservative Malay majorities, the coalition has won every national election since independence. These multiethnic victories have ensured ethnic representation in every governmental cabinet.

In 1971, in response to four days of interethnic rioting in May 1969, the government launched a new economic program that included affirmative-action policies more far-reaching than anything envisioned at the time of the independence bargain. The rioting had not spread beyond the capital (Kuala Lumpur). The official death toll was less than 200; the unofficial toll was several hundred higher. Although this was the first interethnic violence since independence in 1957, and would rank as a mild and isolated breakdown compared with ethnic violence elsewhere, the Malaysian elites were profoundly shocked. They drew the conclusion that economic and education policies would have to be thoroughly revamped to avoid further conflict by changing the ethnic structure of the country's economy. The New Economic Policy (NEP) introduced in 1971, and the adjustments and continuities over the next three decades, represent probably the most thoroughgoing and successful attempt any developing country government has made to design a conflict-avoiding development strategy. Though the NEP has included "affirmative action" preferences similar to those employed in India, the United States and elsewhere, the Malaysian program has aimed at comprehensive structural change unmatched in scope by other countries that have attempted to regress group imbalances through inclusion rather than expropriation. As such, the Malaysian experience has figured importantly in the literature on ethnic conflict, quite apart from its interest to students of economic development for its outstanding growth performance.

The NEP had two overarching objectives. First was the formal aim of all developing countries, to reduce poverty. Second, crafted to fit Malaysia's particular circumstances, was "to accelerate the process of restructuring Malaysian society to correct economic imbalance, so as to reduce and eventually to eliminate the identification of race with economic function."[60] Quantitative targets were set for 1990. The targets included the raising of Malay employment in all industrial and occupational groups to levels proportionate to their share of the overall population, and an increase of Malay corporate ownership from its minor 2.4 percent share in 1970 to 30 percent by 1990.

To accomplish this ambitious restructuring of the ethnic composition of the economy without imposing any costs on the wealth or employment of the Chinese and Indian minorities, the economy would have to grow at a rapid clip over the two-decade period, and the increase in the share of Malay corporate ownership would have to be at the expense of the foreign ownership share, but not through expropriation.

To carry out the restructuring, the NEP called for appropriate policies for "rural modernization"; boosting growth in the economically lagging, mainly Malay, regions; facilitating Malay urbanization; nurturing a Malay entrepreneurial class through interethnic joint ventures and small business support programs. Development in the lagging areas was promoted through large public investment in rice irrigation (the World Bank–supported Muda River project); land settlement projects for rubber and oil palm smallholders; and regional development in the predominantly Malay East Coast province of Kuantan. While these programs passed economic muster, the principal motivations were ethnic and political.[61] The NEP mandated extensive affirmative action policies, interventions favoring Malay access to higher education and greater Malay participation in the markets for labor, land, and capital, where they had previously been underrepresented. The government issued a multitude of targets, quotas, and regulations applying to both the public and private sectors. Private companies controlled by non-Malays had to sell 30 percent of their stock to Malays, at a discount, in order to be eligible for government contracts or to be listed on the stock exchange. New public-sector agencies were created to finance and operate commercial and industrial enterprises, either wholly owned or joint ventures, as instruments for enlarging Malay participation in the modern growth sectors. These were known as "trusteeship agencies." They would accumulate assets, mainly shares of newly formed industrial and commercial enterprises, holding them for future distribution when Malays would be in position to acquire them.

It would be misleading to spell out these policies, and how they have evolved over the past three decades, as a template to apply to other divided societies. The details and adjustments would form a micro-account of particularities too local for formulaic application. Instead, we should identify the basic reasons for the viability of the NEP. First, the policies were worked out with great care and professionalism in a transparent process that included public participation and heated debate. Second, the government sold the NEP as a win-win program for all the society's ascriptive groups; the disproportionate Malay gains were to come out of the *increments* to national economic growth, increments that (the government pledged to ensure) would be large enough to amplify non-Malay incomes as well. Third, the poverty-reduction programs were cast as ethnically neutral; the non-Malay poor would also participate, although the fact that most of the poor were Malay meant that poverty reduction would be tantamount to narrowing the ethnic income gap. Fourth, the affirmative action programs were implemented very flexibly. For example, the 4:1 Malay to non-Malay quota for the civil service was not applied to the professional and technical branches, which were administratively separate from the general civil service and which were important avenues for minority public-sector employment. Fifth, the program was conducted within a framework of orthodox fiscal, exchange rate, and monetary policies. Policy emphases were changed over time as economic circumstances changed. Most important was the shift in emphasis from affirmative action to macroeconomic revival and efficiency in 1986 in response to a slump in overall economic growth.

If any ethnically divided and structurally unbalanced society were today considering a comparable affirmative action strategy, it would probably face a policy debate similar to Malaysia's in the early 1970s. Critics warned of the potentials for unintended and undesirable consequences. The emphasis on economic growth would succeed and would trump over redistribution; the Chinese would end up with an even greater share of the national wealth. (In the early 1970s the development economics community was hotly debating the proposition that redistribution was incompatible with high savings and growth.) Alternatively, GNP growth would fall well below target in any case, not high enough to yield much of a per capita increment to satisfy Malay expectations; some expropriation of non-Malay wealth might emerge that would exacerbate rather than ease ethnic relations. Or the Malay increment would be substantial but would be captured by an insider elite, creating new class divisions within the Malay community. The radical critique viewed the NEP's restructuring prong as "a justification for massively increasing official support for the emerging Malay business class, while its poverty prong is regarded as a propaganda cover for the restructuring policy and not to be taken seriously as a guide to action."[62] Summing up the uncertainties at the NEP's inception, Donald Snodgrass concluded that "while it is plausible to believe, as official ideology contended, that a society with smaller economic disparities among ethnic groups would be a more unified society, it was also clear that the prescribed route to such a state of affairs was fraught with risks of increasing discord. At the very least, the NEP would require careful economic and political management."[63]

It may be interesting to note, nearly three decades later, that the debate (as far as I have been able to determine) did not confront the NEP program with the central objection that would be raised by proponents of today's orthodoxy for developing countries. The fiscal and monetary conservatism, of course, would continue to be applauded. But the affirmative action policies would be criticized for their substantial government intervention into the operation of the country's labor, capital, and land market systems. The interventions would introduce partially administered rather than market-determined allocation of some resources, would impose some constraints on foreign investors, which they would not face in other countries competing for foreign capital, and would introduce significant rent-seeking opportunities in an economy previously known for low corruption and high bureaucratic probity. The essence of the NEP was to establish distributional outcomes intentionally very different from what was most likely (and believed most likely) to eventuate if the market economy were left to its own dynamic devices. In a word, the NEP promised substantial deviations from what became known as "the Washington consensus."

The basic political decisions and broad policy thrusts were local creations. The handful of resident foreign advisers (mostly UNDP-financed) were strongly supportive and provided useful technical analysis. World Bank staff, including then chief economist Hollis Chenery, also endorsed the NEP and provided the usual independent comment and recurrent monitoring that characterized the Bank's relationships with clients not in crisis. Would the World Bank and the development economics community generally adopt the same stance toward an NEP-scale interventionist program today? Despite the skeptical reviews that affirmative action programs in developing countries have had, the Malaysian experience provides evidence of the potentiality for positive results.

The upshot of the Malaysian experience has been most evident in the absence of any racial tensions, any ascriptive perspectives, in the political turmoil and economic setback of 1998 to 1999. One thirty-year retrospective written in May 1999 on the results of the riots and the policy response concluded that

> By any standards, this social experiment . . . has been a success in promoting racial harmony and preventing further bloodshed. . . . [S]ince the present financial crisis erupted nearly two years ago, the country hasn't witnessed even a hint of ethnic tension.
>
> Malaysia's racial tranquillity stands in sharp contrast to the situation in neighbouring Indonesia, where ethnic violence has erupted repeatedly over the past year. So profound have the social changes been that, in the absence of political instigation, most analysts say that a spontaneous outburst of racial violence is now highly unlikely.
>
> Indeed, the regular and occasionally violent street demonstrations that followed Prime Minister Mahathir Mohamad's ouster and imprisonment of his former deputy, Anwar Ibrahim, are seen by some as evidence of the country's underlying harmony. That such demonstrations could take place without a hint of racial sentiment—previously the slightest sign of unrest

often sparked near-panic among Malaysia's minority races—is offered as proof of how much the country has changed.[64]

Also remarkable has been the shift in the focus of political contestation. From before Malayan independence (1957), through the creation of Malaysia (1963), the expulsion of Singapore (1965), and the programs for reshaping the economy and society in the wake of the 1969 riots, the core problem of the Malaysian polity was interethnic relations. In sharp contrast, the political turmoil sparked by the recent financial crisis has been intraethnic, internal to the Malay segment of the population. The reasons were twofold. One source of Malay division has been personal rivalry within the ruling party leadership. The other has been the ability of the main opposition Malay party (known as Pas) to attract voters disenchanted with the problems of corruption, widening income disparities within the Malay community, politicization of the police and the judicial system, and authoritarianism, which have developed over the long uninterrupted rule of the coalition under the dominant Malay party and Mahathir Mohamad, its prime minister. Thus far, the Pas constituency has comprised mainly East Coast Malays drawn to the party's Islamic orientation that contrasts with Mahathir's strong opposition to religious fundamentalism. Because the Malay population comprises a bare majority, the split of the Malay vote between two ethnicity-based parties has meant that neither party can achieve a parliamentary majority without ethnic Chinese minority support. (The contrast with Sri Lanka is striking. With the Sinhalese over 80 percent of the total population, the rival Sinhalese parties have competed for parliamentary majorities without a necessity to form interethnic electoral alliances.) Recognizing this electoral logic, Pas has pursued social policies (for example, respecting public attire of Islamic women) in a manner carefully designed to avoid creating serious anxiety among the Chinese. It remains to be seen if the recent Pas electoral alliance with the opposition Chinese-based party can develop the endurance of the Alliance partnership.

The startling terrorist incidents in July 2000 committed by a tiny and obscure group, allegedly fundamentalist, served as a warning that even Malaysia may not be immune to the kind of religious-based violence seen in Indonesia and the Philippines.[65] The prime minister's play of the racial card in September 2000—a verbal attack on the "extremism" of a nonpartisan grouping of 2,000 NGOs of largely Chinese membership—was seen as an outlandish outbidding move against Pas, and apparently aroused only a tepid ethnic Malay response.[66] Nevertheless, the strength of Malaysia's conflict-avoidance institutions and policies, and the sensitivity of the bulk of the population regarding anything smacking of overt ethnic hostility, makes it likely that extremist ethnoreligious outbidding will remain a marginal phenomenon.

The changes cited by Malaysia watchers as responsible for the abatement of the traditional habit of using interethnicity as the lens for viewing and interpreting fundamental issues are largely economic. Growth of GDP averaged nearly 7.5 percent a year for most of the 1965 to 1980 period, slowing to a 5.2 percent average between 1980 and 1990, and soaring to over 8 percent in the 1990s before the financial crisis in 1998. The percentage of the Malay population living below the poverty income line was a very high 74 percent in 1970. Only 6 percent of all Malaysians were below the poverty line in 1994. (A straight comparison for Malays alone was no longer possible after the government stopped issuing poverty figures by ethnic group.) The Malay share of national wealth rose from 1.5 percent in 1969 to 19.4 percent in 1998. Thanks to rapid overall growth and a relative decline in the share of national wealth owned by foreigners despite large inflows of foreign direct and portfolio investment, the share owned by the ethnic Chinese minority also rose substantially over this period, from 22.8 percent to 38.5 percent. Increases in Malay education attainment were also substantial, laying the basis for the functional diversification of the Malay labor force that was a major objective of the NEP. By the mid-1980s, the unemployment effects of an economic recession were too diverse ethnically to raise issues of communal distribution of market setbacks.[67]

Regional income differentials persisted, however, reflecting regional differences in resource and location endowments, differences that translated into lower per capita income levels for the predominantly Malay populations living in the relatively disadvantaged areas. Whatever the barriers had been to Malay economic mobility—limited education and skill attainment, limited access to credit, ascriptive hiring practices, traditional occupational orientation, and other factors—they had been substantially overcome by the late 1990s, thanks to internal labor mobility, human capital investments, affirmative action programs, and growth of the economy as a whole.

A functional and sectoral distribution of the labor force completely proportional to the country's ethnic composition was never intended. The purpose of the affirmative action and market-intervening programs and policies was to approach proportionality sufficiently to vitiate the common perceptions of ethnoeconomic boundaries and concentrations, to narrow substantially the income gaps prevailing up to the 1970s, and to reduce the imbalance of economic power and ownership to a point where it was no longer a political problem in the eyes of the Malays. These goals appear to have been achieved for the Malay–Chinese relationship. While the ethnic Indian minority has fared less well, posing a continuing challenge of equity, there is no sign that their lagging participation in the country's income growth is causing their radicalization or any ethnic mobilization for mounting a challenge to the state.

As will be discussed further below, Malaysia appears to have retained the flexibility to make substantial adjustments in the affirmative action strategy. Between the progress toward the NEP targets and the increased dependence of the Malay parties on Chinese voters, the stage has been set for a gradual easing or dismantling of the preferences system. In contrast with the first NEP easing in the mid-1980s, which was driven by the needs for macroeconomic adjustment and growth revival, this second round derived from a perception (not shared by rural Malays, to be sure) that the country's competitiveness and economic growth under the new conditions of the world economy would be compromised if the structural inhibitions of the NEP were not further relaxed.

I began this account of Malaysian experience by noting that the country is judged an outstanding example of conflict-avoidance policy-making and management. A comparison with the violent outcomes in many other countries readily supports such a judgment even though, admittedly, the kudos are based on a counterfactual proposition, namely that conflict would have recurred absent the policies and root changes that have been pursued since 1969, and absent the interethnic political coalition that created, and was dependent upon, those policies. In Donald Horowitz's view, "Malaysia's considerable conflict potential has been reduced by the creation of an interethnic center, almost in spite of itself—that is, an interethnic coalition that occupies the middle ground and that, whatever the actual beliefs and sentiments of its members and leaders, fosters interethnic accommodation."[68] Needless to say, these kudos do not imply that Malaysia is a utopia, a country without political, judicial, or economic shortcomings. The kudos also do not imply any overlooking of the fact that some of the policies judged successful in the framework of conflict avoidance have caused problems from other perspectives. For example, the NEP created opportunities for cronyism and insider access to reserved shares, and it has generated considerable Chinese irritation over the higher-education quotas. However, if one accepts the widely held counterfactual proposition, and takes account of the above-average economic growth and poverty-reduction performance the policy framework has helped to bring about, then the presumption is reasonable (incontestable, in my view) that the benefits of the actual outcomes greatly outweigh the costs or possible missed opportunities incurred.

Thailand: Learning and Foresight

Thailand is usually thought of as relatively homogeneous, both culturally and ethnically. About 95 percent of its 60 million people are Buddhist, speak Thai (or a closely related cognate of the Tai language group) as their mother tongue, and identify themselves as ethnic Thai or, in the case of the Sino-Thai, as highly assimilated while perhaps retaining some Chinese traditions. There are a number of small minorities linguistically and/or more or less culturally related to the Thai, such as the Khmer living in provinces bordering Cambodia, and the "Hill Tribes" in northern mountainous areas. The largest minority that is culturally quite distinct (though bilingual) is the Malay Muslims who form a local majority in the southern area bordering Malaysia. Among the "Thai" majority there are many groups that retain distinctive identities of language or dialect pronunciation, traditions, or local religious particulars, but whose bilingualism and overarching adherence to Buddhism make inclusion in "Thai-ness" a comfortable reality for themselves, other Thais, and the state. As of the mid-1980s, one anthropologist could write that

> For the most part, these people are not pushing for formal political recognition for their communities, largely because the way in which *chat Thai* ("Thai nation") is defined makes it possible for people to have distinctive identities and still see themselves and be seen by others as "Thai.". . . Even peoples . . . speaking distinctive domestic languages and following distinctive cultural traditions, have become sufficiently bilingual and bicultural to find no difficulty in also identifying as Thai. This "Russian doll" relationship between local ethnic identities and national identity is easiest for those who adhere to Buddhism and speak Thai fluently as a first or second language.[69]

Three episodes of ethnic conflict stand out in Thailand's modern history, one of which involved an extended violent insurgency. Although these conflicts figure prominently in the Thai literature, Thailand seldom appears in the conflict literature.[70] The reason is that Thai governments managed to develop effective policy responses to mitigate or remove the root causes that might otherwise have fueled more serious conflict than what actually took place. As these episodes flowed to some extent from root causes similar to those operating in other countries that have not avoided deterioration into severe violent conflict, it will be instructive to review the Thai experience.

In the first episode, over a number of years before and after World War II, Thai governments pursued prejudicial and repressive policies against the local ethnic Chinese minority, which could have generated violent response. In the second, Thailand had a simmering low-level conflict that many saw as essentially a Cold War phenomenon, one of the interrelated Communist insurrection-cum-subversion struggles of Southeast Asia that more or less simultaneously challenged the governments in South Vietnam, Cambodia, Laos, Thailand, and Malaysia, in the wake of World War II. The third was a Malay separatist movement in the south.

Ethnic Chinese Exclusion. In the 1930s the Thai military elite who had seized power from the country's ancient absolute monarchy began a program of discrimination against the ethnic Chinese minority comprising roughly 15 percent of the population. In previous centuries, Thai kings had encouraged the immigration of Chinese who would create a commercial sector and man the tin mines, occupations in which neither the Thai royal and bureaucratic elites nor the Thai peasantry evinced any interest. After World War I, the elite began to view the Chinese commercial dominance (along with the European companies that had predominated in the country's banking and international trade) with disfavor, a view not necessarily shared by the peasantry. The elite believed that Chinese merchants and moneylenders were exploiting the farmers and engaged in market-rigging collusion. (Research in the 1950s showed that the allegations of farmer exploitation were bogus. Competition among the Chinese merchants buying Thai small-farmer produce kept the merchants' farmgate profit margins razor thin.) The Thai elite's economic suspicions were compounded by observation of the minority's sympathy with China after the onset of the Sino–Japanese war in 1937. Before World II and then into the early 1950s, policies were promulgated to block Chinese participation in certain occupations, to impose a special tax on the Chinese community, to limit Chinese language usage and Chinese schools, to require adoption of Thai names, to prevent Chinese aliens (who still comprised a majority of the local Chinese in 1940) from owning land, and to establish state enterprises to compete with Chinese-owned business or to preempt the manufacture of new products in the nascent industrial sector.[71] Although the rationale for these policies was ethnic nationalism, not command-economy ideology, the country appeared to be heading down the path of etatism and the undermining of the fiscal and monetary conservatism that had been the hallmark of Thai economic policy for the previous hundred years.

It may be argued that similar racist policies that engendered violent response in other countries would not have caused a violent challenge from the Thai Chinese, given their relatively small numbers, their internal divisions by dialect and province of origin in China, and their concentration in Bangkok under the center of Thai power. In any event, such a what-if was never tested. The Thai military–political leadership was willing to be bought off, the discriminatory and preemptive programs were implemented loosely and ineffectively, and the Thai propensities for compromise and accommodation won out over the impulses for divisiveness and confrontation. If vigorously pursued, the anti-Chinese policies would have hobbled the country's economic development, a more certain what-if, with serious consequences for the second conflict-risk, which emerged during the Cold War. Fortunately, a change of government through a coup in 1957 brought about a policy reversal. The new regime dropped anti-Sinicism, which had never penetrated deeply into Thai society, and the accompanying creation of state (or "bureaucratic") capitalism. In their place the government adopted the basic policy framework and institutions for enhancing development under a market economy system. Without etatism, economic policy became ascriptively neutral; development trumped ethnicity as the central concern of the state, apart from security. The powerful encouragements afforded to the private sector under the new regime and subsequent administrations gave a wide berth to the Chinese business class. The collapse of anti-Sinicism and the many years of Sino–Thai intermarriage and cultural assimilation have brought about the most successful integration and inclusion in Southeast Asia of an "overseas Chinese" ethnic minority. The number of Chinese descendants who speak Chinese as a first, or even second language, or who can read Chinese, has been dwindling for two or more generations.

Ethnoregional Exclusion. The second social threat, the insurgency of the Communist Party of Thailand, had potentialities of a different sort. The initial impetus and the insurgency's financial support came from outside Thailand, and thus were problems of international subversion. The fear that the insurgency might grow into a major conflict derived from the possibility that the insurgency might appeal successfully to important ethnic groups that had grounds for disaffection. The largest of these ethnicities was the Isan, or Thai–Lao. The Isan comprised nearly one-third of the Thai population as a whole, and was (and is) the largest ethnic group of the Northeast region. While the language and cultural distinctions between the Isan and the central and Bangkok Thai may now appear to have been small compared with ethnic marker differences in many countries experiencing conflict, the differences were vivid to both sides, historically and into the post–World War II years. The heavy hand of the central government was imposed on the Northeast only in the late nineteenth and early twentieth centuries. Prior to this time, the Northeast and other outlying regions of the Thai (then "Siamese") state were governed indirectly, through local elites. Siam moved to closer incorporation and consolidation of these regions as a measure to stave off colonial encroachments from France and Britain. Although the Siamese geopolitical program succeeded in maintaining the country's independence, it laid the basis in the Northeast for a rebellion during 1901 and 1902, and for subsequent disaffection and separatist sentiment.

The Communist Party of Thailand (CPT), illegal since 1947, focused on the Northeast starting in the 1950s. The party's Sino–Thai leadership expected to recruit an Isan following based on the region's poverty; its resentments over economic neglect by, and cultural disdain from, Bangkok and the central Thai; and the government's repression of Northeast political leaders.

Thus, although the Cold War context so basic to conflicts in Southeast Asia (and elsewhere, of course) of that era no longer figures in the conflicts of today or the conflicts likely to occupy the international community in the years ahead, the local elements or roots of many of the earlier conflicts are similar to the sources of many post–Cold War internal conflicts. In the Thai case, it was a mix of class and ethnic factors.

> Prior to 1976, the CPT had only very limited success in convincing people that it understood the root causes of inequality and repression in Thai society and that it offered a realistic means to eliminate those causes. For the most part, the people who joined the CPT insurrection were motivated as much by ethnic as by class concerns. In northeastern Thailand, the concerns were those of the Lao . . . populace relative to the dominant Thai; in the North they were those of the tribal peoples, especially the Hmong and Karen; and in the South they were those of the Malay Muslim peoples living in a Buddhist state.[72]

Despite the potentialities these differences and grievances offered for the CPT, and despite the windfall the CPT received when military government repression in the mid-1970s, especially of middle-class university students, drove the young opposition into the ranks of the only organization posing an armed challenge to the dictatorship, the insurrection failed to spark a large response. On the contrary, at its peak in 1979 the CPT had perhaps 14,000 under arms and perhaps 2 million villagers (out of a population of about 45 million) under party influence or control; by late 1982 the CPT was near collapse.

How was this conflict successfully managed and eliminated? Proponents of response by force argued for a number of years with those who believed that other means such as political appeal, regional administrative reform, and/or expansion of economic infrastructure and social services would be more effective. The emphases and substance of Thai government strategy swung back and forth between these views. At times, both strategies were pursued at once, with the military command in one region favoring force and the command in another region favoring reform and local development. Proponents of a nonmilitary strategy to undercut CPT support by addressing root causes of Northeast alienation finally won the upper hand in the late 1970s. External factors also turned favorable, primarily the decision by China to suspend its propaganda and financial support of the CPT. At the risk of oversimplifying a complex history of a conflict that waxed and waned over several decades, the principal domestic factors were as follows:

1. refugees fleeing Communist victories in neighboring Laos and Cambodia bringing to Northeast villagers firsthand accounts of unpleasant effects of Communist rule;
2. the substitution of amnesty and rural development in place of force;
3. retraining of local officials to change the character of official–villager relations, from arrogance and exploitation to cordiality and development program assistance;
4. assignment of the best officials to the provinces involved, in place of the traditional personnel practice of treating the Northeast as a Siberia for the worst bureaucrats;
5. heavy investment in the previously neglected transportation, power, water, and health and educational facilities of the region; and
6. the autocratic methods of the CPT that repulsed the urban students who were seeking (in "the jungle") a democratic alternative to the military autocracy they had fled in the first place.

In sum, external support helped build, then deserted the conflict; the insurgent party understood the rural/ethnic mobilization potentialities, but misunderstood and squandered its potential as an alternative for the students; the government pursued mixed strategies (finally opting for nonmilitary solutions) that addressed Northeast grievances—neglect, poverty, and the exploitation and overbearing behavior of local officialdom—sufficiently to minimize Isan response to the call for conflict mobilization.

The external aid agencies played a significant part in both these conflict management experiences. As far as the donors were concerned, the reversal and cancellation of the anti-Sinic program was an unintended, although inherent and essential, consequence of the strategic policy reform they were advising and assisting on development grounds, and of technically driven aspects of specific sectoral projects. In retrospect, the ethnic inclusion implications and effects of the donor activities are clear and worth citing as examples of conflict-potential alleviation at the roots level. A general development blueprint, including the policy and institutional requirements for a shift toward substantial reliance on private investment and ownership, was drawn up by the World Bank.[73] The USAID funded policy studies and promotional projects aimed at stimulating private, especially foreign, investment. A critical reform component recommended (then monitored) by donor investment-policy advisors was a government commitment not to initiate any state enterprise production that would compete with private enterprises investing in Thailand under the new promotional framework. Resident foreign technical advisors strengthened related policy analysis capabilities of the nascent Thai planning organizations. Very important was the recognition and backing the donors gave to reinforce the intellectual and moral authority of the small first postwar generation of modern technocrats to whom the military looked for definition and management of development governance. The technocrats, virtually all of whom were schooled at European and American universities, included ethnic Thai, Chinese, and Sino–Thai. Their worldview was professional and inclusive. They viewed questions of income and asset distribution, labor force structure, and other economic issues, in the regional, class, and functional terms of standard economic analysis, in contrast to the ascriptive framework of previous economic management back to the 1930s.[74]

At the sectoral level, aid projects were instrumental in weaning government away from direct operation or preemption of functions better performed by markets and private enterprises. For example, under an extensive program of bridge, culvert, and highway construction, USAID introduced the idea of developing a private contracting industry capable of building transportation infrastructure. Before this program was undertaken, all such construction had been carried out by government agencies. The USAID-funded program was designed to assist local contractors, all small firms then capable only of constructing buildings, to replace direct government construction (i.e., to "privatize" road construction, long before privatization became dogma). By dividing highway and bridge projects into numbers of separate small contracts for short stretches of roadway, the infrastructure program was able to produce a secondary institutional benefit, the nurturing of a more efficient private construction sector.[75] The fact that this approach benefited the growth of then mainly ethnic Chinese contractors, facilitating the withdrawal of government from this function, was unintended per se, perhaps even unrecognized by USAID as a significant reversal of the policy of anti-Sinic preemption.

The concern of the Thai authorities and of aid donors (primarily the United States in the earlier years) to sustain stability in the Northeast region dates from the earliest years of post–World War II aid (starting in 1950), well before the CPT initiated armed conflict (1965) and before Charles Keyes's "Russian dolls" model had matured as the Thai ethnic paradigm. In their search for projects in the 1950s and 1960s to raise living standards in the Northeast, the donors (and the Thai government, of course) had few options. The region was entirely agricultural. It suffered from severe disadvantages compared with other areas of the country—poor soil and water, limited production of tradable commodities, locational and transport cost disadvantages, and poorly developed marketing systems. Unlike in the East Pakistan case, the donors sought out investment opportunities despite the virtual certainty, and the accumulating evidence even as early as the mid-1950s, that the rates of return on projects to raise Northeast agricultural productivity would be low, if not negative.

It is generally the case that the costs of installing and operating irrigation projects can be laid out in advance with considerable certainty, whereas projections of expected benefits depend on assumptions (of farmers' water use and choice of agronomic practices, crop patterns actually adopted, future prices, and so forth) that can be defended as "reasonable" within a wide range.

Moreover, the acceptability of the project then depends further on the minimum rate of return the sponsors employ as a standard for economic viability and on technical rules used for arriving at the benefit amounts to be compared with the costs (e.g., for how many years the analyst assumes the project will last). In the face of the gross failures of the first postwar round of small USAID-financed Northeast irrigation projects, the World Bank's first (medium-sized) irrigation project feasibility studies (in 1979, of the Lam Pao and Lam Takhong projects) met acceptability standards by making overoptimistic assumptions about crop diversity and how quickly production increases would be realized, and by understating the real cost of agricultural labor.

In the 1977 feasibility study of USAID's largest Northeast irrigation project, the Lam Nam Oon, similarly optimistic assumptions yielded a rate of return marginally above the cutoff point of unacceptability. The USAID study assumed a project life of fifty years and used an 8 percent discount rate to arrive at the present value of the future benefit stream for comparison with costs. If USAID had used the same assumptions as those behind the World Bank's Northeast irrigation feasibility studies, thirty-year project life and 15 percent discount rate, the projected economic return of Lam Nam Oon would have been unacceptably low.[76] In any case, the resources invested in Lam Nam Oon would have yielded greater benefits to the country's overall economic development at the time if they had been applied in other regions. Whether or not the project analysts deliberately manipulated their assumptions to push the rates of return above the rejection point, it was clear that the donors (subsequently including the Asian Development Bank and others) deliberately invested—if judged by efficiency criteria alone—suboptimally, by their own standards.

These irrigation projects are interesting as explicit illustrations of donor intent and flexibility (i.e., willingness), in a region of high sociopolitical importance, to fund projects with low probability of making effective contributions to poverty reduction. (At best, irrigation could provide only a small contribution to Northeast poverty reduction as the irrigation potential of the entire region was about 15 percent of its arable land.) Other development programs for addressing the relative backwardness of the Northeast region included (inter alia) investments in health and education programs similar to the nationwide efforts to develop the country's human capital. As such, the latter were not exceptional examples of donor response to conflict potentiality. (The human capital investments were arguably more effective than investments to raise output from within the region. As is often the case with resource-poor regions, outmigration of young trained adults and a return flow of remittances from their employment in faster-growing regions—including, in the Thai case, employment in the Middle East and elsewhere—have been major sources of increases in the backward region's per capita income.)

There were two other aid-financed projects in the Northeast region, however, worth particular mention as examples of activities designed to ameliorate what were seen as root causes of potential Isan disaffection. One was a project to establish an in-service academy for officials slated for appointment as district chiefs. Together with training to increase their administrative skills, the academy worked to instill democratic values and to motivate the trainees to substitute honest and sympathetic behavior in place of the traditional authoritarian attitude toward villagers. A large number of the academy graduates were assigned to the Northeast which became the preferred region for career advancement.

The second project was a large rural development effort that provided well drilling, sanitation, rural roads, and other facilities to villages and areas targeted for their apparent or assumed exposure and susceptibility to disaffection. The U.S. aid program in particular included several other projects designed to "win hearts and minds" in the Cold War jargon of the time, some not very effective in their implementation. The Thailand literature contains much controversy on the role of these activities, with some scholars maintaining that Thai culture and history insulated the Isan from conflict mobilization, quite apart from the efforts of these programs to create a sense of inclusion in a previously marginalized region. Others have argued that, notwithstanding such social assets, the relatively low level of insurgent mobilization would have grown had the specific sources of grievance not been addressed.[77] The latter was clearly the view of Thai governments during this period, perceiving the Isan conflict threat as "a crucial element in the determination of Thailand's future." Rural development in the Northeast became a central theme of government development planning.[78] My own judgment is that the two views should not be seen as mutually exclusive. The Thai government (as I have written elsewhere) "recognized the village-level problems that the insurgency could have turned to its purposes, gradually blanketed the insurgent areas with development programs and benefits, and restaffed and retrained the cadre of district officers. The government began with strong assets in villager predispositions and attachments to symbols of monarchy, religion, and country. Whatever it did was apparently sufficient to deny the CPT the social and economic 'asset' potential (of discontent and deprivation) on which a successful insurgency could have been built. Given the important role the U.S. aid program played in this denial process, it appears to deserve the credit accorded to it by those Thais who believe [the aid programs] made signal contributions to the restoration of stability."[79]

In sum, a low-level, violent insurgency was under way; the threat of wide conflict based on Isan economic and social grievances was credible; the government and aid donors made a considerable effort to address these grievances; the insurgency support gave out, and the feared wider conflict was avoided.

Malay Separatist Movement. The third area of potential violent conflict has been the small ethnoregional concentration of Malay Muslims along the Thai–Malaysia border. The area has been troubled recurrently by scattered lawlessness, by the southern wing of CPT activities, and by a movement aiming at separation from Thailand and incorporation within Malaysia. Although the separatist faction apparently developed considerable local support in the 1970s, its external support came from some distant Muslim countries, not from Malaysia. By the mid-1980s this movement also lost local support and withered. The populace and its mainstream political leadership preferred inclusion in the Thai state, while the state and, importantly, the Thai monarchy responded with inclusive measures apparently sufficient to undercut the potential appeal of separatism.

Note the contrast between the Thai and Malaysian cases in the role of economic policy reform and, specifically, the reliance on the operation of markets as a factor to reduce conflict potentiality. In Thailand, government reduced its market interventions and production preemption in order to abandon ethnic-Chinese minority discrimination. In Malaysia, government increased its market interventions and public-sector production activities in order to promote ethnic-Malay majority economic inclusion, in effect creating educational and other exclusions of the Chinese minority. In both cases, the minority was the richer ethnic group.

Underlying the differences of approach in the distributional (not macroeconomic or monetary) economic policies of the two countries were fundamental sociocultural contrasts. The ethnic Chinese in Thailand numbered 15 percent of the population, less than half the proportion in Malaysia; in important cultural respects (religion, cuisine, etc.) the differences between the Chinese and Thai were much less pronounced than was the case between the Chinese and Malays. In both cases, the economic policy responses were designed to narrow differences in income and functional distribution. The Thai strategy reinforced assimilation through inclusion; the Malaysian strategy, facing permanent, sharply defined, ethnic communities, pursued a long-run "separate but equal" outcome through affirmative action. The comparison illustrates an important, if simple, point—namely that conflict-management strategies in divided societies must be tailor-made for local circumstances. Two opposite strategies may both be effective, in their two different contexts. Finally, as far as the Isan minority problem was concerned, the programs of public works and other investment in the relatively backward ethnoregion compared with similar government efforts in the primarily Malay East Coast provinces of peninsular Malaysia.

Bhutan: Accommodation

The small Himalayan kingdom of Bhutan is an interesting example of an ethnically heterogeneous country that has managed its interethnic relations well, but has been overlooked in the conflict literature. Like Thailand, Bhutan is a Buddhist kingdom that avoided colonization, and that encouraged a foreign ethnic group to immigrate for purposes of economic development. Early in the twentieth century, a prominent Bhutanese family invited several elite Nepali families to settle in areas of southern Bhutan that were very sparsely populated.[80] Nepalis had been migrating out of densely populated Nepal for some time in search of arable land in the two districts that lie between Nepal and Bhutan (i.e., Sikkim and Darjeeling). By 1900 the Nepali immigrants had become the majority community in these two districts. By the 1920s a sizable ethnic Nepali population had moved into southern Bhutan. The relations between the Nepalis and the dominant indigenous Drukpas were peaceful and mutually beneficial for over a half century. Under an informal regional decentralization of authority, the Nepalis accepted Drukpa dominance at the center in exchange for considerable autonomy, and relatively greater economic development, in the Nepali areas. In the 1960s and 1970s, Bhutan invited another wave of Nepalis to work under contract on infrastructure projects. Subsequently, the government allowed them to remain, although they were technically illegal, as they were viewed as essential for implementing the country's development program. Until the 1980s the principal disputes were intraethnic, among the Drukpas.

In the 1970s and 1980s, the Drukpa/Nepali relationship was gradually becoming destabilized by ethnic politics and by crises involving Nepalis who had left Nepal to settle in neighboring areas of India. When large numbers of the latter were expelled from northeastern India, they moved illegally into southern Bhutan, which was thinly populated compared with the surrounding states. Concerned by the rise of the Nepali communities to political dominance in Sikkim and Darjeeling, and the threat to Bhutanese culture in the eyes of the Drukpa, Bhutan decided in the late 1980s to tighten its immigration policy and to force the illegal Nepali residents to leave the country. The expulsion was accomplished peacefully, as the government fully compensated those expelled for their property losses, even for land on which they had settled illegally. Although the expelled population was settled in camps inside Nepal, creating a border issue with the government of Nepal, and although for a time Nepali political parties in southern Bhutan had carried out a violent campaign to pressure Bhutan on its immigration policy, the long-term Nepali community in Bhutan has preferred that the camp residents inside Nepal not return to Bhutan. At the same time as the expulsion, the government introduced cultural protection policies similar to those that in some other countries have led to severe conflict; these policies included such as establishing the local language, Dzonka, as the national language, restricting the use of Nepali in southern schools, and requiring a dress code. These policies induced numbers of the legal Nepali residents to leave the country for Assam and West Bengal. A violent Nepali resistance movement in these areas was directed at southern Bhutan—in fact, aiming at the Nepalis who had decided to remain in Bhutan.

Stability has been restored within Bhutan, no doubt helped by government policies that have provided additional economic incentives for the long-term Nepali residents to remain. There has also recently been some peaceful movement of ethnic Nepalis from the south into the mountainous northern areas of the country that heretofore were populated only by Bhutanese. The policy of holding off potential inundation from the vastly more numerous Nepali populations in northeast India and Nepal itself has been successful thus far. It remains to be seen if Bhutan will continue its policy of tolerance and mutually beneficial relations with the local Nepali community, or if elements within the Drukpa elite who favor total expulsion succeed in turning Bhutan's ethnic policies toward hostility.

The Bhutanese experience to date illustrates an interethnic dynamic that has succeeded in avoiding a descent into widespread violent conflict, despite the considerable cross-border provocation. The key factors were (a) political divisions within the two ethnicities, the dominant view in each preferring maintenance rather than destruction of the status quo, and (b) the granting of economic rights to the minority, and the use of economic incentives to secure nonviolent resolution of minority grievances. There are parallels here with key factors in the Malaysian interethnic arrangements.

Mozambique: Preventing Conflict Recurrence

Mozambique is an interesting case for examining the conflict implications of development and reform processes in which donors play a significant part. Ever since the resolution in 1992 of the country's sixteen-year, postcolonial civil war, Mozambique has been favored by the international community for the adherence of the former combatants to the elections and other terms of the accords and for the creditable performance of the government. The country emerged from the civil war as one of the very poorest in the world. As an exception thus far to the common syndrome, that having fallen into civil war once, a country is at high risk to renewed conflict, Mozambique has been an important laboratory for postconflict reconstruction.

During the course of a World Bank study in 1997 of the Bank's role in this reconstruction, several Mozambican interlocutors complained that the privatization and other components of the government's economic program were favoring the region of the dominant (Shangane) ethnic group of the governing party (Frelimo), the country's deep south, and were aggrandizing members of that group's elite. (Frelimo is an acronym for the Front for the Liberation of Mozambique, one of the two combatant parties in the civil war.) The predominance of this ethnic group in the acquisition of privatized state enterprises (excluding selected large enterprises sold to foreign investors) may well have reflected (as asserted by the program's defenders) a dearth of entrepreneurial experience among other ethnicities in Mozambique. Critics also alleged that information about privatization opportunities was not available in areas removed from Maputo (the capital city, also located in the extreme south), that the successful capital-poor buyers could have purchased these enterprises only thanks to bank credit not easily accessible to other groups, and that the buyers were individuals who happened to be connected to the ruling political party. The critics also complained that infrastructure reconstruction, financed largely by donors, had been concentrated in the same southern area. Representatives of the opposition party, Renamo (the Portuguese acronym for the Mozambique National Resistance Party), told the study group that they knew nothing about the World Bank's projects or how beneficiary participation in Bank projects was determined or accessed.

The perception that the Shangane were benefiting disproportionately, at the expense of Renamo-supporting ethnic groups, was especially troublesome, threatening to reopen the same ethnic fault lines that had characterized the long civil war. Some of the complaints may have been unfounded, and some of the apparent allocation bias was unintentional or was driven by objective economic reconstruction priorities. For example, some of the regional differences in reconstruction activity up to that time were due to the lagging implementation of some donors compared with others; provinces had been divided among the donors for area, rather than functional sector, concentration. The highest regional priority had been placed on restoring the southern transportation corridor essential for South African exports, thereby a natural area for generating economic activity for Mozambique. The perception of regional imbalance in the reconstruction process may have been reinforced (a) by the fact that the Renamo-held areas during the conflict, which have remained Renamo electoral strongholds, suffered the greatest destruction, and began the reconstruction process from a lower base than Frelimo strongholds, and (b) by the limitation of World Bank and other aid projects undertaken during the war years to nonconflict areas, again primarily the south, a pattern that took time to adjust. These impressions and outcomes, to some extent only transitional, had created a perception of a reconstruction/reform process that was prejudicial to the interests not of the general nonelite across ethnicities (as in the Russian case referred to below), but to the interests of nonfavored ethnic areas and groups as a whole.

There are no signs of Mozambique moving back toward armed conflict. Both the government party Frelimo and Renamo (the party of the insurgents during the civil war) have adhered to the peace accords in one of Africa's most successful conflict-resolution cases. In the immediate postwar period, Mozambique faced the difficulties common to virtually all recent postconflict situations: demobilizing combatants, resettling refugees, clearing mine fields, distributing humanitarian relief until domestic production of food and other essentials can be revived, reviving economic activity, and conducting an election in a society with low literacy, often no previous electoral experience, and having suffered extensive destruction of its social capital and institutional infrastructure. With major donor assistance, these problems were overcome.[81]

Between the country's comparative political success and the government's responsible economic performance thus far in the postconflict period, Mozambique has gained international recognition as one of Africa's best conflict-resolution and postconflict peacekeeping and redevelopment cases.[82] Nevertheless, nine years (at this writing) is a short period after an eleven-year conflict of unusual ferocity, in a society that is among the very poorest in the world and has existed as a self-governing polity for only twenty-five years following nearly five centuries of colonial rule. Both the fragility of Mozambique's polity and the potential for a return of instability were demonstrated by the second elections, in December 1999, and their aftermath. Based on the increases it won in the nation's legislature, its capture of an additional province, and its narrow loss of the presidential count, Renamo claimed that it had been deprived of victory by election fraud. The party decided to boycott the legislature and to move its headquarters back to the town of Beira, its provincial stronghold. Although Frelimo could have invited Renamo to join in a consociational, power-sharing cabinet after each of the two postconflict national elections (as noted earlier), it has preferred to rule as the sole power ever since the fighting ended, exercising its winner-take-all authority in accordance with the electoral provisions of the country's constitution. This authority includes central government appointment, not popular election, of the provincial governors. The Frelimo government has refused to appoint any governors from the Renamo party even in the provinces with Renamo electoral majorities. Its refusal after the 1999 elections appeared to deepen the opposition's anger over these exclusions.

In a troubling development in August 2000, the government arrested five Renamo members, accusing them of planning a nationwide campaign of civil disobedience.[83] According to one Swedish study (Abrahamsson and Nillson, 1996), there were signs of discontent by 1996 among regional and ethnic elites who felt excluded, both economically and politically. The authors concluded that politics in Mozambique was becoming "ethnicised" and that ethnic groups were showing an early susceptibility to ethnopolitical mobilization. In effect, they sounded an "early warning":

> It is not yet common for the population groups of the rural areas to interpret the inadequate satisfaction of basic needs as an ethnic problem. In the case of the elites the situation is otherwise, and their public agitation in ethnic terms is rapidly being disseminated in public talk. . . . If the [1994] election results can be interpreted in territorial terms and not by socioeconomic differentiation, they provide at least a starting point for continuing territorial mobilisation of voter support in the next elections. Federalist demands can soon begin to emerge from this type of territorialisation of politics, followed later by separatist ones.
>
> We are not speaking of an imminent and acute risk of major subnational conflicts occurring, but it is nonetheless important to keep a sharp eye on the processes that can lead to these tensions, deeply rooted at territorial level, becoming acute contradictions.[84]

Both the government and the donors are aware of the dangers to Mozambique's stability. The donors have been pressing the government to take a more inclusive stance toward the opposition. The 1999 election results were interpreted as a popular reaction to an inadequate flow of resources to the poorest central provinces, a sign that the flow must be increased. Programs in agriculture, rural development, and education are being designed for decentralized implementation. Although these measures appeared to be an attempt by Frelimo to increase its electoral appeal in future elections, it remains to be seen whether the programs produce meaningful "inclusion" of Renamo leadership in the large areas where Renamo maintains majority popular support. The devil will be in the details, especially the extent to which the decentralized, local decision making and implementation can bypass the Frelimo governors. On the one hand, there is an inherent contradiction between the funding and management-decentralizing devices of donor-financed development programs and the political realities of an appointed and centralized government structure under one party's control on the other. Donor efforts to prevent capture of aid resources by the politically dominant tribes in Kenya provide examples of what can be attempted and the resistance such attempts might encounter.

In sum, Mozambique's postconflict experience serves to illustrate the potential dangers of ignoring—in a deeply divided society—ascriptive ownership patterns and unbalanced resource allocations that may result from reform and development processes that are initially conceived, perhaps only by the international agency backers, in technical and financial terms.

Mauritius: Ethnic Power-Sharing and Economic Equity Without Preferences

Mauritius is another ethnically divided country that was at risk to communal conflict but has successfully avoided becoming another entry in the conflict literature. Although it is a small island state in the Indian Ocean with a population of about a million inhabitants, no group of which can claim precolonial "indigenous" presence, the country's experience should not be overlooked as a remote anomaly. Just before independence in 1968, riots between (African ancestry) Creoles and (South Asian ancestry) Muslims—27 percent and 16 percent of the population, respectively; the largest group was South Asian Hindu, numbering 52 percent—appeared to presage a violent future.

Mauritius fortunately inherited from its British colonial period a parliamentary system to which the elites of all groups had become socialized. Despite recurrent economic strains and contentious politics among ethnicity-based parties, the country has avoided any recurrence of violence as a dispute-settlement recourse. Somewhat analagous to the Malaysian experience, the Mauritian political system has been consociational. Governments have been based on interethnic coalitions. Such coalitions have been virtually unavoidable under an electoral system designed to force coalition outcomes. The system was crafted precisely to reflect the country's demographic structure. As a democratic variant that has been more suitable and more conflict-avoiding in its outcomes than any unadjusted adoption of either the American or any West European electoral systems would have been, the Mauritian system serves as an example for the care that must be taken by the purveyors of "democracy assistance."

The series of electoral commissions that established the country's electoral system were careful to avoid democratic structures that might exacerbate the nation's ethnic divisions. For instance, single-member constituencies were considered but were dropped when it was realized that Hindus would be overrepresented. Likewise, the Muslim community pressed for a consociational system of separate voter rolls with a certain number of seats held for each community, but this idea was also abandoned as planners were concerned with promoting national unity, not preserving existing divisions. Thus, the parliamentary system in Mauritius was deliberately structured in a modified consociational fashion, with a nod to ever-present ethnic concerns.

The system contained twenty districts with three members from each district and an additional two from the island of Rodriguez. [A]dditional seats were allocated to "best losers" in order to ensure representation from all the country's major ethnic groups. The eight allocated seats also make it more difficult for one party to gain a majority of seats through votes alone, since more than 10 percent of seats are reserved. They thus encourage parties to run in coalitions. Members are elected through first-(three)-past-the-post rules, which impeded fragmentation, even though with low entry barriers numerous parties put up candidates and have a chance as "best losers." Finally, as in Japan, the system tends to give somewhat disproportionate power to rural districts with lower population than to urban districts.[85]

Also like Malaysia, successive Mauritian governments have pursued export-led development along with compensatory payments and safety nets for segments of the population who have not benefitted equally in the country's rise to second highest per capita income of sub-Sahara Africa. Sound growth-enhancing policies have enabled Mauritius to afford the fiscal costs of the compensatory and safety-net expenditures. Unlike Malaysia, however, the Mauritian compensations have been functionally based (e.g., for unemployed youth, or small-scale sugar producers), not affirmative action systems that would favor any one ethnic community over the others. The exigencies of coalition politics ensured that parties and governments avoided policy extremes, whether defined as Left or Right, or favoring one economic class over another or one ascriptive group over another. In an election in 1995, one party that departed from this pattern lost heavily after playing the ethnic card.

According to Deborah Brautigam (1997), several institutional factors have contributed to the ability of the political system to avoid polarization. There are effective arrangements for policy dialogue between government and representatives of business and organized labor. These have enabled the government to obtain private-sector agreement to austerity policies during periods of economic stress. Such agreements have given government the room "to adjust more rapidly than other African countries to external shocks and high levels of debt while keeping coalitions together through judicious use of side payments to the most vocal losers."[86] At bottom, the society's ability to sustain nonviolent dispute resolution has rested on its institutionalized processes and preferences for elite power-sharing. Mauritius, and Senegal and Botswana, have demonstrated how elite coalitions (or polyarchies) are more inclined than hegemonic regimes or permanent-majority democracies to accommodate ethnic groups in the interests of national unity. Donald Rothchild (1997) attributes this inclination to pragmatic elites' preferences for "cooperative types of encounters," and to their perception that conflicting claims can be reconciled.[87] If such arrangements do not unravel and give way to ethnic hegemony, they provide a growth-enhancing context in which the international agencies can contribute effectively to a country's economic development, and possibly help strengthen the underlying institutional arrangements and the empirical basis supporting the general perception of intergroup distributional equity within the country.

Notes

1. Nafziger and Auvinen, 1997, p. 35.

2. Lawrence Zirling, *Bangladesh: From Mujib to Ershad.* Dhaka, Bangladesh: University Press, 1994, pp. 4–7.

3. Mason and Asher, 1973, pp. 666–667.

4. Ibid., p. 671.

5. Ibid., p. 673, footnote 24.

6. Ibid., p. 675.

7. Ibid., p. 675. This account and interpretation of the World Bank's experience with respect to Pakistan/Bangladesh is reconfirmed in the recent, and second, history of the Bank by John Lewis et al.

8. The two previous paragraphs draw on personal communications with former USAID mission directors Maurice J. Williams and Joseph C. Wheeler, and with Eric Griffel and Townsend Swayze, USAID officials at the time; and on an interview with Wheeler in the U.S. Foreign Assistance Oral History Program, Association for Diplomatic Studies and Training, Arlington, VA, 1998.

9. Agency for International Development, *The Use of Program Loans to Influence Policy.* Evaluation Paper 1A. Washington, DC: USAID, 1970, p. 15.

10. See, e.g., the exhaustive five-volume study by evaluation teams from several OECD donors: *The International Response to Conflict and Genocide: Lessons from the Rwanda Experience.* Copenhagen: The Steering Committee of the Joint Evaluation of Emergency Assistance to Rwanda, 1996. See also Uvin, 1998, and World Bank, 1998.

11. World Bank, 1998, p. 86.

12. Tor Sellstrom and Lennart Wohlgemuth, "Study 1," p. 12, of *The International Response.*

13. "The notion that the difference between Hutu and Tutsi is a racial one probably dates from the colonial period, when the Hamitic hypothesis was introduced. However . . . the images of social and moral differentiation in all likelihood predated

colonization." These images enabled the so-called Hutu social revolution of 1959 to 1962 to take place. The 1957 Hutu Manifesto, written by a group of Hutu intellectuals, "states that 'the problem is basically that of the monopoly of one race, the Tutsi . . . which condemns the desperate Hutu to be forever subaltern workers.' In return, the circle of notables around the Tutsi king wrote that there could never be fraternity between Hutu and Tutsi, for the Tutsi had conquered the Hutu and the latter would always be subservient." Uvin, 1998, p. 31.

14. Leo Kuper, *The Pity of It All.* Minneapolis: University of Minnesota Press, 1997, p. 106, cited in Uvin, 1998, p. 36.

15. Gerard Prunier, *The Rwanda Crisis, 1959–1994: History of a Genocide.* London: Hurst and Company, 1995, pp. 4, 248. Cited in World Bank, 1998, p. 87.

16. World Bank, 1998, p. 91.

17. Ibid., p. 92.

18. Ibid., pp. 84–85.

19. Ibid., p. 111.

20. Uvin, 1998, p. 44.

21. Ibid., p. 113. Italics in original.

22. Ibid., pp. 113–114.

23. Ibid., p. 115. Italics in original.

24. Ibid., p. 118.

25. Uvin, 1998, pp. 109–110.

26. Ibid., p. 229.

27. Ibid., p. 230.

28. Herring, in Esman and Herring, 2001, p. 140.

29. Little, 1994, p. 74.

30. Herring, in Esman and Herring, 2001, p. 155.

31. Ibid., p. 163.

32. USAID cancelled this project in its fourth or fifth year after two American technicians on the project were killed in Jaffna.

33. Herring, p. 148.

34. The description of the Gal Oya experience here is drawn from Norman Uphoff, 1992, and from conversation with Uphoff in November 1999. Uphoff was a member of the Cornell University group that provided technical assistance for this rehabilitation. The technical aspects included irrigation methods, crop protection, and marketing.

35. Uphoff, 1992, p. 6.

36. Ibid., p. 31.

37. Ibid., p. 8.

38. Ibid., p. 76.

39. Ibid., p. 345.

40. Uphoff, personal communication, November 1999.

41. For example, see Albert O. Hirschman, 1984.

42. This account of the Mawaheli Ganga Development Program draws in part on World Bank, 1998, Vol. 5, pp. 134–137.

43. Little, 1994, p. 85.

44. World Bank, 1998, p. 135.

45. Little, 1994, p. 86.

46. World Bank, 1998, p. 145. Italics added.

47. Mason and Asher, 1973, pp. 429–430.

48. The country's full name is Bosnia and Herzegovina. We use Bosnia for convenience.

49. Woodward, 1995, p. 37.

50. Ibid., p. 40.

51. Ibid., p. 18.

52. Ibid., p. 15.

53. Ibid., p. 19.

54. Ibid., p. 50.

55. Ibid., p. 57.

56. Ibid., p. 383.

57. Ibid., p. 384.

58. Ibid., p. 22.

59. Horowitz, 1985, p. 582.

60. From the Second Malaysian Plan, cited by Snodgrass, n.d., from whom the NEP details here have been drawn.

61. "In Malaysia . . . enforcement of ethnic identity has been more important than economic spatial allocation. Thus the promotion of Kuantan on the East Coast as a counterbalance to spatial concentration on the West Coast has been driven more by an ethnic than a spatial goal. (Kuantan is in a Malay-dominated region.)" Harry W. Richardson, *City Size and National Spatial Strategies in Developing Countries*, World Bank Staff Working Paper No. 252, April 1977, p. 37.

62. Cited in Snodgrass, n.d., pp. 2-74–2-75.

63. Ibid., p. 77.

64. *Far East Economic Review*, May 20, 1999, p. 46.

65. *New York Times*, August 13, 2000, p. 8.

66. *Far East Economic Review*, September 21, 2000, pp. 32–36.

67. Unemployment was higher among the Chinese than the Malay males, but relatively lower for Chinese females. See Dipak Mazumdar, *The Malaysian Labor Markets under Structural Adjustment*, 1991,World Bank, WPS 573.

68. Horowitz, in Montville, 1991, p. 458.

69. Charles F. Keyes, *Thailand: Buddhist Kingdom as Modern Nation-State*. Boulder, CO: Westview Press, 1987, pp. 134–135.

70. For example, Brogan's encyclopedic review of about sixty countries involved in all the wars since 1945 has no section on Thailand. See Brogan, 1998.

71. In addition to Keyes, see the classic accounts of William G. Skinner, *Chinese Society in Thailand*. Ithaca, NY: Cornell University Press, 1950; and Richard J. Coughlin, *Double Identity: The Chinese in Modern Thailand*. Hong Kong: Hong Kong University Press, 1960.

72. Keyes, 1987, p. 108.

73. World Bank, *A Public Development Program for Thailand*. Baltimore, MD: Johns Hopkins University Press, 1959.

74. For an account of the evolution of Thai elite thought on economic governance over this period, see Muscat, 1994.

75. See Muscat, 1990, pp. 99–101, for a discussion of these projects.

76. Robert J. Muscat, *Lam Nam Oon: An Irrigation and Area Development Project in Thailand*. USAID, Washington, DC: 1982.

77. For example, see Muscat, 1990, ch. 5, or Somboon Suksamram, *Political Buddhism in Southeast Asia*. New York: St. Martin's Press, 1977, ch. 3.

78. Suksamram, 1977, pp. 58–62.

79. Muscat, 1990, pp. 177–178.

80. This account of Bhutan draws on Leo E. Rose, *The Nepali Ethnic Community in the Northeast of the Subcontinent*, prepared for a conference in Colombo, Sri Lanka, 1993, and on personal conversation with Rose in late 1999.

81. For an account of the implementation of the aid role in Mozambique's immediate postconflict period, see Kimberly Mahling Clark, *Mozambique's Transition from War to Peace: USAID's Lessons Learned*. Washington, DC: USAID, 1996.

82. "It is the ultimate poster child of good economic management." Mark Maloch Brown, administrator of the UN Development Program, *New York Times*, April 30, 2000, p. 9.

83. *New York Times*, August 17, 2000, p. A6.

84. Abrahamsson and Nilsson, 1996, pp. 19–20.

85. Deborah Brautigam, 1997, p. 53.

86. Ibid., p. 56.

87. Rothchild, 1997, p. 43.

3. Development and Conflict

Connections and Precursors

Tolstoy begins his novel *Anna Karenina* with the assertion that "Happy families are all alike; every unhappy family is unhappy in its own way." Every unhappy conflicted country becomes unhappy in its own way. While there have been enough commonalities to give rise to general conflict theories, the differences among, and the complexities of, large-scale struggles have given rise to great variety among these theories. In this chapter I review different approaches students have taken to identify the sources of conflict in developing countries, and the systems that have been designed to give advance warning.

Development, Aid, and Conflict: The Peace Presumption

Because the principal business of the international development agencies is economic development, an examination of the possible relationships between development and conflict is a logical place to begin. It should be noted, for clarity, that these agencies are commonly involved in activities that can be grouped under differentiating terms, while all broadly contributing to "development"—economic management (e.g., anti-inflation stabilization); economic growth (e.g., investment in infrastructure, to promote material or GDP expansion); socioeconomic growth (e.g., investment in health); sustainable development (factoring in environmental protection); economic governance (institutions and government processes that comprise the framework for economic activity). The efforts of some development agencies to promote and support political democracy also are relevant to economic development, even if that is not their primary rationale. Given this heterogeneity of objectives and activities, it is not surprising that explanations of causal relationships between "development" and violent conflict, and by implication between the work of the development agencies and conflict, have also been very diverse.

Development agencies have traditionally acknowledged that development creates tensions, produces gainers and losers, and changes established roles and relationships. But there has been at least an implicit consensus, and explicit justification given to legislators in annual budget processes in donor countries, that development is on balance a positive process for both donors and recipients—positive for its long-run economic benefits and increases in living standards, and for the presumed association among higher living standards, the development of democracy, and a decline in the incentives and willingness of electorates and governments to resort to violence for the settlement of interstate disputes. The presumption that economic development produces peace, or is at least a necessary condition for peace, has become a journalistic commonplace.

Soon after World War II, the connection between development and conflict was the essential justification in the United States and many other donor countries for initiating concessional aid to developing countries. Beginning with the Greek–Turkey aid programs and Point Four during the Truman administration, the improvement of living standards was viewed as critical for winning the "hearts and minds" of populations that might otherwise, spurred by economic hardship and discontent, transfer their loyalties to political forces whose challenges to the social order were endorsed or actively supported by the Soviet Union or its Cold War allies.

In the United States, legislative and programmatic distinctions were made between (nonmilitary) aid (so-called security assistance) to support a government of a country that was an active or potential target of insurgency and subversion, and economic aid (and technical assistance) designed to promote general civilian development (so-called development assistance). Economic aid for security often took the form of straight budget support or the financing of security-related infrastructure; development aid normally financed projects for economic infrastructure, institutional development, expansion of health and education systems, and other sectoral programs that had little or no direct security justification. Because foreign policy concerns have always been a major determinant of the country allocation of American aid, the distinction between the (nonmilitary) security and development categories has been one of form and modes of management and implementation, not essentially conceptual. Thus, over the course of the Cold War, both a successful development process and the aid supporting that process were viewed as major instruments for helping governments win internal conflicts arising from violent challenges from the Left (or, even if essentially ethnic, challenges that could be captured by the Left). They were seen as helping to weaken potential support for insurgencies by reducing discontent and convincing people that they had realistic prospects for rising living standards.

Although it is not the subject of this book, it is important to note the increasing recognition that the characterization of some of the insurgencies as falling into a general worldwide pattern of Soviet-bloc inspiration and stalking horses was simplistic. The roots of some conflicts, on both the challenger and government sides, were essentially local, with the linking up to one major power sponsor or another being opportunistic. The country allocation of Soviet-bloc aid, very different, of course, from that of the Western bilateral development programs, reflected assumptions similar to those driving Western aid, namely that aid would help win or sustain a recipient government's friendly or allied inclination to the donor, and that development would lessen the risk that such a (hopefully allied) government (and its foreign policy orientation) would be internally threatened by economic discontent.

In the search for an understanding of internal conflicts, scholars with different perspectives or disciplines have found many roots and underlying and proximate causes—economic, environmental, cultural, institutional, social, political, religious—in addition to the consequences of international power politics, and of the ambitions, honest intentions, geopolitical calculations, or idiosyncrasies of powerful elites and individuals. There exists no satisfactory general analytic framework that can integrate the disciplinary perspectives, certainly no framework that can attribute relative and measurable weights to these many roots to produce, in any individual case at particular points in time, a warranted prediction that violent conflict is likely to occur. Even when the assembled evidence and scholarly attention on a past conflict is massive, as in the case of World War I, for example, there remain differences of interpretation regarding the causes of the conflict and the weights that should be attached to these causes. In microscopic examinations of the events leading up to the outbreak of many conflicts, scholars (such as J.M. Roberts or Barbara Tuchman, in the case of World War I) can usually identify many turning points in the months and days before war broke out when decisions taken by individual principals, who had authority to choose among alternative courses or even simply next steps, might have avoided the conflict altogether if they had taken one of the alternatives.

At a high level of generality, then, high-intensity conflicts can be seen to arise from the interaction of economic, social, and other factors and forces, with elites who are in a position of responsibility and authority to cope with these forces, either opportunistically or for the general good as best as they can discern it. The rarity with which twentieth-century democratic societies have initiated aggressive wars, or experienced civil war, has been pointed out by many scholars. Authoritarian states are vastly more exposed to the personal idiosyncrasies and calculations of relatively unfettered individual leaders or tiny juntas. However, even under political systems where elites or individual leaders have considerable authoritarian powers, the prevailing economic and social circumstances may go far to determine the available options and the inherent stability or instability of the body politic, and the incentives and openings available for opportunistic dictators or "ethnic entrepreneurs." An instructive and extraordinarily detailed example is provided by Paul Brass (1997) in his examination of interethnic violence in India. Of the five cases Brass explored firsthand, it was unclear if not doubtful that the original incident (e.g., the theft of a revered village idol) behind the subsequent violence had any ethnic or interethnic character or component. As police and political figures from the village on up the administrative hierarchy to national government levels were drawn in to determine the "facts" and interpret (better: "spin," in current American usage) events from their own interest perspectives and for local and larger political agendas, the incidents were painted as essentially ethnic or caste-driven, adding further "demonstration" and exacerbation to the general problems of communal relations in Indian society as a whole. Brass shows how collective violence can emerge or be deliberately generated from even localized, small events, when the wider social context contains potentialities of collective antagonism. Events and development policies and programs can easily be insinuated into the context of underlying social conflict even if these events and programs are inherently conflict-irrelevant.

The assumption that societies and states are less likely in the long run to be prone to internal conflict (or susceptible to calls for overturning the social order) if they enjoy economic development was a generalization of the highest order, one of those "obvious" truths that are more an object of faith than a conclusion firmly grounded in historical analysis. The assumed relationship also lacked precision in its formulation. Is the relationship dynamic or static—that is, does declining risk of violent conflict suddenly kick in when some level of income has been reached? Or is decline a function of the rate of economic advance? Or of a *perceived* rate of improvement, or a period of improvement long enough to create expectations that improvement will continue? Does the link between material circumstances and grievance level hang on the *relative* economic positions (or rates of change) between different ethnic groups? Or are the potentially invidious comparisons of significance related to specific economic functions or kinds of wealth (say, land areas traditionally occupied), rather than comparisons of conceptual economic aggregates?

Even if development and improvement in living standards have been sustained for a long period of time, can a sharp but relatively brief economic reversal, stemming from an external shock (say, an export market collapse), bring on severe conflict despite the preceding growth? Quantitative studies of the correlates of violent conflict have been limited to the modern era, since World War II; is the modern era fundamentally different from previous history, or is it legitimate to test recent statistical tendencies against not-too-distant past conflicts? (For example, the United States on the brink of civil war in the mid-nineteenth century was a relatively high-income, ethnically very diverse democracy, conditions that are statistically strongly associated with absence of civil conflict. Would democratic Spain have avoided civil war in the 1930s if per capita income had been much higher? Not likely.)

The study of the relationships between development and conflict is fraught with additional ambiguities. The terms "development" and "conflict" mean different things in the hands of different authors and in the treatment of different disciplines. As used in economics, development was for many years a relatively limited and precise concept. The presence or absence of development in any period was indicated (and could be measured) by the rise or fall of GDP and income per capita. The anatomy of development in any country could also be measured against patterns of change observed in the experience of the "more developed" or industrially richer countries: the change in sectoral composition of economic output and of the labor force, the rise in worker productivity and increase in capital stock per worker, the increasing contribution of specialization and trade, the increase in investment and research expenditure, the financial "deepening" of the economy and the expansion in banking and financial services functions, and so forth. There were always complications and debates, of course—for example, over the role of population growth, or the costs and benefits of new industry protection at early stages of growth, or the proper role of government as a stimulant or designer of industrial development. But as a process bringing about long-run accumulation of capital and increases in the resources and wealth available to a country, modern development was judged, almost universally, to be a desirable process, historically unprecedented for its ability to raise humankind from the conditions of impoverishment, poor health and short life expectancy, illiteracy, and limited mobility and options in which most people had lived in all previous periods.

The bloom began to fade in the 1970s. Until then, most economists saw development as a macroeconomic process. The profession had focused on development theory and development planning. In the mid-1960s, a conference of leaders in this field reviewed the "most advanced and fruitful techniques, both theoretical and applied, available for analysis of the development process in the emerging nations today." In the studies presented, no mention was made of "poverty" "inequality," or "distribution."[1] When data began to emerge in the 1970s revealing that in many developing countries (perhaps half of those with comparable data) income distribution was worsening, and that in some (a minority of the countries, but including India) the numbers of people in absolute poverty had increased despite growth in per capita GDP, the focus of the profession shifted. Spearheaded by Latin American economists, the 1970s also saw a major intellectual and diplomatic challenge to the international economic structure for its allegedly deliberate bias in favor

of the advanced industrialized nations, especially the United States. The call
for basic revision of the international economic rules of the game was taken
up by leading developing countries, embodied in a program for a "New International Economic Order." But in response to these concerns efforts were
made to redefine policies and to change economic structures, not to jettison
the basic conviction that development should remain an overriding desirable
objective of modern government.

Attacks of different sorts on development itself began to emerge in the
1980s. One school criticized development for causing environmental degradation or "ecocide." Many of the concerns raised by this perspective were
warranted, indeed overdue. Environmental degradation in many forms and
places was recognized as a concrete offset to development, diseconomies
that needed to be seen as reducing measurable economic product, undercut-
ting in some circumstances the sustainability of the development process,
and requiring new perspectives and new policies and program measures.
The extreme attack on development, however, as a heedless process that was
creating possible catastrophic or self-destructive results, and that as a minimum would run up against resource limitations that would stop the whole
development process worldwide, has attracted few adherents. Local limitations on water supply or arable land, in relation to the demands placed upon
them, are certainly realities in many areas, but no global resource limitations
have yet materialized. Artificial shortages that appear to threaten economic
growth may be imposed from time to time on individual commodities open
to cartel arrangements. But even the most successful case to date, the oil
cartel's production cutbacks in the 1970s, was of short duration. Although
the huge jump in petroleum prices caused widespread inflation and put great
economic pressure on the world's poorer and poorest countries, it also induced a large expansion in oil exploration and the opening of new fields not
under the cartel's control. Petroleum prices subsequently fell to levels lower
than those prevailing before the 1970s oil shock, but they remain vulnerable
to manipulation when the major producers decide to cut production and maintain the necessary discipline.

A near consensus of scientific opinion asserts that global warming is under way and that gases released by human activity are a major factor. Global
warming is expected to affect different parts of the planet differently, cause
substantial changes in weather patterns, and bring about a significant rise in
sea levels, affecting low-lying regions where major population concentrations occur. Large-scale shifts in the location of much economic activity,
especially agriculture, may be unavoidable. There would be winners and
losers. But in the time frame of these long-run trends, successful societies
will have accumulated large resources to help them cope, and the continuing

advance of knowledge and technology will likely increase the flexibility and capabilities of humankind. In other words, the best defense against deleterious *global* environmental change is further economic and technological development and flexibility that will increase the capacity of humans to make the necessary adjustments, such as international agreements to reduce greenhouse gas emissions.

If adequate adjustments are not made, it is not difficult to foresee relatively precipitous warming emerging as a wholly new and powerful source of conflict in the not very distant future. For example, low-level migration from densely populated Bangladesh is already an unsettling problem in the northwestern panhandle areas of India. A rise in sea level could push the coastline of the Bay of Bengal deep into Bangladesh, drowning large areas that are now supporting huge numbers of people. If outmigration is not a feasible safety valve, Bangladesh could face intense internal competition and conflict over its diminishing arable land. Dutch solutions to sea encroachment that might be feasible for littoral areas of wealthy countries may not be feasible for developing countries that do not make substantial economic and technological development in the next few decades. In short, the high levels of development and the technologies currently in use in the major industrialized nations of the world could (if insufficiently adjusted) cause immense problems for relatively poor countries that suffer from a combination of high weather-change and/or sea-rise risk on the one hand, and inadequate economic and technical adjustment capacity on the other. The development of the winners, instead of helping to pull the exposed developing countries up out of poverty, would be generating vast new obstacles for the losers. Rather than draw out scenarios of the possible instabilities and conflicts, which would take us far afield, we leave the subject here with the hope that realization of such potentialities will bring the international community to agreement on an effective avoidance strategy.

Development-Conflict Connections: Exacerbation or Amelioration?

In the limited literature on the relationships between development and conflict, one finds a common view that development, on balance, has exacerbated rather than ameliorated conflict. If valid, this would be a defect more grave than ecocide, given the fact that the conflicts within developing countries have occasionally taken the form of genocide, have sometimes lasted for long periods and caused heavy casualties, and have often triggered extensive economic damage and wiped out years of economic and social advance. In this view, the recent history of developing countries would run as follows: colonial containment/suppression of internal conflicts, and creation of unequal status among diverse ruled groups; initiation of self-rule, independent politics and economic development and "modernization"; deepening of (and creation of new) internal divisions and competition for economic assets and over the policies and fruits of development; failure of the polity to develop mutually acceptable alternative policy sets; descent into violent conflict; large-scale human and physical capital destruction, wiping out much of the accumulated development. Economic development would be an inherently self-destroying process for the large group of countries recently emerged from colonial status. Such a paradigm would also put a heavy burden of responsibility, even if inadvertent, on the international development agencies helping to promote and finance this development.

Scale and virulence obviously must be taken into account in attempting any judgment. Economic development unavoidably has differential effects among all populations. At any point in time, recent changes and outcomes will have produced relative winners, relative losers, and absolute losers. If resulting tensions and perceptions of injustice are played out in a context of inclusive politics and policy adjustments, to ensure that losers can have credible expectations of better future outcomes (or at least "fair" chances), then conflict can remain nonviolent, nonchallenging to the legitimacy of the state, nondemonizing, nonessentialist in character. In such a context, development can be seen as a process that in its dynamism generates material advance and continuous undermining of any status quo, a process not ineluctably leading to large-scale violence and self-destruction, but rather opening up an array of potential outcomes depending on the political system and political leadership under which economic actors go about their business.

Some losers have no expectations of inclusion or justice. If they are marginal in numbers and location (e.g., Amazonian Indian tribes in Brazil whose traditional lands are lost to developers, or "tribals" displaced by irrigation projects in India), their discontent is unlikely to develop into high-intensity conflict that challenges the state.

The World Bank has succumbed to criticism over projects (mainly irrigation and roads) that have resulted in involuntary displacement of "indigenous" or "tribal" people who do not wish to move or who have been given alternative land or monetary compensation as an incentive which the recipients consider insufficient. Although the World Bank has developed policies aimed at ensuring more equitable outcomes in cases of displacement—it has hired anthropologists to examine such situations before projects are locked in, and has retreated from projects that threatened to have inequitable consequences—implementation results have been mixed. It is ironic, however, that the development agencies have focused their response to situations in-

volving threats to the most powerless and marginal groups, thereby garner-
ing critics' approval, while paying relatively little attention until recently to
the inequalities and exclusions affecting large, nonmarginal ascriptive minorities. As our subject here is conflict, not developmental justice in general,
we will not focus on the problems of excluded micro-groups. There have
been cases we need to examine below, however, where presumably development-enhancing population movements and resettlements have exacerbated,
or threatened to exacerbate, interethnic relations on a scale clearly relevant
to intense conflict potentiality.

Many scholars see increasing complexity and differentiation of interests
and associations as one of the most powerful products of economic development conducive to a gradual waning of ascriptive bases for conflict. Development tends to vitiate one- or two-dimensionally characterized identity.
People whose traditional sense of identity and self-interest had derived almost entirely from their ethnic group membership begin to see themselves as
having numerous nonascriptive characteristics and interests. As development
draws ever larger numbers of people into multiple affiliations, they find themselves allied in crosscutting relationships with people of other ascriptive or
class identity with whom they may have had no previous relationship, or no
relationship of common interest, or toward whom they might have had only
negative and prejudicial feelings, before the development process began to
shake up their traditional circumstances and worldview. Students of ethnicity
and the politics of ascriptively divided societies stress the increasing risk of
violent conflict, the greater the extent to which ascriptive division coincides
with economic and other divisions within a society. The obverse of this proposition is that the risk of violent conflict should diminish as other affiliations
that cut across ascriptive lines emerge with increasing salience. And it is
precisely modern economic development that most powerfully proliferates
arrays of affiliations and heterogeneous sources of identity.

Not surprisingly when dealing with macro generalizations on the incentive structures and behavioral dynamics of masses of people in many different societies, there are other scholars who doubt the empirical validity or
forcefulness of the proposition that development reduces conflict by creating complex and offsetting interests and loyalties. One counterargument asserts that ethnicity is unimportant as a source of antagonism in premodern
societies where life is geographically limited and identity is based on kinship. It is only when development widens the economic and social scope of
life and creates commonality of values and wants that ethnic solidarity becomes a tool in a widening competitive arena.[2] Even if this proposition is
true, however, it does not follow that higher risk of conflict is an inevitable
result. Ethnic solidarity organizations like language societies and chambers

of commerce among the overseas Chinese in Southeast Asia served as an early form of civil society, mediating between government and the Chinese minorities in a constant search for accommodation and social tranquility. In urban areas, ethnic networks can help migrants find housing and employment, thereby easing the transition from traditional agriculture to modern wage-labor.

Donald Horowitz cites many examples of differential responses to the opportunities opened up by economic development, with many groups judged to be backward, allegedly suffering from a set of values and behavior patterns not consistent with the requirements for material advance under modern development conditions.[3] In virtually every society one finds ethnic groups stereotypically characterized as lazy, unintelligent, inefficient, and lacking initiative. More advanced or dominant groups may be characterized as aggressive, enterprising, intelligent, frugal, and better organized for collective advancement. It is also common for the backward group to share the invidious characterization of themselves, although they may see some of the characteristics as positive, as traditional elements of a culture with its own superior values. There are also many examples of groups that have undergone rapid changes in values as part of a successful adaptation to and participation in modern development. Nevertheless, it is undeniable that different groups may be more or less favorably situated at the start of the development process, with different endowments of location, resources, or a favored or subordinated history under a colonial administration.

The idea that some cultures are inherently more compatible than others with the requirements of modern development has a respectable history of its own. Although the modern development of countries with predominantly Catholic (or Buddhist) populations undercuts any modern relevance of Max Weber's thesis that the "Protestant ethic" was more suitable for capitalist development than the Catholic (or other economically nonaggressive religions), there are many examples of groups still immersed in cultures that teach prescientific conceptions of the world, inculcate distrust of all who are outside narrow circles of kinship, penalize individualism and nonconformity, or constrain individual economic mobility by sanctioning rigid social stratification. The development process may well work to the disadvantage of such groups. There are also many examples of (often immigrant) minorities, such as Lebanese in parts of Africa, who have concentrated in providing marketing services for largely agricultural indigenous populations and are thereby positioned to take more aggressive advantage of the diversified opportunities offered by economic development. If we label the relevant attributes of such minorities (commercial acumen, financial risk-taking, urban orientation, etc.) as "cultural" characteristics, then these groups can be described as bearers of a culture more compatible with, or efficacious for, modern economic development.[4]

Eric Nordlinger (and others he draws upon) sees little evidence that the loyalties, arising in the course of economic development, to shared affiliations other than ascriptive (i.e., other than race, language, ethnicity, religion) have had enough *salience* anywhere to offset the power of the ascriptive. Even if they had such salience, the groups in question would have to feel (or be "triggered by") the power of these offsetting affiliations *simultaneously* with the calls to ascriptive loyalty for the latter to be offset effectively. Some experience (from Nigeria of the early 1960s in this case) demonstrates that groups can compartmentalize their interests and loyalties, coalescing across communal lines for some economic issues at some times, but reverting back to their primordial communal (tribal in this case) identities after the secondary association episode has passed.

Belgium presents an even more striking contradiction. For approximately the first 120 years after Belgium achieved statehood, the economically and politically disadvantaged Flemings accepted the basic national goal of "Belgianization" as defined by the Francophone Walloons, although not without resentment, including the adoption of French as the ticket for social mobility. Belgianization, coupled with the more rapid industrial development of Wallonia, "led to reinforcing (rather than crosscutting) relationships among the socioeconomic, religious and ethnic cleavages."[5] Between the ethnoregionally dualistic character of Belgian economic development, and the ability of the Francophones to co-opt and acculturate many of the Fleming elite, development deepened the ethnic division. The Fleming response to this pattern of relative economic exclusion emerged early, in the 1850s. But rather than challenging the legitimacy of the state, the Flemings employed political and economic collective action to achieve gradual gains in representation and economic strength, a strategy facilitated by the conflict-management orientation of the state. Although this collective action was being pursued by Flemings, "ethnic relations were rarely addressed directly and never in a concerted fashion until the rapid, quite sudden rise of the cleavage to saliency, between 1958 and 1961."[6] The ethnic cleavage arose, paradoxically, from the fears of the Walloons after World War II that they were suddenly descending into economic and political decline compared with the Flemings. The old industrial structure of Wallonia emerged relatively undamaged from the war, but obsolete. Flanders was now better positioned for postwar industrial development. Under these reversed fortunes, new ethnic political parties emerged and "Belgianization" collapsed as the national project. Rather than separating (or fighting), the two Belgian wings redesigned the state, creating language-based regions with substantial autonomy and a structure requiring a completely new form of political interaction.

In sum, the Belgian experience up to World War II appears to be a case that turns Nordlinger's generalization on its head. Although development long reinforced the ethnic divide, the historic Fleming response was collective action within the institutions of industrialization (e.g., collective bargaining), without falling back on ascriptive identity as a mobilizing concept embracing the entirety of their dissatisfactions.

In the context of today's developing countries, the deniers of development's salience appear to have fallen into a circular argument that misses the essential point. Nordlinger sums up the argument:

> When the requirements that contradictory values be of nearly equal salience and almost simultaneously triggered are added, the hypothesis gains in plausibility but loses in scope of applicability. In fact there may be very few societies in which these and other aspects of the explanatory variable are found together. Yet this problem would not be crucial were it not that the hypothesis' scope is reduced practically to the vanishing point when applied to deeply divided societies. . . . Such societies contain very few crosscutting loyalties, values, issues or group memberships; politically relevant detachments almost always form a mutually reinforcing pattern.[7]

The circularity is obvious: the experience to date of these societies cannot be cited as evidence against the crosscutting hypothesis since crosscutting social formations have not yet emerged. In other words, economic development and modernization have not yet advanced to the point where the hypothesis can be applied or tested.

Nordlinger cites Northern Ireland as a case where industrialization has taken place but where class loyalties are not strong enough to cut across the religious lines of conflict. But surely there are also countries and ascriptive groups where historic ethnic divisions remain unmistakable as sources of separate identities but where the salience of crosscutting affiliations and rational choice alternatives has been powerful enough to offset calls for secession or to violence in the name of group injustice or to obtain ascriptive objectives. Recent examples could include Quebec, Scotland, northern Italy, and the Basque provinces of Spain. In addition, the literature on ethnicity often points out that group homogeneity is frequently more apparent than real. Large groups of humans are virtually certain to be marked by internal factions, power rivalries, heresies that may seem obscure or trivial to outsiders, dialect differences undetectable by nonspeaking outsiders, subregional and local loyalties, and other fissiparous particularisms. Throughout history, commonality of religion, say Christianity as a whole, or Catholicism, Islam, or Buddhism, often (probably most often) has not been ascriptively powerful enough to overcome the interests and motivations for rulers and groups sharing the same faith to engage in violent conflict. Much depends on circumstances and time. Groups apparently homogeneous when confronting each other, as with Muslims and Christians at various times, have been violently heterogeneous at other times, as with Shiites and Sunnis, or Roman Catholics and Protestants. Even a coincidence of religion and modern nationalism may be overridden by crosscutting political philosophies and class interests, as was the case in some countries occupied by Germany during World War II where local reactionary groups or classes welcomed the forced advent of fascism.

A striking firsthand observation of the override power of class interest is provided by Harold Nicolson, the British diplomat and diplomatic historian. In June 1938, by which time (after German rearmament, the fascist interventions in Spain, the German takeover of Austria, etc.) Nazi intentions were unmistakable, and frequently cited by Winston Churchill as a fundamental danger to Britain and the rest of Europe, Nicolson wrote in his dairy:

> People of the governing classes think only of their own fortunes, which means hatred of the Reds. This creates a perfectly artificial but at present most effective secret bond between ourselves and Hitler. Our class interests, on both sides, cut across our national interests. I go to bed in gloom.[8]

The fact that neither economic class interests nor the other crosscutting interests that development can engender (e.g., loyalties to nonascriptive political parties, or membership in civil society organizations concerned with issues of governance, social welfare, environment, sports, consumerism, etc.) have overridden ascriptive loyalties in many developing countries in conflict is more an indication that the objective bases for such affiliations have still been weak because economic development has still been at an early stage. It would be a mistake to conclude that nonascriptive interests and affiliations are *generally* incapable of overriding ascriptive divisions or of strengthening motivations for nonviolent conflict management in situations where ascriptive divisions are sources of contestation.

It is also critical to recognize that the period of postcolonial economic development, within the historically unprecedented system of international promotion of development through resource transfers and technical assistance, has been relatively short. In many of the former colonies, the coincidence of racial or ethnic divisions with economic class divisions was created by colonial policies that favored one group over another and/or promoted immigration of ethnically different manpower to meet specific labor supply requirements not filled (for whatever reasons) from the indigenous population. Thus, many former colonies inherited a superimposition of economic functions with ethnicity, a pattern that has proved in some cases to be highly combustible. If segmentation and discrimination persist, development could intensify economic conflict through continuing denial of access to expanding opportunities in the labor market.

Conversely, economic development over time can generate the expansion in economic functions, the increases in employment opportunities, the (non-discriminatory) provision of education of the same content to all children and youth regardless of ethnicity, through which ascriptively defined people can gain access to all sectors and functions, and break traditional patterns of intergenerational occupational immobility, thereby reducing the salience of ascription as a category relevant to a whole range of potentially conflictive issues.

In fact, even more can be said for the potential contribution of economic development to conflict management. A strong case can be made that economic development has been a powerful force, perhaps the most powerful force yet experienced, for eliminating violent group, class, or ascriptive conflict as a method for settling intrastate differences in the modern world. Economic development has produced this happy outcome through its association with the evolution of stable democratic systems built on the rule of law and the guaranteeing of human rights (i.e., systems designed for inclusiveness and nonviolent resolution of, or compromise over, conflicting interests). Unlike authoritarian regimes that tend to repress opposition and aggrieved minorities, democratic governments are likely to favor processes—of open debate, bargaining, representation, decentralization, and power-sharing—that obviate any need of minorities to resort to violence.

Democratic societies have also shown a superior ability to adjust to economic crises or recessions. Dani Rodrik has observed that democratic conflict management institutions have been far more important for the ability of economies to weather turbulence than conventional economic analysis has recognized.[9] Economic crises are on most of the lists of "early warning" as signs and triggers of impending conflict. Although democracy is not a necessary condition for *early* economic growth (one need only cite several outstanding cases of rapid modern economic growth under nondemocratic, or quasi-democratic, systems to make this point—China, Malaysia, Singapore, and Taiwan, South Korea, and Thailand prior to the recent democratic evolution of the latter three), Robert J. Barro (1991) has shown that higher per capita output is strongly associated with increasing levels of democracy. Liberal democratic values and high-income open economies combine to widen the options available to individuals, to increase personal mobility both spatially and culturally, and to expand access to education. Successful economic development also contributes to preferences for negotiation and compromise by raising the potential costs of violent conflict. As wealth accumulates, people have more and more to lose if the golden goose gets throttled.

Nevertheless, democratic transition is no automatic panacea. Where strong authoritarian regimes are replaced by inexperienced and fragile democratic governments, secessionist challenges to the state or interethnic confrontations, previously forcefully controlled, may spring into action. Post-Suharto Indonesia has been a case in point. Democratic systems can take different forms, some of which in deeply divided societies have exacerbated rather than ameliorated political conflict. As the comparison of Sri Lanka with Malaysia shows, whether or not political parties are ethnically exclusive or combined in cross-ethnic coalitions can be critical to determining whether a parliamentary system widens or lessens ethnic division. We return to this subject below in our examination of development agency efforts at conflict prevention.

Though the great majority of the developing countries that have undergone internal conflicts have had authoritarian forms of government, dictatorship per se does not necessarily produce civil war. The degree of risk that the acts of an authoritarian regime will engender violent conflict among different social groups (as contrasted with riots or other violent popular reactions against the regime) will depend on the nature of the regime. Under totalitarian regimes characterized by elaborate state apparatus and comprehensive state domination and control (e.g., Nazi Germany), the regime's repression ensures that no potential internal conflict (except against its own internal targets) can be realized. Under a tyranny (e.g., Uganda under Idi Amin), the individual dictator pursues his own aggrandizement, employs ruthless repression to maintain power, and may sow the seeds of conflict by playing his own ascriptive base against opposition groups. In contrast, a benevolent despot (e.g., the Thai dictatorships of 1958 to 1972) may be only mildly repressive and kleptocratic, avoiding divide-and-conquer tactics and attempting to promote the (nonpolitical) interests of the population. Periods of transition from one governance form to another, especially from more to less repressive regimes, may experience increasing risk of internal conflict as the forced constraints on underlying divisions are loosened, compared with the enforced stability of successfully repressive dictatorships.

Liberal democratic values that define individuals in their civic identity, and stress the human rights of individuals equal under the law, can also reduce the relative salience of traditional ascriptive group identities and associations. In some contexts, however, these same values can produce the very opposite result, at least for some period. India's elaborate system of preferences for specified disadvantaged ascriptive groups (lower castes, tribes) gives members of these groups favored access to education and other tracks to social and economic mobility. Where such systems prevail, there is a strong incentive for members of such groups to exploit their ascriptive identity, and for other groups claiming disadvantaged status to establish comparable ascriptively based rights.

Milton Esman has provided a convenient summary of the three schools of thought one finds in the scholarship on economic development and conflict.[10] One school asserts that economic growth facilitates ethnic conflict management. Economic expansion makes a positive-sum game possible. All groups can benefit without deprivation to any single group. Economic disparities can be reduced and accommodation facilitated. Conversely, economic stagnation and decline are inauspicious for conflict management. A second school of thought asserts the opposite: economic growth aggravates ethnic conflict. Growth raises expectations and discontents, sharpening resentments of the relatively disadvantaged. The early stages of modern economic growth typically widen the inequalities of income and wealth. The relatively disadvantaged may perceive a widening gap between their aspirations for personal income growth (feeding on the palpable material progress of the relatively advantaged) and their expectations of what they deem likely to happen to themselves. Increasingly strident demands are perceived as increasing threats by the relatively advantaged. If income distribution starts out uneven across ethnicities, with some ethnically defined group(s) concentrated in the lower rungs and others in the higher rungs, the increasing disparity (and its resulting widening of the gap between aspirations and expectations) can be a major source of conflict, especially if these relationships are made known and used by elites for ethnic mobilization. Increasingly strident demands are then perceived by the relatively advantaged as increasing threats.

Another variant of the aggravation thesis concerns the speed of economic change: "rapid" economic change gives a society less time to cope with the consequent social strains and adjustments than would slower economic expansion. The problem with such a generalization is that it would have to explain why the most rapidly growing economies in recent decades have been among those most successful in mitigating social stress and avoiding violent conflict (i.e., Taiwan, South Korea, Thailand, Malaysia, Singapore). More attention has been given to speed of economic change when governments (supported, influenced, pressured, or forced, as it is often construed, by the IMF) implement a turnaround to reverse a set of unsustainable and dysfunctional policies, so-called structural adjustment.

The third school of thought Esman cites asserts that economic growth does not affect ethnic relations. Ethnic conflicts originate from other, primarily political, causes. Economic growth or, more generally, economic performance, is "essentially irrelevant." Conflicts are waged "for different stakes." This school appears to dominate the academic literature on ethnic conflict and on conflict resolution. One can read serious studies of contemporary conflict (some are cited in the bibliography and have been invaluable for researching this book) with few references to economic conditions or policies, and even fewer (frequently no) references to the international development banks or aid agencies. There are certainly cases where economic rationality appears to have been abandoned altogether, where conflict has been pursued, and disastrous tactics employed, regardless of the consequences for the material conditions and prospects that would face any expectant victor. In a conflict driven by a combination of ethnic paranoia and Maoist class-warfare theory, the Khmer Rouge deliberately destroyed Cambodia's educated classes and all centers (libraries, schools, etc.) of knowledge and technology, in the absurd belief that the country would be better positioned to achieve regional power without these assets. During the twentieth century's largest conflict, Germany continued to allocate transport, manpower, and other resources to the destruction of militarily insignificant European Jewry despite the country's worsening resource position in the face of surrounding military reversals. Some of the regions that separatists would inherit if successful, like the arid Tamil area of northern Sri Lanka, might have poorer economic prospects than if they remained, at peace, in the country they wish to leave.

In fact, according to Donald Horowitz, most secessionist movements in Africa and Asia "involved regions that stood to lose economically from autonomy or independence." Horowitz denies the salience of economic issues altogether in many conflicts. "It remains difficult to tie significant aspects of ethnic conflict to economic interests. On the contrary, what emerges quite clearly is the willingness of ethnic groups to sacrifice economic interest for the sake of other kinds of gain."[11] Horowitz immediately qualifies this generalization by noting that secessionist elites may expect to end up better off by being dominant in a new poorer country than by being subordinate in the less poor country they want to quit. For such elites, the potential economic gains (at the expense of their trusting followers) would appear to have salience.

Where Horowitz does see economic factors as relevant, he accords them secondary importance. "Economic interest may act either as an accelerator or a brake on separatism. Yet, among the most frequent and precocious secessionists—backward groups in backward regions—economic loss or gain plays the smallest role, ethnic anxiety the largest."[12] As with so many generalizations on the causes of conflict, there are important exceptions where the salience of economic interests (not just the interests of the secession-minded elite) has been unmistakable. Economics was a major reason behind the secession of Bangladesh from Pakistan; in that case it was evident that the much poorer East would be better off separated from the extractions of the West. Separatists in southern Sudan could reasonably expect to be better off independent and in total control of the oil fields in that part of the country. As we have seen in the Malaysian case, the leadership of the Malay and Chinese communities believed economic inequalities were the country's core issues. In the end, Horowitz avows that economic measures are potentially relevant for conflict prevention.[13]

A number of statistical studies have been made that correlate economic factors with political instability and/or conflict, and economic growth. These cross-country studies employ various measures of instability and of economic or social deprivation, using countries as a whole as the units for measurement, not internal interethnic disaggregation. A review of this particular literature, covering the period from 1960 to the late 1980s, concluded (with all the necessary caveats respecting the variables and models used) that significant correlations between income inequality and sociopolitical instability had been demonstrated. The research results

> suggest an argument that might help explain different investment and growth performances in different parts of the world. Several countries in Southeast Asia have had very high growth rates in the post–World War II period. In the aftermath of the war these countries had land reforms that reduced income and wealth inequality. Furthermore, and perhaps as a result of this reform, these countries have been relatively stable politically, compared with, for example, Latin American countries. The latter, in turn, have had much more unequal income distribution, more sociopolitical instability, and lower growth rates. From a normative point of view, these results have implications for the effects of redistributive policies. Fiscal redistribution, by increasing the tax burden on investors, reduces the propensity to invest. However, the same policies may reduce social tensions, and, as a result, create a sociopolitical climate more conducive to productive activities and capital accumulation. Thus, by this channel, fiscal redistribution might actually spur economic growth. The net effect of redistributive policies on growth has to weigh the costs of distortionary taxation against the benefits of reduced social tensions.[14]

At a very aggregate level, these studies capture a quantitative relationship among economic inequality, sociopolitical instability, and foregone growth, in effect confirming the observations in the political conflict literature where the conclusions are drawn from a marshaling of case studies and detailed examination of the many (economic and noneconomic) forms of inequality and how they have played out in the politics and group psychology of deeply divided societies. The conclusion that the macro benefits for growth and for sociopolitical stability of fiscal redistribution may outweigh the sum of the micro costs of the redistributionary distortions is of the utmost importance. In the many cases where the instabilities have led to violent conflict or open warfare, the benefits of any redistributive program that might have restored sociopolitical stability would have been vastly greater.

By contrast, I have found no more overstated and succinct denial of the essential causality of noneconomic factors than the view advanced by the International Food Policy Research Institute (IFPRI):

> Conflicts in counties such as Burundi and Rwanda are frequently characterized as the results of tribal or political issues, when, in fact, the underlying causes are natural resource degradation, extreme poverty, and widespread food insecurity. Such conflicts in turn breed further food insecurity, poverty, and natural resource degradation, continuing a vicious circle of hunger and instability. Technologies and policies capable of improving food security will decrease the probability of conflict. The interaction between conflict, food security, natural resource management, and agricultural research deserves more attention from the food policy research community.[15]

Former U.S. President Jimmy Carter, one of the most prominent figures dedicated to conflict prevention, agrees with the view that food insecurity is a major underlying cause of conflict. Drawing on a report prepared by the International Peace Research Institute in Oslo, Carter described the report as having found that

> most of today's wars are fueled by poverty, not by ideology. The devastation occurs primarily in countries whose economies depend on agriculture but lack the means to make their farmland productive. . . . The report found that poorly functioning agriculture in these countries heightens poverty, which in turn sparks conflict. This suggests an obvious but often overlooked path to peace. . . . In the name of peace, it is critical that both developed and developing countries support agricultural research and improved farming practices. . . . The message is clear: There can be no peace until people have enough to eat. Hungry people are not peaceful people.[16]

Although it is reasonable to assume that people living in poverty may be responsive to calls to violence against whatever authority or other group they believe is responsible for their plight, some of the countries cited as examples provide only ambiguous support, at best, to this generalization. India is said to have escaped "widespread violence in large measure because the Indian government made food security a priority." The fact is, caste violence and the armed conflicts in some states over time might well be called "widespread." Although food security has been a priority objective in India, an estimated 350 million of India's 1 billion people still fall below the country's poverty line. The conflicts in Sri Lanka and Sudan have arisen out of the reaction of subordinate ethnicities to policies of the dominant ethnicity that have been hegemonic in one respect or another. It is doubtful these conflicts would have been avoided had poverty been lifted but the governments had continued to pursue the same policies otherwise. In fact, Sri Lanka stands out as an outlier, a poor country much praised by development agencies in the 1970s for its determination to alleviate poverty and for the success of its "basic human needs" programs in raising levels of well-being of the poor. (This policy rarity among developing countries was much criticized by these same agencies as fiscally unwise welfarism in the 1950s and 1960s, before poverty alleviation emerged as a development objective that should be attacked immediately rather than left for the fullness of time.) The meeting of basic needs and the solicitude for the poor shown by successive Sinhala-dominated Sri Lankan governments did not inoculate the society against conflict arising from other causes.

In sum, these latter views argue that, contrary to the assertions that conflict arises from political/ethnic/cultural causes, the real source of violent conflict can be traced to the *absence* of the economic development that can eliminate extreme poverty and food insecurity. The Sri Lankan case aside, one can easily cite severe conflicts in countries where living standards are very low (basic human needs are grossly undermet), and where development and modernization have barely gotten under way, such as the tribal areas of Burma, or Chad and southern Sudan. If such cases do not demonstrate a hard rule that absence of development will cause conflict, they do appear to undermine the theories that development is a general cause of conflict, or at least serve to illustrate that every theory of conflict will have its exceptions.

A related explanatory model sees population pressure and environmental resource scarcities as the causes of living standard collapse and warfare. Such either/or statements pitting economic, political, social, religious, racial or other classifications of human characteristics and behavior as mutually exclusive, or individually sufficient, causes of conflict are too simplistic and reductivist for the complexity of the problem (other IFPRI papers treat the food/conflict relationship at greater length and are more nuanced, pointing out that studies of environmental scarcity and conflict suggest no simple causal relationship, but an interaction between economic conditions and political conflict over human rights abuse and social inequalities).[17] Singapore provides one illustration of interactions among economic and noneconomic causes of social division and conflict (nonviolent in this case) between its Chinese majority and small ethnic Malay minority: "[D]ifferences in the cultural framework within which Malays and Chinese organize their economic lives, especially with regard to entrepreneurship, have put Malays at an economic disadvantage in Singapore since independence in 1959, and have supported the idea that Malays are culturally inferior which, in turn, has been a source of discrimination against them."[18]

Despite the fact that the relative importance of (individual!) economic factors as contributory causes of any specific conflict cannot be meaningfully quantified, they are always identified as present, as will be evident below when we review the current spate of conflict modeling. At this point, one reference will suffice to illustrate the contributory role of economic rivalries and the problem of separating out causes in a "thick" analysis of a complex situation. The conflict in the Congo has involved a multiplicity of state and nonstate belligerents: the (former) Kabila regime in the Congo; three neighboring countries (Burundi, Rwanda, Uganda) that intervened with their own armed forces and that are supporting different rebel groups; Zimbabwean military forces that supported Kabila; numerous (Congolese and non-Congolese) Hutu, Tutsi, and other insurgents fighting each other and aligned with or against Kabila (including the rejuvenated Hutu "genocidaires"); two other governments (Sudan, Angola) also intervening to promote their own interests deriving from relations with other participants; local militias in the Congo protecting local interests; and minor military support for Kabila from Namibia, Chad, and Libya. In sorting out this thicket of actors and interests, a recent account of this extraordinarily complex set of interrelated hostilities described the economic and social roots as follows:

> The free-for-all over Congo's vast natural resources fuels the conflict. Some belligerents are using state military budgets to finance their involvement in the war while individuals close to the leadership plunder. . . . [A]ll parties to the conflict are exporting minerals to help defray war expenses . . . , reducing the potency of donor leverage for peace.
>
> Competition for land, resources, and favored positions in a poverty-stricken environment fuels rivalries between Tutsi and non-Tutsi populations. The prevalence of minerals and export crops throughout rebel-controlled territories and the value of land in areas such as Masisi in North Kivu province increases the stakes. Economic collapse and demographic pressure feeds insecurities and resentment, providing a fertile ground for recruitment into various military forces.[19]

As should be clear even from this brief overview, it is too early in modern history to extract a definitive general theory of the relationships between economic development and social change on the one hand, and the evolution of institutions and abilities (and preferences) for managing nonviolent resolution of group differences on the other. One cannot but agree with the many students of conflict that our understanding is still deficient. Any effort to reduce the likelihood of conflict must deal in the end with individual conflict-prone societies, each with its unique configuration of ethnicities, institutions, history, and economy. An awareness of the complexities and general tendencies across the range of divided societies can only serve as background to the attempt to understand the individual case, at a point in time, that should be made by any international development institution whose involvement may be relevant to a country's conflict dynamics.

Democratic Optimism

Despite all these difficulties of theory and uniqueness, the apparent success of the high-income liberal democracies in managing conflicts within and among themselves can give us confidence, or at least support a guarded optimism, that the forces and characteristics of modern economic development will draw increasing numbers of countries into successful conflict mitigation. This book is written on the optimistic assumptions that many (but certainly not all) conflicts in our age can be mitigated, that the development process can be deliberately managed and shaped to prevent material interest differences from degenerating into violent conflict, and that the international development agencies are perforce significant actors in that process. At a minimum, they should adopt the Hippocratic oath: Do no harm. Avoid supporting policies and projects that exacerbate conflicts in deeply divided societies. Perhaps deliberate attention on their part to their past and potential effects on conflict can help them to realize a contribution that may have been largely only latent thus far. Even where antagonisms are exacerbated by symbolic or ethical issues (acceptable public garments, holidays, sexual behavior, status symbols, "official" religion, etc.) that are outside the terms or competence of the development agencies, material incentives and outcomes— very much within the terms of these agencies—may often serve as universal offsets. Money and material benefits may be fungible with noneconomic factors.

It is prudent to remain "guarded" in such optimism for obvious reasons. From an historical perspective, these fortunate, high-income democratic countries have reached this stage only very recently, with some of them in our own generation having engaged in deplorable collective conflicts and atrocious criminal behavior, as defined in the Geneva Conventions. And even if an ethnic or ascriptive identity has been attenuated or unmilitant over time, it is likely to remain latent and susceptible to a revival of salience and to assertive or defensive political mobilization. Contemporary examples, to cite only a few, include Zionism, Palestinian nationalism, Quebec separatism, Scottish nationalism, Buddhist–Sri Lankan militancy, Bosnian Muslim nationalism, Taiwanese identity, the subordination of Muslim identity to (East) Bengali ethnonationalism, Chechnyan nationalism, and the resurgence of ethnic salience in Belgium after 1958. Naturally, many forms of cultural revival serve to enrich provincial identities, such as Celtic language movements in France and the U.K., but they are well short of the salience that could nurture separatism or violent expression.

Should we draw optimistic conclusions for the possibilities for conflict management from the fact that most societies have gone through periods of domestic peace, or pessimistic conclusions from the obverse fact that most societies have gone through alternating periods of conflict, both internal and with other societies? Reflecting on the group self-restraint inherent in modern democratic states, the Spanish philosopher Ortega y Gasset was pessimistic:

> The political doctrine which has represented the loftiest endeavor towards common life is liberal democracy. . . . Liberalism is that principle of political rights, according to which the public authority, in spite of being all-powerful, limits itself and attempts even at its own expense, to leave room in the state over which it rules for those to live who neither think nor feel as it does, that is to say as do the stronger, the majority. Liberalism . . . is the supreme form of generosity; it is the right which the majority concedes to minorities and hence it is the noblest cry that has ever resounded on this planet. . . . It was incredible that the human species should have arrived at so noble an attitude, so paradoxical, so refined, so acrobatic, so anti-natural. . . . It is a discipline too difficult and complex to take firm root on earth.
>
> Share our existence with the enemy! Govern with the opposition! Is not such a form of tenderness beginning to seem incomprehensible? Nothing indicates more clearly the characteristics of the day than the fact that there are so few countries where an opposition exists.[20]

Writing in mid-1930s Europe, Ortega saw the threat of majority intolerance and absolutism in political terms—that is, as the rise of totalitarianism based on mobilization and manipulation of undiscerning masses. Nevertheless, the specter of illiberalism toward the "other" applies equally in the more contemporary circumstances where the stronger group in control of the state defines itself (or is manipulated to define itself) ethnically.

Sigmund Freud was equally pessimistic over the prospects for social peace. His pessimism was based on a view of human nature just as bleak as Ortega's, but expressed more in terms of the individual human per se:

> Men are not gentle creatures who want to be loved, and who at the most can defend themselves if they are attacked; they are, on the contrary, creatures among whose instinctual endowments is to be reckoned a powerful share of aggressiveness. . . . *Homo homini lupus.* (Man is a wolf to man.) Who in the face of all his experience of life and of history will have the courage to dispute this assertion? . . . In circumstances that are favorable to it [aggressiveness], when the mental forces which normally inhibit it are out of action, it also manifests itself spontaneously and reveals man as a savage beast to whom consideration towards his own kind is something alien. Anyone who calls to mind the atrocities committed during the racial migrations or the invasions of the Huns, or by the people known as Mongols under Jenghiz Khan and Tamerlane, or at the capture of Jerusalem by the pious Crusaders, or even, indeed, the horrors of the recent First World War—anyone who calls these things to mind will have to bow humbly before the truth of this view.[21]

Freud's qualification—that the wolf emerges when circumstances are favorable to it, and when the normally inhibiting mental forces are out of action—is central to any attempt to understand conflict or to devise methods of mitigation or avoidance. As pointed out above, circumstances at most points in time normally contain a wide range of possible outcomes. By the time circumstances have been allowed to culminate in a crisis, the range of options may suddenly narrow to exclude conflict alternatives. At the level of the individual citizen or group member, the violence-inhibiting "mental forces" can be shut down. Peter Gay has described how European nationalisms swept aside all the ascriptive-crossing identities and loyalties that nineteenth-century economic development had created:

> As early as 1879, American sociologist William Graham Sumner had declared that the world was a "unit" where "the barriers of race, religion, and nationality are melting away under the operation of the same forces which have to such an extent annihilated the obstacles of distance and time." The decades that followed appeared to bear out Sumner's sanguine assessment. . . . And yet, cosmopolitan sentiments collapsed in July and early August 1914, as in the battle of loyalties nationalism blotted out all the others. Love of one's country and hatred for its enemies proved the most potent rationalization for aggression the long nineteenth century produced. . . . A human life is a life of multiple roles. A man is—all at once—a worker, a Roman Catholic, a Frenchman, a good husband and father, a stamp collector, a supporter of the local soccer team. Most of the time, these diverse identifications coexist peacefully. But there may be moments of crisis when a choice becomes imperative, and in the summer of 1914

the choice was a militant nationalism. Its most spectacular casualty was the organized international workers' movement, which showed itself helpless before patriotic appeals and patriotic excitement. For years, socialist parties had vowed to disrupt any effort by their governments to send workers into slaughter from which only the capitalists would profit. . . . Then came Sarajevo. For weeks, socialist leaders frantically negotiated to avert war. But once the war had been declared, they abruptly turned patriot, discarding their commitment to the workers of the world.[22]

This particularly fateful collapse of cross-national, nonascriptive affiliations was an example of the power of imminent threat perceptions to sharpen the ascriptive lines between *Us* and *Them*. But it did not deny the reality of the cross-ascriptive trends or in general the potentialities of affiliative complexity to enhance the prospects for conflict management under noncritical conditions. And as conditions are normally noncritical during the periods, measured in years, before most conflicts degenerate into high violence, the problem for conflict management is to foresee the possibilities for escalation and to develop policies and programs designed to promote affiliative complexity and to reduce the salience of deep divisions or, more precisely, the imbalances underlying these divisions, be they economic, social, or whatever. This is where the particular characteristics of the development process come into play.

Some Development Particulars: Illustrations of Conflict Effects

The argument thus far regarding the relationship between development and conflict must leave the reader unsatisfied, especially the "development practitioners" who deal in the specifics of the development process and may find only limited enlightenment from general theories that attempt to subsume within one model or construct the myriads of policies, programs, projects, sector and subsector transformations, technological changes, market operations, institutional innovations, and so on, which together comprise the totality of the development process. A closer look at some of these components is needed if we are to get closer to the real-world activities of the international development agencies and the development professionals, and attempt to explore the relevance and implications of these activities for conflict. In fact, many aspects of the development process have been relevant to conflict in many countries. These aspects—specific policies, programs, projects, many of which have involved the international development agencies—have sometimes exacerbated and sometimes ameliorated conflict. Context and the manner of implementation also have made big differences; a conflict ameliorating program in one set of circumstances can be an exacerbating factor in other circumstances.

Structural adjustment is a term of art for a special case of developmental change. Structural adjustment is a very modern process, dating only from the late 1970s as a deliberate subject of economic analysis and of international agency attention. Of course, the process of development since the Industrial Revolution has everywhere entailed continuous change in economic structure. What distinguishes recent "adjustment" is its reference to a substantial shift in certain economic policies, designed to take effect over a relatively short period of time (say, two to five years). Structural adjustment became a major subject of World Bank lending when many developing countries found their economies destabilized by the effects of the oil price "shocks" of the 1970s. These effects included severe inflation, a ballooning of external debt, rising fiscal and external deficits, and overvalued currencies. The accumulation of economic imbalances proved unsustainable. Major policy adjustments became unavoidable as countries approached the limits of foreign creditor willingness to continue financial transfers without an improvement in the prospects for restoration of economic and financial balance and strength. Governments willing to commit to the required policy adjustments received substantial financial support, especially from the IMF and World Bank. That support helped pay for otherwise unsustainable import levels and provided budget support for governments forced to contract public-sector expenditures.

The adjustment programs typically included monetary tightening (e.g., banking system credit constraints, decontrol of interest rates), fiscal deficit reduction (through government expenditure reductions and revenue increases), exchange-rate liberalization, and a wide range of structural reforms designed to facilitate a return to macroeconomic balance and to strengthen an economy's long-run competitiveness and efficiency. The structural reforms typically entailed fundamental changes in economic and development management philosophy, often amounting to a break with prevailing antimarket ideologies. Programs ranged over state enterprise regulation, pricing, and privatization; tax systems; rationalization of import tariff and barrier regimes; industrial efficiency, competition, and protectionism; and banking-sector reform and equity market development. To focus the analysis and policy change requirements in specific sectors, such as industry, agriculture, and the social sectors, general balance of payments and adjustment loan programs began to be supplemented by "sector" adjustment loans. Some bilateral donors also provided adjustment financing, while both multilateral and bilateral donors offered technical assistance to help governments design and monitor the policy-change programs.

The extent of the changes entailed by these programs, the distance countries had to travel from government-controlled to market-based systems, and from subsidized to market price systems, varied from country to country. The distance was greatest in those countries, mainly starting in 1989, that embarked on *transition* from thoroughly centrally planned, socialist systems, to market-based, capitalist economic systems. Both structural adjustments in market-based or mixed developing economies, and economic transition, have been complex processes, hotly debated over issues of timing, sequencing, efficiency, and distributive impact. Both processes were essential for the further economic development of the nations involved. The socialist or command economies had reached a dead end; the mixed or market lower-income economies were too destabilized and distorted to resume sustainable development without adjustment.

The reform programs designed, and the conditions imposed, by the IMF and the World Bank, and the subsequent performance of the redirected economies, have been studied and critiqued at length. Both the World Bank and the IMF have drawn lessons from evaluations of the outcomes, and they have adjusted their advice and requirements over time in favor of greater flexibility and of giving more attention to softening the effects of these programs on vulnerable groups.[23]

A major argument on transition has centered around the question of optimal speed and sequencing. Some have argued that the entire package of transition policy and institutional change should be introduced at once (an economic "big bang") to deny the vested interests of the old regime the time to mount an undermining reaction. Others argue that the complexity and historic novelty of the required transformation call for a gradual process, getting the sequencing right between things that need to be done first and later changes that depend on prior institutions and policies being in place. Poland is commonly cited as evidence for a "big bang" approach, in contrast with the transition process in Russia. In any event, to date the *economic* transition in Eastern European countries has not generated large-scale violent conflict in the form of vested-interest defense or class violence by the economically deprived. The breakup of the Soviet Union has been followed by violent conflicts in the Caucasus and Central Asian regions; though economic resource issues are important in some of these conflicts, they are problems of control rivalries, unleashed ethnonationalisms, and religious fundamentalism, not emanating from transition processes per se. The breakup of Yugoslavia, and the attendant conflict, stands out as an exceptional case of reversed federalism, as noted earlier.

As far as structural adjustment is concerned, there has been vigorous criticism by the United Nations Children's Fund (UNICEF) and others arguing that adjustment has unfairly imposed heavy burdens on the poor; adjustment programs should be redesigned "with a human face." The validity of this criticism must vary by country. Some research on adjustment in Africa has shown that the programs did not harm the poor (nor significantly benefit them); cutbacks in social-sector budgets, for example, did not reduce the level of services available to the poor as large numbers of them, especially in rural areas, had hardly been touched by such services in the first place.[24] While the "IMF-riots" were reactions to the real pocketbook issues of lost subsidies, the urban beneficiaries of the subsidies had generally been relatively favored compared with the rural poor. Policy adjustments that improve the rural/urban terms of trade, such as devaluation of an overvalued exchange rate, and decontrol of artificially elevated prices of domestic manufactures and artificially repressed domestic food prices, can raise incomes of poor agricultural producers to higher levels that were unattainable under the policy structure of the years preceding the adjustment process.

In short, the social impact of structural adjustment has varied case by case, with the effects on different groups depending on how the adjustment process affects their sources of income and the goods and services they normally purchase.[25] Thus, the short-run effects on absolute or relative poverty do not run uniformly in one direction or another. In the longer run it is clearer that the effects on aggregate growth of income and on the ability of an economy to address and alleviate poverty are positive, if only because the preadjustment policy structures could not sustain growth or in many cases even reverse decline. The riot reactions were episodes of transitory low-level violence, not leading to mobilization between ascriptive or class groups, or mobilization against the government. To draw more useful conclusions regarding the possible effects of structural adjustment programs, reinforcing or ameliorating sources of social or ethnic conflict, it will be necessary to examine some of the specific policy components. We return to this subject below.

The Rwanda case is an example of how the development process, or major components of that process, can increase the capacity of (and opportunities available to) the state to promote the hegemony of the dominant ethnicity, even contributing to violent conflict. In such cases, development can be construed as having *enabled state repression and/or minority exclusion* to a greater extent than would have been possible otherwise. Under conditions of modern economic development, the technical capacity of state organs to carry out state policies naturally increases over time. The bulk of international technical assistance aims to increase government capacities, under the assumption that these capacities (in agriculture research and extension, public health, education, economic infrastructure, etc., and in general public administration and governance) would be applied to promoting the general welfare of the recipient countries. If a government is pursuing hegemony and exclusion that is inequitable and that raises the risk of internal conflict, the country would be better off if the government's technical capacities were too weak to implement its policies effectively. The Thai case provided an example. The government's program to marginalize Thailand's ethnic Chinese business class failed partly because it had no alternative but to hire local Chinese managers to run the very state enterprises that were supposed to supplant and preempt Chinese firms. By the time technical assistance to strengthen the government's capacities across the board got under way in the 1950s, the discriminatory policies (which went beyond the enterprise sector) were being abandoned. It can plausibly be argued that if the vast program of training government personnel had gotten an earlier start (either by the government itself in the 1930s, or by foreign aid immediately after World War II), government incapacity would not have hobbled the anti-Sinic program.[26]

In addition to growing technical capacity, development can also generate increasing revenues for government, depending on the elasticity of the tax structure. In some cases, one can plausibly argue that the increased flow of aid associated with "good" policy performance, or aid drawn to countries appearing to offer developmental "success," may have exacerbated conditions leading to conflict where the recipient government has exclusionary objectives. As Peter Uvin argued in the case of Rwanda, aid can inadvertently provide an elite with the incremental finances it needs to carry out a conflict-promoting agenda.

Ever since ancient times, a quickening of economic activity has everywhere been associated with *urbanization*. Whether as trading locales or as sites for industrial conglomerations taking advantage of economies of concentration, urban centers with regional or foreign linkages have been both sources ("growth poles") of general development and beneficiaries in terms of the opportunities and amenities they have provided their residents. In modern economic development, the proportion of a country's population in agriculture declines universally. The nonagricultural sectors (other than mining) tend to concentrate in urban areas, whereas employment opportunities and other attractions of urban life, especially in metropolises like Mexico City and Bangkok, draw vast numbers of migrants. Large urban centers are likely to bring together people from various regional and ethnic or cultural backgrounds, migrants from home areas where the ethnic composition was less varied, often monolithic. While urban migrant populations of one ethnicity or region of origin often cluster in their residential areas, they will be thrown together with people of diverse origin through work or other urban activities. Differences between rich and poor may be much greater than in rural areas, while the new rich may display their success in conspicuous consumption.

The effects of urbanization on interethnic relations can go either way. If the competitive aspects of urban life heighten the prejudices or predispositions to interpret relationships as exploitative and to view the "other" with mistrust and antagonism, the potentialities for mob psychology, for ethnic entrepreneurs, and the ready access to ethnic targets may increase the likelihood of violence. A current example can be found in Karachi, Pakistan, where there has been an ongoing violent relationship between Sindh residents and Muhajir migrants. The interethnic riots in Malaysia in 1969 were confined almost entirely to Kuala Lumpur, the capital. Conversely, before the recent collapse of Yugoslavia, Sarajevo had a long history of peaceful coexistence and intermarriage among its Muslim, Croat, and Serb residents. Sarajevo would appear to be one among many examples of urban ethnic mixing leading to greater tolerance, understanding, and appreciation of cultural diversity. (The reader should not conclude that Sarajevo also demonstrates the fact that urban multiculturalism may not be permanently impervious to ethnic conflict; the Serb residents who abandoned Sarajevo during the recent civil war did so reluctantly, forced out by the non-Sarajevan Serb military.)

Ethnic ties often help migrants find initial employment and adjust to urban life, reinforcing rather than weakening ethnic separation. One study asserts that in Africa urban ethnic heterogeneity has not acted to bring about assimilation or to break down the different ethnic value systems brought from rural hinterlands. As one observer has noted: "Non-ethnic institutions (such as trade unions) tend to be weak, while the urban elites have adopted a dual role—acting as sophisticated Westerners on the one hand and maintaining contacts with their home backgrounds and with traditional values on the other. In some Asian countries, heterogeneity has been a source of conflict."[27]

The alternation of periods of friendship and hostility in the history of many cities suggests that a destruction of amicable communal relations must result from changes in other factors that would likely produce conflict regardless of the patterns of residence and location. Urbanization per se is not a useful explanatory variable for understanding the Hindu–Muslim and intercaste riots that have been endemic in India since independence. These riots have occurred in large and small cities and in villages. In addition, "analysis of variance cannot explain why riots have become endemic in cities such as Meerut and Aligarh, among others, while other cities and towns with demographic and other characteristics even more favorable for riots have experienced far fewer such riots or none at all."[28]

In multilingual countries *language* differences, or efforts of governments to promote one language as the official one or the culturally dominant one in the name of pursuing national unity, have often been major sources of division and conflict. Economic development heightens the importance of language as a determinant of individual participation in the "modern" sectors and in government, and of group status. Many tongues spoken by relatively small populations are in a process of extinction as living languages, their speakers being irretrievably drawn to fluency in a majority, or major world, language. Throughout the Third World, knowledge of an international language (often the former colonial tongue) conveys major advantages over those who speak only the local languages; these advantages, for example, are seen in foreign trade or investment relationships, dealings with the international development institutions, or acquiring knowledge of modern science and technology. As development proceeds, rising levels of skill, knowledge, and communication expertise become increasingly essential as sources for raising productivity and income. Even among the world's richest nations, in Western Europe, multilingualism is the norm in the smaller-population countries.

Language can become a deeply divisive issue. Governments may promote the dominance of one language by granting it sole "official" status, requiring its use by civil servants or in citizens' dealings with government and in judicial proceedings, requiring it as the language of school or university instruction, or even by introducing sanctions against the use of proscribed languages. Forceful promotion of a dominant language as a method of achieving national unity—in effect, coercive assimilation of the speakers of the subordinated languages—can provoke the very divisiveness and conflict the policy is designed to prevent. In contrast, prudent language policy can be an effective tool for conflict management. For example, continued use of the colonial language as the *lingua franca*, or as a second official or legal language where one local language is given such status over other local tongues, may satisfy speakers of minority languages that their status and interests are not being subordinated. Alternatively, sole official status of the language of a dominant majority may be accepted by minority language groups if the use of the latter is given wide scope and not denigrated in any way. Esman has argued that long-term national cohesion may be best served by this sort of combination of sole official language, a required subject in the schools, alongside liberal use of the secondary languages.[29]

Migration has been a major factor in human history. Warfare has commonly marked the movement of whole peoples intent on economic betterment by usurping the land and wealth of others. The demographic composition of many developing countries today is the result of colonial-era migration policies that were intended to promote the colonies' economic development. The slave trade that transported masses of Africans to work the plantations of the Western Hemisphere was, of course, involuntary. In the nineteenth century, several colonial powers encouraged voluntary migration to promote the economic development of colonies they judged lacking sufficient commercial or professional classes or agricultural labor. Much of the contemporary conflict in developing countries has been occurring in postmigration societies that have yet to develop a new multicultural coherence or satisfactory power-sharing arrangements.

Modern economic development can also entail population movement other than urban migration. Such movements might involve resettlement of people from a densely populated area to one previously unoccupied and unexploited, or resettlement into an area already occupied but presumed to be underpopulated in relation to the land or other resources available for exploitation. Movement can be individual and spontaneous as people respond to what they perceive as better economic opportunities, or it might take place as a result of government encouragement or official resettlement programs. In late nineteenth- and early twentieth-century Spain, spontaneous internal migration from rural Castile to the industrialized areas of Catalonia and the Basque provinces contributed to destabilizing separatist movements. Although Basque nationalism historically had been weaker than Catalan, the depth of some Basque intellectuals' concern over demographic dilution of Basque culture and identity was greater, thereby contributing to the conditions that led to Basque terrorism. Modern Basque history and conflict would arguably have been quite different were it not for the apparent effect of immigration on the radicalization of Basque nationalism.[30]

In another example, the complex of issues feeding the Muslim insurgencies in the southern Philippines has been driven largely by the migration of Christian Filipinos from the more densely populated northern islands. The gradual reduction of the Moros to a minority in their previously homogeneous Islamic areas is the result of the migration encouragement begun by the American colonial administration and continued by independent Philippine administrations. In Indonesia, interisland migration also appeared to be a rational development policy for a country with some areas having dense agricultural population working very small landholdings and other areas having unoccupied arable land. The migration has brought together peoples of different religious and other identities, in some cases fueling violent conflicts that are adding to Indonesia's current problems of destabilization and of separation movements. (Although international population movement encouraged by government, such as the "guest worker" migrations to the advanced European economies as they recovered from World War II, or the large organized movement of Asian workers to Middle East oil producers in the 1970s and 1980s, may also cause ethnic tensions in the host countries, these consequences of modern development are outside the scope of this study.)

Additionally, recent migration of lowland Vietnamese settling on land in the country's Central Highlands region has resulted in violence between the migrants and the indigenous ethnic minorities. In this case, destruction of outlawed churches serving the Protestant minorities has added a religious complexion to the unrest.[31]

Government programs may involve forced or voluntary movement. Population displacement can take place in either rural or urban areas. Government-sponsored rural voluntary movements are most commonly associated with projects that offer people who are landless, or who are farming marginal holdings in densely settled "old" areas, the opportunity to resettle in newly opened irrigation or other land development programs. Involuntary displacement has often been a feature of irrigation or hydroelectric projects that entail the buildup of reservoirs and a consequent inundation of occupied lands. While resettlement in irrigation or land development programs has typically been voluntary on the part of the beneficiaries, it can have an obverse involuntary character for communities of prior occupants who may view the insertion of settlers as a threat to their holdings or cultural homogeneity. Urban development programs often require involuntary movement, especially in the case of slum clearance.

Indonesia provides a number of examples of conflict arising from recent migration that was officially promoted for economic development reasons. The inhabitants of West Kalimantan province on the island of Borneo have long resented the presence of migrants from Madura Island who were resettled under an official program dating from the 1960s, a program financed with donor support. In early 1999, no longer under the tight control of the authoritarian Suharto regime, the indigenous Malays and Dayaks massacred large numbers of the Madurese migrants. The government bowed to the indigenes' pressures, sequestering the Madurese and sending some back to Madura. The problem flared up again in early 2001 when "widespread rioting, looting and beheadings" required a massive response by the Indonesian military and police and further removals of Madurese refugees by the Indonesian navy. With the number of fatalities since 1999 reportedly in the thousands, this violence would classify as a civil war under the common criterion of at least one thousand fatalities a year.[32] In the Moluccan Islands there were long-standing Christian–Muslim tensions over perceptions in each group that the other was shutting them out in trade and education, respectively. The tensions were exacerbated when Muslim inmigration in the 1980s tipped the population balance against the Christians. Communal bloodletting in 1999 and 2000 claimed more than 5,000 victims.[33] The differing dynamics of migration and its social consequences in the northern and southern Moluccas are worth noting in detail.

In the south, political power had long been the domain of Christians. They were favored by the Dutch during the colonial era and carried that legacy forward when independence was achieved. After the migrations of the Soeharto years, immigrants from South Sulawesi . . . made up roughly a quarter of the population of the capital Ambon City. Their arrival tipped the confessional balance in favor of Islam and was accompanied by a rise in the political and economic fortunes of individual Moslems. In the 1990s, as part of President Soeharto's efforts to win the political support of Moslem groups, he began appointing Ambonese Moslems to the governorship. . . . As a consequence Moslems came to dominate the bureaucracy.

As in most parts of Indonesia, local politics has been intimately connected with patronage, access to resources and abuse of power. As power and bureaucratic weight have shifted from Christians to Moslems, so have money and opportunity. Christians in Ambon felt that they were being overwhelmed. . . . Just as in the south, North Maluku's conflicts have been aggravated by migration. . . . For instance, numerous battles have broken out between the Makian and Kao ethnic groups in the last 25 years, entirely due to the migration policies of the Soeharto years. . . . Cultural differences, competition for limited resources and a forced transfer of traditional Kao land to the Makian guaranteed a legacy of conflict between the two communities.[34]

In addition to heightening local resource pressures and political competition, migration also indirectly raised these areas' susceptibility to violence by contributing to the collapse of the traditional local conflict resolution systems.[35]

The Indonesian case is particularly apt because of the substantial support transmigration received from the World Bank and because its inequities and violent consequences (and resulting international criticism) forced the Bank to withdraw from this activity. This was apparently a case of missed opportunity, or, to be more precise, opportunity avoided. If the World Bank had applied (and the government implemented) the Bank's own policies respecting resettlement and the treatment of indigenous people, the outcome would probably have been very different and more beneficial to all participants.[36]

It is through the land pressures that have been generating many of these population movements that *population growth* emerges most clearly as a root of conflict. As Ismail Sirageldin has pointed out, however, demographic pressure can become either a source of conflict or a facilitator of development depending on the success and distributional outcomes of a country's development process. "Countries that postpone their fertility transitions will only increase the size of the demographic momentum, increase its impact on system vulnerability and reduce the potential for sustainable development."[37] For many years, wherever governments have been receptive, the development agencies have been assisting programs designed to slow population growth and bring the fertility transition forward in time. Donors have long emphasized in their development-assistance programs female education, maternal and child health, and family planning—the principal factors that have been affecting fertility levels. Because demography has already been a major concern of the development agencies, recognizing its relationships with conflict risk does not lead us to any new program conclusions for a conflict-prevention agenda.

Forced movement involving substantial numbers of people has generally been a political rather than economic phenomenon. So-called ethnic cleansing has been a political–military policy consequence of the failure of (or the perpetrators' disinterest in) conflict prevention, not a problem that can be charged to economic development per se in any meaningful way. Nevertheless the development agencies have been called upon to play a major role in alleviating the plight of people who are being, or have been, displaced by force. Resolution of the problems of forced movement is sometimes tied to the achievement of postconflict stability, that is, the prevention of another round of violent conflict, which would generate another round of displacement.

Conflict Modeling and Prediction

I turn now to some of the most recent attempts to develop models of conflict causation and forecasting. Faced with the complexities and multiple chains of causation behind every episode of modern internal conflict, many students have been developing models intended to sort out the more from the less important and to distill systematic patterns. Some of this work aims at description and explanation. Other work has been designed to provide policymakers with "early warning" of potential or impending conflict in specific situations. Economic factors figure in most of these models.

I focus on the more recent research, which is not necessarily superior analytically to earlier work, but which does have the advantage of building on the earlier work, and of taking account of the most recent conflicts and changes in the character of international response. As a point of departure I use the results of a large project of the World Institute for Development Economics Research (WIDER) and Queen Elizabeth House at Oxford University. The thirty-nine scholars contributing to the project wrote both case studies of conflicts in fourteen countries and the Transcaucasian region and thematic chapters on many aspects of the origins and prevention of conflict. The project's conclusions have been summarized by one of the authors, Jeni Klugman.[38] Strictly speaking, the subject of the WIDER project is "complex humanitarian emergencies" (CHEs), a recently coined category, defined as multidimensional manmade phenomena (i.e., some combination of intrastate

war, forced migration, hunger and disease, and essentially political and politicized crises). For analysis of conflict, CHE might be too broad a concept because it embraces countries suffering from a "poverty crisis" but free
of violent conflict. In fact, however, despite its title, the WIDER project
focuses only on countries that have had internal war—along with disease,
hunger, and/or population displacement.

For any practitioner or development agency policymaker desiring to contribute to conflict prevention, or at a minimum to avoid exacerbating the
problems underlying deep internal divisions, a broad knowledge of conflict
experience and of the general explanatory frameworks is essential. Nevertheless, an important caveat limits the practical applicability of any framework that purports to provide a *generally* valid analytic scheme, and of
virtually any empirical generalization, including those from quantitative statistical studies that couch their findings in the language of probabilities. The
caveat is simply this: in the real world of trying to prevent violent conflict,
one deals with individual conflict-prone countries, one at a time. Every case
has its own local history and some unique social, political, and idiosyncratic
characteristics.

In a recent study of a number of African cases, undertaken by the OECD
Development Centre, the authors capture the centrality of economic factors
and the balance of generality and local specificity. "The approach adopted
here explicitly acknowledges that socio-political instability has highly
economy-specific roots. Case studies, nevertheless, reveal many complementary elements and lead to some common insights that help to explain the
wide spectrum of socio-political outcomes within the same geographic region."[39] Every framework and generalization has its exceptional cases; application of causality concepts drawn from a large number of cases may be
misleading and distorting, and interventions that might be helpful in many
other cases could be ineffective or worse in any particular situation at hand.
The general frameworks and the supporting literature are important for ensuring that the analyst and practitioner avoid simplistic thinking and take
account of the potential applicability of conclusions from other experiences.
But there is no substitute for intimate knowledge of the specific society where
an outside agency has an opportunity and responsibility to help prevent violent conflict.

External agency responsibility cannot be ducked: the assumption long
held (or at least asserted) by many development practitioners and agencies,
namely that development assistance can be technical-neutral, in effect insulated from political conflicts in the surrounding society, has never been valid.
Mary Anderson observed that aid cannot be neutral in the midst of an ongoing conflict: "When given in conflict settings, aid can reinforce, exacerbate,

and prolong the conflict; it can also help to reduce tensions and strengthen people's capacities to disengage from fighting and find peaceful options for solving problems. Often, an aid program does some of both: in some ways it worsens the conflict, and in others it supports disengagement. But in all cases aid given during conflict cannot remain separate from that conflict."[40] Just as humanitarian aid cannot avoid affecting the dynamics of a violent conflict, so development aid cannot avoid affecting the underlying dynamics or root causes of conflicts in the years before they turn violent.

Returning to Klugman's summary, the author begins by distinguishing between root causes and triggers. "Conflict usually occurs when some 'trigger' event occurs in a situation of underlying vulnerability to conflict, arising from persistent economic and political differences among groups. The trigger necessarily involves some change—such as a sharp worsening in relative deprivation of a particular group." (Some analysts believe it beneficial to distinguish between triggers and accelerators. A *trigger* is defined as a unique event, such as an assassination, that immediately precipitates violent conflict. An *accelerator* is an earlier event, such as Klugman's "worsening in relative deprivation," which worsens the grievances and relationships, thus increasing the probability that a trigger event will occur and precipitate violent conflict.) Commonly found prior to violent conflict are certain necessary conditions, including (1) the *mobilization* of the contending groups, often facilitated by a history of earlier violence (e.g., Rwanda), and often deliberately accomplished by political leaders as a means to achieve power; (2) political and economic *inequalities* facilitate mobilization; absent such inequalities, group identification is likely to be weak and "remain a cultural rather than political or conflict-creating phenomenon"; (3) absence of alternative sources of income (i.e., unemployment), which would otherwise make the private cost of violence unattractive for followers; for leaders, in many cases, violence was a means for private accumulation (ethnicity merely a tool), while followers may be drawn by opportunities for loot (Liberia), if not by ideology (Cambodia).

The foremost root cause, according to Klugman, is *horizontal inequality*, that is, inequality between groups, in contrast to vertical inequality among income classes of individuals. Horizontal inequality can be economic, social, and political, often mutually reinforcing. For example, social inequality tends to limit access to economic opportunities that can reduce economic differences. Access to education, land, or the military may be key. Horizontal political inequality is nearly universal in conflict countries, with power monopolized sometimes by a majority, elsewhere by a minority. Invariably, the group monopolizing political power also benefits unequally from control of economic resources—government employment, revenue access, asset control. High poverty is found commonly among subordinate groups, thus facilitating their mobilization and resort to violence. Persistent economic failure induces dominant elites to resort to corruption and discrimination against the politically marginalized.

Severe conflicts are commonly preceded by a *crisis of state legitimacy.* In some cases a strong and repressive government has lost legitimacy among groups provoked to conflict. In others, weak and "eroded" states have left a vacuum in which violence has erupted. State disintegration is usually a long and degenerative process, sometimes initiated or enhanced by economic decline, and commonly entailing deterioration in public goods and services, such as education and transport infrastructure. In much of Africa, state legitimacy has eroded in the absence of democratic institutions. Conversely, democratic elections can induce political parties to play an "ethnic card," worsening ethnic tensions.

Worsening of economic conditions correlates with conflict eruption. Together with widening disparities, the main causal events are an increase in uncertainty about economic prospects and a weakening of public goods and services. Macroeconomic crises can also act as triggers (as in the Central American conflicts) when there is no consensus as to how to distribute the burden of adjustment in a society already characterized by deep economic inequality. The WIDER conclusions about worsening economic conditions and conflict appear to be ambiguous. On the one hand, Klugman notes that "standard stabilization and adjustment packages, through demand restriction and . . . liberalization of markets and reduction in the role of the state, can make parts of the population susceptible to mobilization by threatened elites." On the other hand, IMF and World Bank conditionality, "sometimes thought likely to promote conflict because of its harsh effects on vulnerable groups" through cutbacks in consumer subsidies and public services, was found generally not to have triggered ("directly provoked") conflict, except for minor episodes after some IMF agreements.

For some countries, these conditionalities were irrelevant altogether because the adjustment programs were never carried out. There appears to be an important distinction here respecting the extent and duration of violence commonly attributed to structural adjustment and the IMF. The WIDER project finds no conflict triggering; other studies focus on the frequent occurrences of the so-called IMF riots, mass urban protests most often triggered by adjustment program cuts in food subsidies, and resulting food price increases.[41] These findings are consistent because there is seldom a politicized connection between riots over market price increases for food (which are inherently nondiscriminatory among ascriptive groups of food consumers), on the one hand, and discriminatory and comparative grievances that form the basis for ascriptive group mobilization, on the other. (Again, Yugoslavia was an exceptional case; the IMF-led adjustment program was a contributory factor, as we have seen, through a strengthening rather than a reduction of central state authorities at the expense of the ascriptive-based republics.) For countries implementing such packages, WIDER recommends that the policy package include distributive measures to lower the risk of conflict. In fact, it has become common practice to include social safety net projects in the aid package.

Sudden *external economic shocks* (e.g., large shifts in the terms of trade) can worsen economic conditions, possibly leading, as just argued, to heightened possibility of conflict. Somalia and Nigeria are cited as examples. However, the WIDER project included an econometric test of possible causal relationships in 124 countries for the period 1980 to 1995, which found, among other things, no association with external shocks. The test did confirm significant correlation of CHEs with low economic growth and worsening income inequality (as measured by the Gini coefficient [an index of the extent to which the actual distribution of income in a country deviates from perfect equality]), slow growth in food production per capita (which does not appear to be an added finding for this research because in Africa stagnant food production would be an important component of low economic growth or decline rather than an additional independent variable), consumer price inflation, and a history, or "tradition," of past conflict. The test's use of income class (vertical distribution, which is what the Gini measures) for its association with CHEs is puzzling, for the text clearly states the conclusion that horizontal rather than vertical inequality is among the root causes, and is "foremost" at that. Finally, the research concludes that the presumption that *environmental decline* (and associated poverty) has been a cause of CHEs is not supported by the evidence. Nevertheless, environmental problems can worsen economic conditions, thereby increasing people's vulnerability. Conflict over water sharing has not been of a magnitude to be labeled a cause of CHEs, but has contributed to separatism in the Punjab in India and the Sind in Pakistan.

Even if we make allowances for the unavoidable omission of detail in any summary of underlying research as large as the WIDER effort (my summary truncates it even more, of course), the model illustrates some points common to many conflict paradigms. First, given the range of differences among conflict cases there are examples of conflict situations where conditions have departed from the model in important respects, implying that the model, if it had been used before the fact as a predictive tool, might have overlooked such cases. Although environmental degradation has led to local unrest and to the formation of activist NGOs (and "green" political parties in some industrial countries), it has not been shown to be a direct cause of general conflict. Nevertheless, several models include such degradation as a factor that can contribute to the catchall of general economic decline. As compared with vertical income inequality, horizontal inequality is more prominent in conflict models than in standard economic descriptions of country circumstances. Models vary in their causal typologies, but commonly agree on the importance of distinguishing between root causes and triggers.

Besides the WIDER framework, a number of additional efforts are under way to develop systematic or quantitative conflict models. Some of these efforts are the work of individual scholars; others are institutional products developed by teams of researchers. Most of these are intended as "early warning" guides. Virtually all are based on a causal structure, even if only implicitly in the choice of the relevant phenomena that merit monitoring as precursors of violent conflict.[42] Conversely, triggers (e.g., an assassination), early warning signs (e.g., sudden suppression of civilian rule), and statistically correlated factors (e.g., an association between low openness to international trade and high risk to conflict) that might signal violent conflict potential may have only a symptomatic rather than generative relationship with underlying structural causes.

Take, for example, the finding that the risk of conflict in a country is higher (other risk factors already accounted for) if the country has undergone a prior conflict. To my knowledge, the research thus far has not examined the degree to which such risk, at any point in time, might be raised by two previous conflicts rather than one, or multiple conflicts extending back through time. Does a history of successive conflicts reinforce the finding? Is there a kind of statute of limitations in the contemporary relevance of conflicts several generations past? Or should one assume that a certain number of repetitions indicates that renewal of warfare is unavoidable? The Moro Muslim rebellion in the Philippines is perhaps the longest-running, recurrent conflict in the world. As pointed out in the preface, it dates back four centuries. Does this history produce a dynamic that somehow renders all possible accommodations short of secession so unsatisfactory to the Moro that they will reject inclusion forever?

Based on the *Minorities at Risk* project, sponsored by the U.S. Institute for Peace, Ted R. Gurr has developed a model to assess which ethnic groups are most likely to rebel against their state. Gurr describes the *Minorities* project as the first research into communal conflict that, rather than being based on one or a small set of case studies, builds on information and data on all the (233) minority groups in the world that met two criteria: (1) "The group collectively suffers from, or benefits from, systematically discriminatory treatment vis-à-vis other groups in a state. Such differential treatment may be a consequence of widespread social practice or deliberate government policy or both." (2) "The group was the focus of political mobilization and action in defense or promotion of its self-defined interests at some time between 1945 and 1989."[43] Of course, not all minorities meet these criteria; groups in Tanzania, Switzerland, and elsewhere live in nondiscriminatory environments. The criteria may be thought of as root causes, as necessary but not sufficient conditions for generating violence. The criteria embrace both those groups that discriminate and initiate hegemonic (or worse) violence and groups that are discriminated against and adopt a violence program as a response. As Gurr and Harff added in a subsequent paper, for a completely causal, or predictive, model, these structural criteria need to be supplemented with dynamic factors that propel one group or another toward violent conflict, namely the accelerators or triggers. The structural model classifies groups as high risk, medium-high risk, or medium risk to conflict. The accelerators/triggers might be such things as attacks on the group, escalation of the group's demands and rhetoric, an increase in the militancy of the group's elite, or opportunities opened up by disunity or a weakening of the state's elite.

A relatively massive quantitative approach, involving a large number of academics and data collection and manipulation experts, is the State Failure Project supported by the Central Intelligence Agency (CIA). This project is intended to give early warning of crises as much as two years in advance. The definition of "state failure" focuses on severe erosion of state authority. Failure is identified by extent and by type (i.e., revolution, ethnic war, genocide/politicide, and disruptive regime change). Although the concept of the phenomena being studied by each of these first three approaches is different (complex humanitarian emergencies [CHEs], crises involving ethnic minorities, state failure), implying at least that some countries and conflicts in one data set may not qualify for inclusion in another, there is, in fact, substantial overlap. For example, it would be hard to imagine a severe violent interethnic, or state–minority conflict that would not qualify as a complex humanitarian emergency. For a contrary example, the conflict in Sri Lanka should not qualify as a case of state failure because the elected governments have retained their domestic and international legitimacy and their ability to rule over the majority of the country's area.

The State Failure Project drew a quantitative model from multivariate analysis of 617 variables, of which 31 were statistically significant for differentiating between states that did and did not suffer some type of failure. Among the significant variables were the openness to trade, already mentioned; infant mortality (a marker for quality of life); level of democracy ("partial" democracies being more vulnerable to failure than full democracies or autocracies); and "youth bulge" in ethnic conflicts. An adaptation for sub-Saharan Africa included variables such as urban share of population and presence of ethnic discrimination.

A. Jongman and A. Schmid of PIOOM (Interdisciplinary Research on Root Causes of Human Rights Violations) also begin by collecting a large data set for statistical manipulation. The data are indicators of human rights status and violations. Their approach is more dynamic than the previous exercises, however, as the indicators are recurrently updated (to create a time series to indicate trends and turning points) by field monitors using a common checklist. Although the objective is described as understanding root causes of, and identifying early warnings of, human rights violations, many of the countries in conflict, or at risk to conflict, would be covered.

By contrast, however, a human rights net would also cover countries that have gone through extended periods of serious violation where the very harshness of state suppression prevented any violent countermobilization (e.g., Argentina, Chile, China, Soviet Union). The PIOOM checklist includes the basic characteristics of stable, legitimate social systems: democracy, minority rights, orderly transitions of power, judicial independence, free press, would-be class or ethnic destabilizers lacking wide support, no paramilitary, no abrupt economic deterioration. Stages of increasing tension and rising conflict are characterized by degrees of deterioration in these characteristics. The PIOOM approach appears to rely on informed judgment brought to bear on a country-by-country basis, rather than a search for quantitative triggers drawn from averaging or multivariate techniques. It is more a typology than a general explanatory scheme, designed to serve as a pragmatic "watching brief."

For our perspective there is no need to detail the other predictive models summarized by Klugman.[44] As most are intended to be operational tools for crisis monitoring and policy response decision making, they call for continuous updating of the input data. Their large databases appear generally to record structural and event information on causes, changes, and triggers, and to categorize countries by stages of escalating risk.

A model prepared for USAID by Creative Associates is interesting because it is designed for use by practitioners and policymakers at all levels, including diplomats, military personnel, aid officials, NGO managers, and "development planners."[45] The model divides intergroup relations into five stages: durable peace, in which conflicts (differences of interest) may be latent or manifest; stable peace—conflicts (competitions) are manifest but regulated; unstable peace—unregulated conflicts, tensions, and possibly irregular armed forces and sporadic violence; crisis—tense confrontation of armed forces; war—low-intensity, anarchy, or all-out. As conflicts tend to evolve gradually through these "intermediate" stages, so the relevant potential interventions will vary. Between root (systemic or structural) causes, and immediate or triggering causes, the model defines an intermediate category of proximate or enabling factors. Whereas triggers are specific events, proximate causes are "problems in the social, political and communicative processes and institutions" that "influence" whether systemic conditions evolve into violent conflict. Conflicts tend to have a "life cycle" as they move through the intermediate stages into violence, and then de-escalate, often in stages of resolution that are also differentiated for identifying pertinent interventions— crisis management and dispute resolution, peace enforcement, peacekeeping, and postconflict peace-building.

The model lists ninety policy tools for conflict prevention and mitigation. In addition to diplomacy (such as good offices, formal conferences, sanctions, recognition or its withdrawal), nonofficial methods (NGO diplomacy, nonviolence campaigns, etc.), military measures (arms embargoes, military reform, preventive peacekeeping forces or intervention, etc.), political measures (party and election support, human rights monitoring and promotion, civil society development, power-sharing promotion, etc.), judicial and legal measures (war crimes tribunals, legal system reforms and strengthening, etc.), and communications and education (peace media, journalist training, civic education, training in conflict management and resolution), policy tools for conflict prevention also include economic and social measures. Among the latter are development assistance, economic reforms, private investment, humanitarian assistance and resettlement, economic cooperation and intercommunal trade, and two forms of pressure, namely economic sanctions and aid conditionality. *Sanctions* are shown as relevant for addressing immediate or triggering causes, *conditionality* as relevant for triggers or addressing proximate or enabling causes. All other developmental "tools" address systemic or structural causes. The guide then lays out an analytic process that moves from status description to the setting of preventive goals to the defining of specific measures to achieve the stated goals. The factors and problems recommended for attention are generally the same as those identified in the various early warning models.

Many of the insights of the studies I have cited are reconfirmed by a recent Dutch research project into the causes of conflict, based on fourteen country case studies. Though the Netherlands Institute of International Relations project unearthed some commonalities, it found that each conflict was locally and historically specific, with a "bewildering variety of factors and circumstances that conspire to make a situation conflict-prone."[46] It points out the importance of understanding the different starting points at independence, the different colonial histories and social configurations. In a slightly different take on categories of causes, the Netherlands Institute differentiated between root ("pivotal") factors needing resolution for a settlement, and factors that escalate and precipitate conflict, namely mobilizing factors, aggravating factors (which add weight to pivotal or mobilizing factors; e.g., small-arms proliferation), and trigger events. The study found that weak institutional capacity of government (to mediate, provide services to reduce dissatisfactions, or maintain sovereign authority) had contributed to the outbreak of violence. By attributing inadequate provision of services (implicitly, by benign governments) to capability shortcomings of public-sector service organizations, the study identifies a factor that is commonly addressed by development assistance programs and that might be worked on more aggressively where service dissatisfactions are feeding deep general grievance.

Getting from Causes to Interventions: Dense Reality versus Salient Focus

In agreement with the models above, most students of conflict in general, and individual conflicts in particular, believe that the causes (not necessarily the triggers) of conflict are multiple. In contrast, some students see multiplicity as obscuring the (presumably identifiable) limited number of causes that have been powerful enough by themselves to be sufficient conditions. Multiplicity would then confuse any attempt to identify the critical sources and would lead to a false sense that a much wider range of policies and interventions may be relevant than is actually required. There is a parallel here between the differences in negotiation strategy described by Kevin Avruch—the narrow, Realpolitik bargaining among the hostile leaderships versus the comprehensive resolution of underlying differences at many levels. Multiplicity of causes implies that resolution requires multifaceted negotiations and programs; critical subset implies that resolution efforts should focus leverage and resources on a limited number of critical issues.

A recent analysis of the conflict in the Congo provides an example of the multiplicity school. It cites three categories of issues essential for peace: "equitable distribution of power throughout the Congo; integrated, coordinated and multifaceted counterinsurgency campaigns against the nonstate actors. . . ; and a coherent strategy for addressing the boiling cauldron called Kivu [the easternmost region of the Congo.]" It calls for addressing these issues at "multiple levels." For example,

> The question of citizenship status of Congolese Tutsi populations remains explosive. A comprehensive social, legal, and economic strategy must be fashioned for this issue, including community meetings on coexistence, civic education, free movement of people, economic development, secure

land tenure, protection of individual and group rights, and local defense mechanisms.[47]

In a conference volume on conflict on the African continent, including country and cross-cutting studies, the multiplicity of causes is laid out in some detail. The prominent Africa scholars Francis M. Deng and I. William Zartman (1991) cite various domestic and external causes that have taken different configurations and relative weights in individual countries. The intrastate causes fall into three groups. First, there have been conflicts over natural or other resources, with individuals or groups competing for control over the resources or for "greater distributive justice" respecting national wealth. Second, there have been conflicts "over the definition of 'self' in the struggle for self-determination," the "core" of the conflicts in Sudan and Ethiopia/Eritrea. Third, there have been conflicts fueled by competing ideologies.[48]

In the same volume, Raymond W. Copson cites "ethnic cleavages or other deep social divisions," poverty, and "repressive policies and other political excesses on the part of African governments." He stresses the relative poverty of competing groups rather than the absolute level of deprivation, and the "resentment" felt by the relatively disadvantaged, or exploited, as they have observed these inequalities.[49] Although Copson does not make the point explicitly, his examples of political excesses illustrate a point that for many models also remains only implicit, namely the often critical role of individual rulers and their personal decisions to compromise or to repress, to bridge or to exacerbate and manipulate ethnic divisions so as to avoid or to precipitate conflict. The idiosyncrasies or fanaticism of individual rulers may have wide scope to determine the course of group conflicts in states where power is centralized and not constrained by rule of law or by a well-developed civil society. In other words, the causes include economic and material, psychological and sociological, and intellectual factors. The implication is that the multiple causes of conflict in Africa cannot be understood in their totality, or disentangled and weighed, if seen through the lens of only one or two disciplines. And efforts to prevent or mitigate these conflicts by addressing the apparently critical causes identified by one discipline or another (say, economics or political science) are likely to be simplistic and insufficient.

Most of the social and economic interventions called for by all these analyses would commonly be included in development programs anyway, whether or not a country was conflict prone. For people who doubt the effectiveness of foreign aid, or who see (nonhumanitarian) aid as only a marginally useful instrument of foreign policy in the post–Cold War world, the long-term links among economic development, democratic evolution, and the decline of violence as a means of conflict resolution should amount to a powerful argument for foreign aid in the self-interest of donor nations. At such a general level of analysis, however, without specifying just how the interventions might relate to conflict and might be shaped deliberately to enhance nonviolent outcomes, the recommendations are not programmatically powerful.

Although the few econometric studies that have attempted thus far to identify factors leading to conflict, or correlated with conflict to be more precise, using rigorous statistical analyses, have made suggestive beginnings toward separating the more salient causal relations from the less important, they also have yielded only limited guidance. Like the WIDER econometric study, Auvinen and Nafziger's research found significant association among slow economic growth or decline in GNP, a low level of economic development, and warfare (or complex humanitarian emergencies).[50] They found ("less clearly") that income inequality ("relative deprivation") and slow growth in food production were also sources of conflict. The associations with inflation and IMF funding were ambiguous. Two noneconomic variables included in their analysis, military "centrality" and a tradition of conflict, were "robustly" associated with humanitarian emergencies. Although the strength of these correlations varies depending on the numbers and kinds of variables included in the models, the statistical tests employed, and the data sets from which the variables are drawn, the general conclusions agree with much of the nonquantitative political science research. From this level of generality, however, one cannot expect detailed guidance for preventive intervention. Thus, the authors conclude that the international community should support economic growth, help reduce disparities in income and wealth, assist adjustment to economic disequilibria, promote good governance, and reduce trade in arms.

Recent work by Collier and Hoeffler (2000) illustrates how econometric analysis of conflict falls into the antimultiplicity camp. The purpose, of course, is to separate the more significant factors from the less significant through statistical treatment of variables that are selected to represent data (from as many conflict countries as possible, given data availability and comparability) on presumably conflict-relevant phenomena. This is an important line of research. The effectiveness of international conflict-prevention efforts depends in part on the choice of factors such efforts try to influence in any given situation. If it were known with some certainty which factors were unlikely to affect the outcome to any significant degree, external influence and resources could focus on the factors of importance. The Collier/Hoeffler research is still "work-in-progress" as indicated by their reservations regarding the quality of the data, their experimentation with different models, and the usual questions raised by the choices of individual variables used in the statistical analysis to serve as proxies, or representations, for social and political phenomena. A number of their findings are counterintuitive and inconsistent with (if not dismissive of) "conventional" findings that have gained wide acceptance in the literature on conflict, ethnicity, and state failure.

For example, the researchers found no significant relationship between income distribution and conflict. Further, in a comparison of two models, one postulating "greed" as the explanation for rebellion, the other postulating "grievance," they found grievance had low explanatory power.

> Our results thus contrast with conventional beliefs about the causes of conflict. A stylized version of these beliefs would be that grievance begets conflict, which begets grievance, which begets conflict. With such an analysis, the only point of intervention is to reduce the level of grievance. Our model suggests that what is actually happening is that opportunities for primary commodity predation cause conflict, and that the grievances which this generates induce diasporas to finance further conflict. The policy intervention points here are reducing the absolute and relative attraction of commodity predation, and reducing the ability of diasporas to fund rebel movements.[51]

The driving force in the Collier/Hoeffler research is "greed." Rebels initiate conflict in order to aggrandize themselves. The leaders go for the big prize, control over primary export earnings. The rank and file join for employment. It would follow that "rebellion depends on the financial and military feasibility of predation during combat."[52]

The reach for policy advice based on such research seems a bit premature. To generalize across a large number of conflicts is to eschew differentiation among types of conflicts and to exclude advice tailored to individual circumstances and exceptional cases, such as African cases "when a radical faction seizes power to eliminate corruption or to implement fundamental socioeconomic and political changes."[53] Or cases where conflict begins out of one party's conviction that no other recourse is available to perceived fundamental threat, despite the absence of an export prize or weaponry other than machetes (as in Rwanda and the Mollucas). Or where the military power of the state is overwhelming, and "feasibility" to an outsider might be judged dubious (as with Aceh province in Indonesia). On this latter point, Nafziger and Auvinen (1997) believe that severely repressed groups ("desperate bargainers") can be driven to launch civil war despite its apparent infeasibility as a winning strategy.

> Desperate underdogs will fight regardless of the consequences if they feel they have nothing to lose. South Africa's black population had been driven to such a position by the apartheid regime. The country would have lapsed into civil war no matter how strong the repressive machinery of the white

establishment was and no matter how little hope there was for the African National Congress coalition to win militarily.[54]

Paul Collier has also shown that heterogeneous countries with large numbers of ethnic groups, each representing a small fraction of the total population, are less likely to have civil war than countries with fewer ethnicities. In the latter cases, presumably (as Horowitz noted earlier), it is more feasible for a relatively large ethnic group, or an alliance of a very few groups, to attempt to establish hegemony. However, selecting a different set of variables as hypothetical causes of conflict can lead to very different explanations of individual country cases. Thus, Collier (2000) cites the absence of civil conflict in highly ethnically diverse Tanzania as an illustration of his statistical finding. Auvinen and Nafziger (1997) cite the relative evenness of income distribution ("shared poverty") as a possible explanation of the absence of destabilization despite Tanzania's economic stagnation.

The Fallibility of Conflict Forecasting

Many of the difficulties of modeling or predicting conflict have been illustrated by failures of the U.S. "intelligence community" to anticipate internal warfare, as in the cases of Rwanda and Yugoslavia.[55] A striking example was a mid-1999 publication of a conflict *tour d'horizon* prepared every eighteen months by the interagency National Intelligence Council. Based on the "coordinated views of analysts and experts from agencies across the Federal Government," the exercise attempts to foresee the likely direction (worse, status quo, or better) of ongoing and potential complex humanitarian emergencies (CHEs). The publication identified twenty-three countries then experiencing CHEs and another nine at risk. Indonesia was listed as an ongoing emergency because of economic crises and its need for food aid the previous year. Conditions were projected to improve between mid-1999 and end-2000. Somehow, the warning methodology and the culling of experts' views missed the conflict (and major CHE) that erupted in East Timor not long after the assessment was issued, and that had been predicted by the press in early 1999.[56] I see such discrepancies not as indications of incompetence, but as unsurprising examples of the fallibility of short-term prediction. Immediately after East Timor exploded, a group of Indonesia scholars and watchers admitted that, "As recently as August 30 [1999], when the East Timorese went to the polls on a day relatively free from violence and intimidation, it was possible to hope that an opportunity existed for Indonesia's democratic transition and economic recovery to progress side by side with self-determination for East Timor. That hope was shattered by the atrocities permitted and committed by the Indonesian military in East Timor."[57]

A critical Rand Corporation analysis characterized the predictive methodologies of the intelligence agencies as

> large-scale inductive models that statistically "grind up" enormous amounts of data, ranging from health and mortality statistics to the number of people under arms, in an effort to develop useful predictors of political violence. Such predictors, if at all finally available, merely describe correlations between some class of data and political violence. They do not establush a *causal* link between the variables included and the social outcome they seek to explain. Not surprisingly, such inductive models cannot ask questions that bear on the problem of *how* deprivation and discontent lead to strife.[58]

The Rand alternative is syncretic, a guide to judgment on a case-by-case basis. It is a staged analysis that moves from strife preconditions; through political mobilization by "identity entrepreneurs," changes in the power balance and resource availabilities, outside aid, and "tipping events"; to political confrontation, where bargaining and the role of the state determine whether there is nonviolent resolution or a breakdown into armed conflict. The analyst would use the framework to follow the course of events. Economic, anthropological, political, institutional, geopolitical, and other phenomena would be taken into account. The outcome never is predetermined (as simplistic historicism would assert: "these people are always at each other's throats"), but is contingent on many decisions, influences, chance happenings, and idiosyncratic personalities.

One cannot come away from a reading of the burgeoning "warning" materials and the beginnings of econometric examination of conflict without strong reservations. First, for most of the forecasting efforts "early warning" is a misnomer. The genre should more accurately be characterized as putative *late* warning systems. Much of the data fed into these systems applies to events (or accelerators) and triggers that are eleventh-hour happenings. Intergroup trust has already collapsed and violence is already under way or being prepared. We should reserve the notion of *early* warning to causal factors and indicators that are evident at least, say, a year prior to the breakdowns that take the parties to the brink, and over. A notional five to ten years would be much better as an intellectual orientation to true early warning. This is not to assert that such "warning" would serve as a predictor in any specific case. Rather, it would be interpreted as signaling a plausibly unfavorable outcome, a "heads-up." Based on experience elsewhere, the particular case could evolve into violent conflict. Current divisions, policies, and institutional arrangements should best be examined in this context.

Second, most investigators admit that the state of the art is still primitive. Some examples:

Conflict researchers by and large lack the ability to forecast adequately specific types of conflict, despite having identified hundreds of factors that in various combinations may contribute to the development of conflict phenomena. The problem is that large-scale empirical efforts may identify a handful of general variables that increase the likelihood of conflict but tell us little about what types of crises with what magnitude are likely to occur. . . . At present, "early" warnings are rarely early, seldom accurate, and moreover lack the capacity to distinguish among different types of conflict or crises.[59]

After virtually every major relief operation there are calls for the development of an effective early warning system of mass refugee flows. Despite such calls, there is no such system in place.[60]

Already in the 1960s Israel Charny called for an early warning system to prevent genocide. Three decades later we still do not have such a system. . . . In the field of human rights we still have no early warning system.[61]

Nevertheless, in recent years the warning enterprise has been growing in subtlety and has benefited from the obvious conviction on the part of the researchers and organizations involved that the ills they are addressing are among humankind's most egregious, and that they are developing public-policy instruments that could be of substantial value for human welfare. The fact that there is a great deal of overlap among their various constructs has encouraged rapid dissemination of ideas, data banks, and draft papers (and Web sites). There is probably some wasted money and effort in this profusion owing to the different missions of the interested organizations and different disciplinary frameworks of individual researchers. Thus, separate conceptual and data-gathering systems have been created aiming at "early" warning of different aspects of violent conflict: internal population displacement; external, that is, refugee, flows; political terror; political violence (politicide); large-scale human rights violations; general minority risk; state failure; civil war; complex humanitarian emergencies; and genocide. There are clear differences among these phenomena. Internal and external population displacement differ in their cross-border and international effects. Minority risk or civil war seldom transmutes into genocide. But all these phenomena are correlates of violent conflict; they often occur in the same conflict and might be tracked or "forecast" by a single model that could effectively capture conflict escalation processes, as suggested by Alex P. Schmid, of PIOOM.[62]

Third, care should be taken to avoid assuming that collection of ever greater volumes of data, and the appearance of increasing quantification of the analyses, ensures that we are getting closer to having robust conflict theories and increasingly reliable conflict forecasts or numerical indicators of conflict-risk probabilities. Perhaps because the state of the art is still primitive, increasing resources seem to be going into construction of warning models and statistical formulations of conflict risk. We should recall von Hayek's warnings about the fallacies of misplaced quantification, from his 1974 Nobel Memorial Lecture on "The Pretence of Knowledge":

> Unlike the position that exists in the physical sciences, in economics and other disciplines that deal with essentially complex phenomena, the aspects of the events to be accounted for about which we can get quantitative data are necessarily limited and may not include the important ones. . . . And while in the physical sciences the investigator will be able to measure what, on the basis of a *prima facie* theory, he thinks important, in the social sciences often that is treated as important which happens to be accessible to measurement. . . . Such a demand for measurable magnitudes quite arbitrarily limits the facts which are to be admitted as possible causes of the events which occur in the real world.[63]

There is a further technical difficulty. Even if the investigator identifies a relevant variable that appears quantifiable in a straightforward·manner, the measured events may actually be ambiguous as an indicator of the phenomenon they are intended to represent. A history of political instability, for example, is a common precursor of violent conflict. Some investigators have created indices of instability based on the frequency of revolutions and/or coups. Such an index would miss the potential for conflict in a country that had undergone a long period of authoritarian government that had successfully repressed discontent or frustrated local ethnonationalisms (e.g., in Zaire/ Congo, or among ex-USSR republics). It would also falsely predict conflict if a country had a long history of coups by military rivals riding along on the surface, so to speak, of an underlying history of social stability and technocratic/bureaucratic continuity, as was the case for many years in Thailand. In short, an effort to nail down a general sociopolitical concept can misconstrue complex realities that vary substantially from country to country.

Illusive but Real: Nonmaterial Motivations

If any demonstration is needed of the relevance of von Hayek's point to the investigation of the essentially complex phenomena of societies in conflict, one can refer to the important role of psychological, ideational, and ethical factors among the causes, or enabling conditions, leading to the two worst conflicts and largest genocide of the twentieth century. In his effort to understand how the bulk of the German population and elite were drawn to support the Nazi agenda, historian Fritz Stern wrote at length about his "belief that National Socialism was the great moral drama of our time, and that the vulnerability of Germans, especially of the German elites with their claims to superior education, responsibility, self-awareness, and a sense of history, to Hitler's triumph was a fateful theme in that drama." Stern argues that "for many Germans, National Socialism in its deliberate pseudo-religious form appeared as a great temptation, as a promise of national salvation that harked back to earlier hopes and delusions. 'Temptation' in the essay title suggests the irrational elements in submission." Stern observes that World War I inculcated "ideological simplicity and vast distrust. The Germans did not have a protracted or unifying course in politics or self-government. The emotional vocabulary continued under Weimar; in many ways National Socialism was a continuation of wartime politics and psychosis by other means and under different circumstances."[64] Stern also records the captivation, in World War I and in the years leading up to World War II, of the intellectuals and of their suspension of critical thought under the spell of emotional nationalism.

> "Self-imposed" conformity, often unconscious, kept pace with Hitler, and nowhere was this more striking than in the German universities, which had always boasted of their autonomy. This self-surrender of the intellectual elite recalls Sigmund Freud's sense of why in the Great War "the best intellects" demonstrated "their uncritical credulity towards the most disputable assertions. . . . Students of human nature and philosophy have long taught us that we are mistaken in regarding our intelligence as an independent force and in overlooking its dependence on emotional life. . . . Thus, in their view, logical arguments are impotent against affective interests. . . ." These "affective interests" had as much to do with the self-surrender to National Socialism as other interests; cold calculation or opportunism offers only partial explanation. . . . Despite [Nazi] attacks on the traditional rule of law and on the honor of scholarship, most professors—as they had in 1914—immediately and passionately espoused the national cause, the German renewal. This outpouring of support was of course in part a product of human weakness, of fear of reprisal, of careerism. But opportunism alone does not explain this behavior.[65]

There was a similar outpouring of elite and popular enthusiasm for war in Europe in 1914. Stern describes how a "war-starved" Europe responded to the outbreak with "unprecedented exaltation." "The famed spirit of August 1914 expressed a great yearning for a different world, a world of action, sacrifice, unity, a release from bourgeois boredom. War as the redeemer, unifier, cleanser—that was one of the great delusions of our century." No less a person than Thomas Mann admitted in 1915 that "we had seen the trial coming—and still more, in some way we longed for it, felt in the depths of our heart that the world, our world, could not go on like this any more. We knew that the world of peace . . . horrible world, which no longer is, or no longer will be, after the great storm passed by. Did it not crawl with spiritual vermin as with worms? Did it not ferment and stink of the decaying matter of civilization?"[66]

In his magisterial study of nineteenth century Europe's intellectual history, entitled *The Cultivation of Hatred,* historian Peter Gay concludes by writing about the culmination in broad enthusiasm for, and belief in, violent conflict:

> The [1914–1918] war had not come wholly without warning. For decades, imaginative novelists and underemployed military men had forecast sanguinary conflicts between nations and races. Some of these dreamers wrote to castigate human self-destructiveness, others to belabor a bourgeois order badly in need of a fighting tonic. . . . This literature reflected, and fostered, ingrained bellicose attitudes, whether drawn from a Social Darwinist defense of conflict in human affairs or an avant-garde irritation with effeminate commercial civilization. The pacifist ideology, though it had enlisted eloquent advocates, was feeble in comparison; spokesmen for pugnacity, schooled to see mortal violence as a great teacher, apparently had a solid majority behind them."[67]

Several years before the Nazis took power, the student population was "enthralled" by National Socialism. As Fritz Stern observes: "[T]he student elections of 1928–1930 were decisively pro-Nazi, far in excess of the party's national electoral strength. The students had grown up in the deprivation of the war; their teachers—authoritarian figures—had contempt for the [Weimar] republic. . . . [T]he young infected their teachers as well. The teachers' envy of the young, the admiration for their 'idealism,' while they were embarrassed by their own bourgeois tenured security, was considerable."[68] In effect, Stern sees generally shared intellectual failures and distorted emotional proclivities as central for an understanding of the ease with which National Socialism mobilized the population behind its violent agenda.

The vast scholarship on the causes of the two world wars is seldom, if ever, drawn upon in the literature on contemporary internal conflicts of developing countries. The parallels may be few, although the general conflagration included intrastate conflicts, such as the Spanish Civil War, the warfare among resistance armies in Yugoslavia and China, and conflicts between resistance movements and collaborationist regimes in some occupied countries. I cite these references to the impetus to conflict flowing from intangible, emotional, and psychological motivations only to recall the obvious point that such conflict motivations not easily captured as quantifiable data or variables can be powerful forces. As historian Paul Kennedy notes:

> In an anarchic world that lacks a single sovereign power to order its destinies, tribes, cities, empires and nation-states have jostled alongside each other, and all too often gone to war with each other for a whole variety of motives—for land, for trade, for gold, because of dynastic or religious or ideological rivalries, out of fear of being overtaken or a desire to overtake.[69]

Conclusion: Multiple Causes Call for Multiple Interventions

Deng and Zartman have written about the "complex pattern of causation" behind Africa's conflicts. Among the major internal factors, they cite "ethnic cleavages or other social divisions . . . religious cleavage . . . a region's relative impoverishment . . . degradation of unemployment and underemployment . . . repressive policies and other political excesses." The persistence of repressive governments and violent guerrilla movements in "uncompromising stances" has frustrated the efforts of would-be outside mediators.[70] In the face of such arrays of motivations and sources of conflict, many of which in any one situation are likely to be present and of varying (and uncertain) relative importance, it is not surprising that the search for international responses and remedies has generated calls for multiple interventions.

A good example is the final report of the Carnegie Commission on Preventing Deadly Conflict, issued at the end of 1997. The Carnegie Commission proposes the widest possible range of measures aimed at prevention when conflict appears imminent, and at prevention by addressing root causes. In the face of imminent conflict, the commission urges (in addition to forceful measures, if necessary) strengthening of early warning capabilities, preventive diplomacy, economic inducements or sanctions, aid conditionality (or what others have called "peace conditionality"), and the creation of new international machinery to serve as dispute-resolution good offices for intrastate economic disputes, analogous to the interstate role of the World Trade Organization.

To address international and internal root causes, what the Carnegie Commission calls "structural prevention," the report proposes both international and internal measures. Recommendations concerning such things as controls on weapons of mass destruction, conventional arms control, regional security arrangements, avoidance of third-party exacerbation and meddling in internal disputes, and creating just regimes and police and military adherence to rule of law—are all of obvious importance but beyond the scope of this study. There can be little doubt that if these various measures and institutional arrangements were generally in place, the efficacy of the rest of the commission's proposals—which concern internal root causes beyond fears of insecurity—would be enhanced substantially.

The commission report posits a direct connection between material deprivation and risk of conflict.

> Existing in a secure environment is only the beginning, of course. People may feel relatively free of from fear of attack, but unless they also have the opportunity to maintain decent living standards, discontent and resentment can generate unrest.
>
> Too many of the world's people still cannot take for granted food, water, shelter, and other necessities. The slippery slope of degradation—so vividly exemplified in Somalia in the early 1990s—leads to growing risks of civil war, terrorism, and humanitarian catastrophe.[71]

The critical connection with receptivity to violence may be through people's perceptions that their government is standing in the way of improvement in their conditions, both absolute and relative.

> Well-being entails access to basic necessities, including health services, education, and an opportunity to earn a living. In the context of structural prevention, well-being implies more than just a state's capacity to provide essential needs. People often are able to tolerate economic deprivation and disparities in the short run because governments create conditions that allow them to improve their living standards and that lessen disparities between rich and poor.[72]

To improve living conditions and create confidence that government is enhancing rather than blocking people's prospects, the commission recommends widely shared economic and social development. The perception of fairness is more important than material progress itself. "The resentment and unrest likely to be induced by drastically unbalanced or inequitable economic opportunity may outweigh whatever prosperity is generated by that opportunity."[73] Development also needs to be sustainable, as mass violence can erupt from disputes over resources that are scarce or depleting. Countries need strong rule of law, sound legal regimes to protect human rights, participatory governance, and social accommodation of diverse groups. Such accommodation should include freedom to practice religion, educate people in minority languages, and pursue individual cultures. International assistance of various kinds can help countries develop the requisite legal and other governance systems, civil society organizations, and responsible free media. Religious leaders should be called upon to promote tolerance and interfaith dialogue and to censure fellow religionists who espouse violence. Important contributions to greater understanding of the causes of violence, and to promoting tolerance, dispute-resolving institutions, and a "culture" of nonviolence, should be made by the scientific, educational, and business communities, and by the media. Donors should enhance development prospects through measures like increased aid and debt relief.

The Carnegie Commission endorses a set of judgments taken from reports by the World Bank and UNDP on how economic and social development should be approached. The judgments are standard calls for pro-growth and poverty-reducing policies. "These judgments reinforce the Commission's belief that diligent programs that help cultivate the human resources of a country, in ways that ensure widespread access to economic opportunity, will help create conditions that inhibit widespread violence."[74] As an article of faith, the presumed connection—pro-growth and poverty-reduction (i.e., development and distribution) policies that create the kinds of socioeconomic conditions that inhibit (widespread) violence—is too complex to be accepted without examination or qualification. Development and distribution policies are numerous and heterogeneous. Even if intended to favor the poor, it is unlikely they would all, under all developing country conditions, have the happy result of ensuring peace. What is surprising is that early prevention, through development assistance deliberately shaped to address root causes of internal conflict, has received relatively little attention beyond generalities and hopeful proposals.

Notes

1. Gary S. Fields, "Income Distribution and Economic Growth," in Gustav Ranis and T. Paul Schultz, eds., *The State of Development Economics*. Oxford: Basil Blackwell, 1989, pp. 459–460.

2. Tellis et al., 1997, p. 7.

3. Horowitz, 1985, ch. 4.

4. The small community of ethnic German Mennonites who have lived in Kyrgyzstan for generations (some are descendants of settlers from over two centuries ago) provides an interesting example of cultural characteristics, sustained over many years, more materially efficacious than those of the host society. The community is known for hard work, thrift, and orderliness. Their homes are recognized as superior investments, better built and maintained than the homes of other ethnicities in the country. *New York Times*, October 11, 1999, p. 4.

5. Martin O. Heisler, "Hyphenating Belgium: Changing State and Regime to Cope with Cultural Division," in Joseph V. Montville, ed., *Conflict and Peacemaking in Multiethnic Societies*. Lexington, MA: Lexington Books, 1991, p. 181.

6. Ibid., p. 182.

7. Nordlinger, 1972, p. 99.

8. Cited by Blanche Wiesen Cook, in *Eleanor Roosevelt*, Vol. 2. New York: Viking Penguin, 1999, p. 502.

9. Dani Rodrik, "The Asian Financial Crisis and the Virtues of Democracy," in *Challenge* (July–August 1999): 44–59.

10. Esman, "Economic Performance and Ethnic Conflict," in Montville, 1991, pp. 477–490.

11. Horowitz, 1985, p. 131.

12. Ibid., p. 259.

13. Horowitz, n.d.

14. Alberto Alesino and Roberto Perotti, "The Political Economy of Growth: A Critical Survey of the Recent Literature," in *World Bank Economic Review* 8, no. 3 (September 1994): 367–368.

15. International Food Policy Research Institute, *IFPRI 1998: Essays*. Washington, DC.

16. Jimmy Carter, "First Step Towards Peace Is Eradicating Hunger," *International Herald Tribune*, June 17, 1999.

17. See Cohen and Feldbruegge, n.d., p. 3, and Messer et al., 1998, pp. 9–13.

18. Tania Li, *Malays in Singapore: Culture, Economy and Ideology*. Singapore: Oxford University Press, 1989, p. 182.

19. Prendergast and Smock, 1999, pp. 7–8.

20. Ortega y Gasset, *Revolt of the Masses*. New York: Mentor Books, 1950, p. 55.

21. Sigmund Freud, *Civilization and Its Discontents*. New York: Norton, n.d., p. 65.

22. Peter Gay, *The Cultivation of Hatred*. New York: Norton, 1994, pp. 518–519.

23. For a good one-volume overview and evaluation of structural adjustment programs, see Carl Jayarajah and William Branson, *Structural and Sectoral Adjustment: World Bank Experience, 1980–92*. Washington, DC: World Bank Operations Evaluation Study, 1995.

24. David E. Sahn et al., *Structural Adjustment Reconsidered: Economic Policy and Poverty in Africa*. Cambridge: Cambridge University Press, 1999.

25. Jayarajah and Bronson, 1995, ch. 6.

26. Muscat, 1994, pp. 54–65.

27. Harry W. Richardson, *City Size and National Spatial Strategies in Developing Countries*. World Bank Staff Working Paper No. 252. Washington, DC: April 1977, p. 37.

28. Brass, 1997, p. 51.

29. Esman, 1992, p. 393–395.

30. Basque nationalism "lacked the political clout of its Catalan counterpart. With little support from the local industrial oligarchy, its cultural, linguistic, and political roots were less secure. The most eminent Basque intellectuals . . . scorned Basque as a literary language. Native Basques had a strong sense of community but, unlike Catalonia, the Basque provinces could not count on the memory of a single political unit with a glorious past. Sabino de Arano . . . the founder of Basque nationalism and its party, the PNV, saw the Basque-speaking community as being threatened by a flood of migrant Castilian speakers . . . who came to work in the mines and factories around Bilbao. To save this community from adulteration Sabino de Arano invented a national unit, which he called Euzkadi, which would separate from Spain. . . . Catalan nationalism, given its wide social support and secure linguistic and cultural roots, had no need to resort to violence." Raymond Carr, *Spain: A History*. New York: Oxford University Press, 2000, pp. 228–229.

31. "Vietnam Admits to More Unrest Among Minorities in Highlands," *New York Times*, February 9, 2001, p. A5.

32. "Indonesia Clashes," *New York Times*, February 26, 2001, p. A6.
33. *Far East Economic Review*, February 24, 2000, pp. 32–33.
34. International Crisis Group, 2000, pp. 2–3.
35. Ibid., p. 2.
36. The experience is described briefly by Daniel R. Gibson in "The World Bank and Displacement," in Esman and Herring, 2001, pp. 38–39.
37. Sirageldin, 1994, p. 20.
38. Klugman, 1999.
39. Goudie and Neyapti, 1999, p. 10.
40. Anderson, 1999, p. 1.
41. E.g., John Walton and Charles Ragin, "Global and National Sources of Political Protest: Third World Responses to the Debt Crisis," in *American Sociology Review* 55 (1990): 876–890.
42. My summary of these models draws partly on the convenient review in Verstegen, 1999.
43. Gurr, 1998, pp. 6–7.
44. Accelerators of Genocide Project, B. Harff, University of Maryland; Life Integrity Violations Analysis (LIVA) project, H. Fein; Protocol for the Assessment of Nonviolent Direct Action (PANDA), D. Bond, Harvard University; Conflict Early Warning Project, P. Brecke, Georgia Institute of Technology; conflict patterns/stages analysis, P. Schrodt and D. Gerner. Some focus narrowly on a brief time span prior to a violent outbreak, differing from each other more in the recording and manipulation methods than in the structural or event data they judge relevant. One is designed to forecast (or at least identify the precursors of) only the most extreme form of conflict —genocide. There are also warning models and data bases developed by the United Nations, the World Bank, and a few governments. Humanitarian Early Warning System (HEWS), U.N. Department of Humanitarian Affairs; model of the German Federal Ministry for Economic Co-operation and Development; model of Pauline Baker, Fund For Peace; model of the Forum on Early Warning and Emergency Responses (FEWER), a consortium product; pilot study for an early warning system, Swiss Foreign Ministry.
45. Creative Associates International, 1997.
46. Netherlands Institute of International Relations, 1999, p. i.
47. Prendergast and Smock, 1999, pp. 8–9.
48. Deng and Zartman, 1991, pp. xvi–xviii.
49. R.W. Copson, "Peace in Africa? The Influence of Regional and International Change," in Deng and Zartman, 1991, pp. 25–27.
50. Juha Auvinen and E. Wayne Nafziger, "The Sources of Humanitarian Emergencies," in *Journal of Conflict Resolution* 43(3) (June 1999): 267–290.
51. Collier and Hoeffler, 2000a, p. 25.
52. Collier and Hoeffler, 2000c, p. 14.
53. Ted R. Gurr, "Theories of Political Violence and Revolution," in Deng and Zartman, 1991, p. 170.
54. Nafziger and Auvinen, 1997, p. 54.
55. Tellis et al., 1997, pp. 2–3.
56. *Far East Economic Review*, February 11, 1999, p. 18.
57. East Asian Institute, Columbia University, *Transition Indonesia: Perspectives of American, Japanese, and Australian Observers*, September 1999, p. 14.
58. Tellis et al., 1997, p. 4. Italics in the original.

59. Barbara Harff, "Early Warning of Humanitarian Crises: Sequential Models and the Role of Accelerators," in Davies and Gurr, 1998, pp. 70–71.

60. L. Clark, *Early Warning of Refugee Flows*. Washington, DC: Refugee Policy Group, 1989, p. 1.

61. Alex P. Schmid, "Indicator Development: Issues in Forecasting Conflict Escalation," in Davies and Gurr, 1998, p. 39.

62. Ibid., pp. 40–41.

63. Friedrich August von Hayek, "The Pretence of Knowledge," in *The American Economic Review* 79, no. 6 (December 1989): 3.

64. Fritz Stern, *Dreams and Delusions*. New York: Random House, 1989, pp. 140–141.

65. Ibid., pp. 168–169.

66. Ibid., pp. 141–142.

67. Gay, *Cultivation of Hatred*, 1994, p. 517.

68. Stern, *Dreams and Delusions*, 1989, p. 160.

69. Paul Kennedy, "American Grand Strategy, Today and Tomorrow: Learning from the European Experience," in Paul Kennedy, ed., *Grand Strategies in War and Peace*. New Haven, CT: Yale University Press, 1991, p. 167.

70. Deng and Zartman, 1991, pp. 225–227.

71. Carnegie Commission, 1997, pp. xxxi–xxxii.

72. Ibid.

73. Ibid., p. xxxii.

74. Ibid., p. 86.

Part II

Toward an Agenda for Conflict Prevention

4. Relevance and Assessment

To address root causes of conflict, the Carnegie Commission report recommends stronger measures to cope with security problems, to strengthen systems of justice, and to promote well-being and development. It calls for upgrading the state's capacity to provide access to basic needs (health, education, water, shelter, etc.) and improving both the policies and the attention that governments devote to raising living standards and reducing disparities. In its call for greater international efforts to promote economic growth and reduce poverty, the Carnegie Commission cites, in very general terms, a few interventions: economic organization that enhances broadly distributed growth; a focus on women and children; resolution of conflicting claims over scarce resources (food, water) and natural resource endowments (e.g., oil); reducing environmental degradation and the pressures of population growth; developing good governance. "In sum, improving well-being requires a multifaceted approach. It means mobilizing and developing human capacities, broadening and diversifying the economic base, removing barriers to equal opportunity, and opening countries to participation in the global economy and the international community."[1] Unfortunately, recommendations at this level of generality do not provide additional practical guidance. All of these activities have long been the staples of international development programs.

As is the case with much of the prescription literature, the Carnegie Commission assumes economic development will be conflict-reducing. The recommendations also reflect the ease with which a prescription can move from "development" to an emphasis on one or a handful of factors based on a surface plausibility of strong relevance. For example, the commission states: "There is great preventive value in initiatives that focus on women and children, not only because they are the main victims of conflict, but also because women in many vulnerable societies are an important source of community stability and vitality."[2] No one would quarrel with the observation that women and children are the main victims of many conflicts and that they deserve international attention. However, for reasons we will examine below, the argument that women are an important source of community stability, and therefore are a natural conflict-opposing constituency that can be strengthened in this role by aid resources and projects, is less compelling as a guideline for international assistance.

The examination of conflict thus far has thrown up numerous structural characteristics, policy areas, and conflict-management processes where the work of the international agencies has been, or could be, relevant in shaping outcomes. It is important to avoid any simplistic assumption that potential relevance of any one or set of the interventions or activities reviewed here will automatically translate into general conflict reduction. In some circumstances—of timing, conflict intensity, extremist politics, or fundamentalist religious movements—the mandates, policy and project agendas, and capabilities of the international development agencies are totally overshadowed by forces that can be addressed only by international diplomatic and security processes. It would be unrealistic to believe that development-assistance programs might have been construed to prevent conflict in societies where rule of law has never been reestablished (or initially established in modern independent history) and where power is recurrently contested by warlords; or in countries with a long history of internal violence, where conflict can be said to be a "normatively justifiable" characteristic of the political culture;[3] or in countries ruled by authorities who reject the modern material development paradigm; or during periods when countries are ruled by vicious and/or hermetic regimes.

It is also difficult in practice to know when an apparent opportunity holds realistic promise of root-cause amelioration. Aid-assisted socioeconomic measures might be inadequate to the opportunity if not accompanied by effective diplomatic and political interventions, or an international effort of many dimensions may be powerless (short of military intervention) to change or block local political forces intent on violent contestation. The African nation of Burundi is a case in point. At independence in 1962, the Tutsi minority (16 percent of the 6.2 million population) retained the governing power they had held for four centuries except for the (German-British-Belgian) colonial period that had begun in 1899. The Tutsi military rejection of the first (1965) election results, in which the Hutu won a large legislative majority, initiated years of revolt, political assassination, massacres, and deepening ethnic polarization and extremism. A window of opportunity seemed to open in 1988 following an army slaughter of about 20,000 Hutu. The donors pressed upon the latest Tutsi regime a package of political and economic reforms. As described by Stephen R. Weissman, it is "almost unthinkable" that a political settlement could be developed in Burundi without "substantial international support, including a deft mixture of carrots and sticks."

However, the effort made when the window appeared to open failed because it relied on an electoral form that was majoritarian rather than a power-sharing form, and because the "moderates" with whom the international community negotiated did not command the allegiance of their more extremist constituencies. Needless to say, in such a politically flawed "settlement" the economic measures, and the leverage applied, were marginal and ineffectual. It remains to be seen whether the power-sharing arrangements, installed on November 1, 2001, after lengthy negotiations led by Nelson Mandela, will fare any better. The violence launched within days by Hutu groups that had refused to participate in the negotiations was not encouraging.

In other conflict-prone countries, however, well short of genocide, major issues of contention are likely to be affected by the programs of the development agencies. The dynamics of contention may still allow sufficient time for these agencies to help develop mutually acceptable solutions and conflict-avoiding alternatives. Given the large numbers of donors and projects in typical developing countries, and the wide range of potentially conflict-relevant factors, it would be surprising if many aid activities did not touch contentious issues and conflict sources. As examples, in Tanzania more than forty donors were supporting over 2,000 projects in the early 1990s. Kenya and Zambia in the mid-1980s had sixty to seventy donors with about 600 projects.[4] Such arrays of activities commonly engage virtually every government ministry, working in nearly every sector and area of a country.

In what follows, I try to sketch out an agenda covering subjects and activities that are relevant to conflict and that are the normal bread-and-butter concerns of the development agencies. Some subjects are more suitable to multilateral agencies, either by mandate or by the comparative advantages they have developed over time. Others are more suitable for bilateral aid agencies, reflecting their less constrained mandates, their aid orientation, or historic relationships with particular recipient countries. An important point stressed above bears repeating: the pursuit of the policy and project activities in this agenda may often affect conflictive relationships even if the involved agency has been oblivious to these conflict-dimensions altogether, under the illusion, and with the intent, that its aid is underwriting a politically neutral "technical" activity. As the Bangladesh secession example demonstrated, perverse unintended consequences are reprehensible even if they arise from sheer oversight or from an analytic framework that artificially separates the economic or technical from the political and social. How severe the divisions are, how antagonist the relationships, what the specific points at issue are, what kinds of interventions or policies or projects may be salient—all will vary from country to country and from time to time, and they can best be determined, or suggested, by a systematic assessment.

In discussing any particular structural or distributional feature, and how an agency might be relevant and attempt some ameliorative action, I do not mean to imply that in general this problem or that structural feature is likely to be a sufficient cause of severe conflict, or that any single intervention will be powerful enough itself to counterbalance all the forces that may be pressing toward conflict. Rather, I assume that each of the potential interventions will be relevant in some instances, irrelevant in others, more salient in some and less in others. Some combination of interventions and policies will probably be advisable in most cases to develop a program adequate to create expectations and trust that credible positive-sum accommodations are feasible and are being created with international support.

Much of what follows builds on some guidelines Milton Esman has laid out in his valuable paper on foreign aid and ethnic conflict.[5] Esman suggests that development agencies search for appropriate *allocation formulas* in their choice and design of policies or projects. The first formula involves *common interests*. "The ideal policy or project set produces positive sum outcomes for all the parties concerned." Avoid interventions "that will be perceived as benefiting one community at the expense of another." His second formula favors *divisibility*—that is, projects that can be provided in separate components, thereby offering benefits to different communities residing in different areas. Third, Esman suggests searching for programs that create *interdependence*, "where a division of labor between ethnic communities rewards cooperative rather than competitive behavior." He cautions that allocation of aid-financed or aid-supported benefits (scholarships, jobs, privatization of state enterprises, etc.) according to neutral criteria of merit or market competition may correct or reinforce systemic ethnic distortion, depending on the circumstances. Technical neutrality does not guarantee an optimal social outcome. Competitive criteria, proportionality in allocation, or compensatory preferences may each be most suitable in different contexts. In any case, donor choices should be made in consultation with government and with all the ethnic communities that might be affected. "[T]he search through dialogue for common interests and mutual accommodation can increase the legitimacy of the process and reduce the likelihood of conflict."[6]

For any development agency, the feasibility and appropriate form of interventions will vary depending on where a country's authorities stand along the spectrum between benign, accommodating, self-aggrandizing, clientalistic, hegemonic, or repressive. None of the following discussions of individual activities or subjects are meant to be comprehensive. I will not try to summarize the many lessons of policy and best practice that can be found in the extensive literature available on each of the subjects. The purpose here, instead, is to explore how each subject might appear in a new light when looked at from the perspective of conflict exacerbation or prevention.

Conflict Assessment

An essential requirement for taking conflict-relevance into account in a specific country is knowledge of local social and political conditions. To create a basis for intelligent planning respecting potential conflict prevention, or to avoid exacerbating or deepening interethnic divisions, a conflict assessment should be made, covering the following ground. First, the assessment should review both the country's recent history and its major changes and long-run trends. An understanding of past violent conflict, if any, along with lingering consequences, would obviously be very relevant. Second, it should outline the structure of ascriptive, regional, and political divisions within the society, giving close scrutiny to socioeconomic tensions (economic, religious, linguistic, political representation, educational, etc.) that contribute to grievance and divisiveness along structural fault lines. As debatable as some of the conclusions might be, an analysis of the potential effects on these divisions of policies or projects still in the proposal or development stage could alert the agency(ies) to a need for options that could reduce potential negative effects or introduce positive conflict-amelioration effects or offsets.

Third, the assessment should explore issues of ethnic politics. Are the contending groups mobilized along ethnic lines? Or are they subdivided, with some factions drawn to conflict-ameliorating, cross-ethnic alliances? Are economic, geographic, or cultural factors reinforcing or attenuating these enmities and alignments? What is the status of economic, professional, or other interest groupings that cross ascriptive lines? What are the goals of the contending elites and the dynamics of their relationships with their nonelite followers? Understanding the goals and rhetoric of contending elites (whether dominant or challengers) is critical for assessing conflict risk and the urgency of, and scope for, ameliorative interventions. These goals will be more or less open to accommodation and feasible satisfaction depending on where they sit along the range of objectives between inclusion adjustments and zero-sum extremism—that is, between economic concessions (e.g., budget allocations, revenue-sharing, job preferences); political structure concessions (e.g., power-sharing, political process reforms); degrees of autonomy; federal reconstitution; capture of the government; hegemonic repression; secession; ethnic cleansing; genocide.

Fourth, what is the role of the state—mediator and promoter of the general welfare? Captured by a dominant group, and partisan or exclusionary? Hegemonic over subordinate groups? Are any of the dynamics that Donald Horowitz has identified as underlying severe ethnic conflict present: (a) fear of competition; (b) ethnically based political parties, and politics pervaded by ethnicity; (c) powerful juxtapositions and stereotypes; (d) intraparty competition that induces jingoistic outbidding; (e) nonnegotiable, zero-sum postures?[7] Fifth, an evaluation of the conflict relevance and effects of past assistance programs in the country could be especially useful for guiding a fresh look at the implications of ongoing programs and for forward planning. Taking the past experience into account, which activities appear to be the most salient for both promoting development and addressing conflict potentialities? Which have the potential to exacerbate the country's divisions? Integrating political and economic analyses poses an obvious challenge to development agencies whose expertise is traditionally economic, technical, and only in some respects social. The assessment analyst can draw on an extensive literature on the politics of deeply divided, ethnically diverse, developing countries.[8]

Sixth, the assessment must analyze the economics of the society's fault lines. The literature on poverty in developing countries is enormous. Unfortunately, much of it sheds little light on the *intergroup* income status and trends that are the relevant phenomena for most internal conflict. Standard quantitative poverty analysis is based on the distribution of income by *class* (income brackets), across an entire country population. Commonly drawing on data collected in household surveys, the analysis divides the population according to income-level gradations. Although the analysis will show what percentage of the population earns each level of income (for example, in a country with a highly skewed distribution of income, Brazil in 1989, the richest 10 percent of the population earned 51.3 percent of total country income, while the poorest 10 percent earned a mere 0.7 percent; put another way, the richest decile of the population had a per capita income seventy-three times greater than those in the poorest decile),[9] it seldom breaks down this information (or related data that may be collected about household wealth, health, educational attainment, and other indications of living standards) into ascriptive groups. Household survey data and gross product accounts are commonly designed to yield regional comparisons. Comparative regional analysis may stand in for group analysis if the groups are highly concentrated in particular regions or provinces. The approximation may only give indications, however, if ethnic majority regions contain within them local minorities.

A manual on social benefit-cost methodology issued by the United Nations in 1978[10] provides a good example of how this economic, as opposed to political or ethnological, framework for data collection and analysis carried over into the conception and appraisal of investment projects. The manual spells out how the expected income flows to the relatively poor can be given greater weight than comparable flows to the less poor. Such weighting may alter the selection of projects in favor of those expected to yield more equitable distribution. The manual points out that governments may want to attach extra value to "basic needs" that will accrue to people in "target income groups," but it conceives of potential target groups only as the (undifferentiated) poor, or as members of functional classes like labor or small business, or as the inhabitants of a poverty-stricken region. Poor-region weighting, and the implied regional bias in project location decisions, would translate into an ascriptive group weighting in the many countries where backward or subordinated ethnic groups are geographically concentrated, but the manual does not extend its conception of disadvantaged groups to embrace the ascriptively defined.

A similar limitation is found in all the contributors to a volume on cost-benefit analysis put out by USAID in 1980.[11] One researcher offers an example of a poverty group–ranking method for rural projects that lists the very poor, poor, small farmers, well-off, and very wealthy.[12] In an IMF technical manual for analyzing public expenditure policy issues, the discussion of income distribution and of fiscal policies for its improvement treats a population as an assemblage of individuals.[13] Distribution that is described by the Gini coefficient and other measures that define group cohorts only by income class buries the ethnic distinctions that are essential for understanding the political economy of divided societies.

The project appraisal techniques used by the development agencies have varied in their complexity and in the extent of their adoption in practice, and they have been criticized on many methodological and practical grounds in an extensive literature. Perhaps the best commonsense defense for using a systematic analysis is that it forces the analyst to take account of all the relevant aspects, and to specify the reasons for and costs of choices that deviate from the arithmetically optimal. The group distribution effects that I am proposing be added to the analytic requirements for project appraisal (by those agencies that still perform systematic appraisal) merely extend the existing distribution perspectives to cover a type of benefit-group differentiation that in many contexts exceeds in importance all other standard benefit-group categorizations. At the same time, I would be remiss if I ignored the cautions in the U.N. guide:

> Once the analyst begins adjusting values of the goods per se for social reasons, even economically disastrous projects can be made to show "good" social rates of return. Furthermore, the borderline between "social" and "political" is thin; it is easy to end up maintaining that politically expedient projects, regardless of how economically wasteful they may be, are "socially" justified.[14]

Nevertheless, the U.N. guide urges the analyst on, arguing that use of the methodology makes it possible to specify the cost, or return forgone, of "pursuing objectives other than pure economic efficiency." In a further comment for "purists who think that economics should be devoid of political or subjective judgments," the guide notes that the normative considerations it outlines "are problems of the real world, and investment decisions are made in this world, not in the world of theoretical abstraction. Ignoring these issues will not make them go away; it will only make the advice of the economist partially useful at best and irrelevant to the decision maker at worst."[15]

Where different ethnic groups are highly concentrated in separate areas, analysis of regional economic differences may give an accurate picture of ethnic relative economic status. An analysis of interregional resource flows can be particularly useful. As illustrated by the East–West Pakistan and Sri Lanka cases, and by the violent response in ethnoregions in Indonesia, Nigeria, and elsewhere, where the local population receives only a fraction of the national revenue generated from local oil or gas fields, interregional resource balances structured by central government can be fundamental sources of grievance and conflict. Even if a total resource balance analysis is not feasible, partial balances may be estimated from central government revenue and expenditure accounts respecting a region in question, supplemented by estimates of net flow effects of other policy instruments (like an industrial protection regime or foreign exchange policy). Such analyses may reveal systematic imbalances long before the level of ethnoregional grievance emerges as a conflict "signal." If the imbalances are inadvertent, the analysis could alert a government to the need for corrective policy change, and be the basis for donor assistance to help accomplish that end. If the imbalances are deliberate, the analysis can be the basis for placing the issues on the table for negotiation between government and donors, or for whatever action the donors judge appropriate.

Analyses of economic sectors or labor-force components may also paint a reliable picture of ethnic differentials in an economy where ethnicity and function tend to coincide. Though ethnic functional concentration may have originated from colonial government policy, ethnic segmentation is often continued by employers who maintain informal practices of occupational discrimination in hiring. In economies where the same functions are performed by different ethnic groups (i.e., where there is interethnic competition in the labor markets), there is often a segmented wage scale that can be identified that discriminates against workers from low-status ethnic groups.[16] In some countries survey data on demographic and social characteristics may reveal ethnic disparities.

For example, according to the 1998 *Human Development Report* issued by the U.N. Development Programme (UNDP), life expectancy among South African whites was sixty-eight in the early 1990s, and among blacks only fifty-four years. In Malaysia, poverty incidence among ethnic Malays was 24 percent compared with 6 percent for ethnic Chinese. Poverty as measured by the UNDP's human development index could be shown to vary widely by language groups within Namibia.[17]

In any deeply divided society where the conventional available data do not lend themselves to ethnic characterization, an effort needs to be made to develop empirical information and indicators that will make reliable judgments possible on the differentials and trends respecting the most fundamental cleavages. More than economics, the work of anthropologists and sociologists should be drawn upon for information about interethnic relations where economic functions such as farm-gate produce buying, agricultural lending, intermediate marketing, village shops, urban retail marketing of specific product lines, or modern-sector business ownership are commonly identified with particular ethnic groups. Functional separation may actually promote good interethnic relations if it focuses competition within rather than between ethnic groups. Rural ethnic Chinese merchants have traditionally had smooth relations with Thai farmers; intraethnic merchant competition kept marketing margins low, while Thai villagers saw advantage in marrying the children of the local Chinese merchants.

Conversely, functional separation may fuel conflict if one group perceives that another is extracting monopoly or monopsony (sole purchaser) rents, or, on a larger scale, if another group is seen as dominating the economy or parts of it. Indonesia is an example of a country with a small ethnic Chinese minority, prominent in local trade but most conspicuous in major industrial enterprises (favored by the Suharto regime), which has been subjected to occasional pogroms.

In general, assessments of conflict potential should draw on the "early warning" literature, looking for signs that may be present in the country being studied. In addition, the analyst needs to be alert to some of the longer-term factors we discussed earlier from the scholarly work on conflict and ethnicity that may be significant in the particular society. An important example might be internal migration (which cuts across several of the development activities below), either from densely to thinly populated areas or from backward to more prosperous areas and that brings together previously separated ascriptive groups.

An assessment of the scope suggested here probably would need to be done only once every several years, especially if independent researchers are regularly taking the social pulse and watching for "early warning" signs. However, donors working in a deeply divided society should maintain a "watching brief," alert to changes or interventions whenever they occur and that have the potential, perhaps only after a lag of some time, to affect group asymmetries or grievances. Take, for example, the problems, perhaps crises, that may overtake a developing country when it is hit by an unforeseen economic "shock." Such shocks are commonly external events such as the sudden oil price rises of the 1970s, or a sharp worsening of the terms of trade because of a collapse of the world prices of one of its major exports. Shocks can destabilize even those countries that have been conducting prudent economic management (i.e., nations not candidates for structural reform programs). The government can take various policy measures to ride out the unfavorable events, cushion the domestic impact, and restore its macroeconomic balances. The choice among alternative policies takes a high degree of judgment and must be tailored to the particular circumstances and the expected future course of the shock factors. Because loan funds from the IMF and the World Bank commonly are an important element of the response package, both institutions commonly are deeply involved in the crafting of policy responses to external shocks.

A conflict watching-brief perspective would keep the IMF and World Bank alert to the conflict-relevant implications of shock response policies, or of macroeconomic management policies generally. These problems and policy responses are often short-term in nature, temporary departures that are reversed as a crisis passes or as ordinary cyclical changes swing back and forth. For the art of macroeconomic management there are important distinctions between the regular annual cycles and occasional refinements in periods of relative economic stability, the crisis management demands of shock instabilities, and the more far-reaching overhaul requirements of structural adjustment where a complex of reforms is needed to remove basic obstacles and change the long-term orientation of an economy. However, the same policy instruments are commonly employed in "normal" times, in crisis management, and in structural adjustment; the distinctions in how these instruments are used arise from differences in *duration* (e.g., shock management may require only brief departures from long-run best practice), *severity* (e.g., the extent of a shock-induced drop in incomes), and *phasing* (e.g., the timing of specific policy changes dependent on related institutional changes, under structural adjustment). The conflict-prevention and group-distribution perspective should be applied to ensure that the potential relevant consequences of any recommended policy change are not overlooked, regardless of the nature of the macroeconomic episode.

Finally, there are practical and sensitive questions: Who should make long-term conflict risk assessments? How should such assessments be used or distributed, especially if they conclude that there is perceptible risk? Could publication of an unfavorable conclusion have the perverse effect of actually damaging a country's prospects for avoiding conflict by discouraging investment? Donor government agencies are likely to have fewer constraints on conducting sociopolitical risk assessment. The research work of multilaterals is largely transparent, and the decision to undertake and/or distribute country research is commonly subject to consent of the country's government. Much would depend on the sources of a country's divisive problems, and on the character of its government. If government is not a party to the country's social divisions and hostilities, not itself predatory and partial, it might be receptive to the insights and policy suggestions such an assessment might produce. Sensitivity could be less if assessments were done by an independent academic or research institution, which could be domestic or foreign. Objective scenario building that estimates the economic losses a potential conflict could entail, especially the losses to the segment most likely to initiate violent conflict, might enliven a search for alternatives less damaging to the parties' economic self-interest.

Notes

1. Carnegie Commission, 1997, p. xxxiii.
2. Ibid., p. 84.
3. As in Colombia, according to Nafziger and Auvinen, 1997, p. 57.
4. World Bank, 1999, p. 14.
5. Esman, 1997. A slightly revised version appears in Esman and Herring, 2001.
6. Ibid., p. 12.
7. Horowitz, in Montville, 1991, p. 457.
8. Two good examples are Esman, 1994, and Horowitz, in Montville, 1991.
9. World Bank, *World Development Report*, 1996, Table 5.
10. U.N. Industrial Development Organization (UNIDO), *Guide to Practical Project Appraisal: Social Benefit-Cost Analysis in Developing Countries*. New York: 1978.
11. John D. Donahue, ed., *Cost-Benefit Analysis and Project Design*. Bloomington, IN: USAID and Pasitam, 1980.
12. Ibid., p. 104.
13. Ke-young Chu, and Richard Hemming, eds., *A Guide to Public Expenditure Policy in Developing Countries*. Washington, DC: IMF, 1991, pp. 119–128.
14. UNIDO, *Guide to Practical Project Appraisal*, 1978, p. 77.
15. Ibid., p. 75, footnote 109.
16. E.g., wage discrimination against lower ("scheduled") caste and tribal workers in Gujarat, New Delhi, and elsewhere in India, and against African workers in Kenya, is cited in Michael Lipton, *Labor and Poverty*. World Bank Staff Working Papers, No. 616, 1983, p. 83.
17. United Nations Development Programme, *Human Development Report*. New York: Oxford University Press, 1998, p. 34.

5. Inducing Nonviolent Politics and Conflict Management

Top-Down: Reengineering Politics

American foreign aid began as a straightforward instrument of Cold War competition. In the 1950s, economic assistance was provided to democracies and dictatorships alike, to sustain allied relationships and encourage "Third World" governments not to become Soviet clients. In the 1960s, the Kennedy administration increased foreign aid in the belief that development and modernization would lead naturally to democratic evolution in authoritarian developing countries, thereby inoculating these societies against any lure of revolution or communism. As this concept appeared to fail in delivering its promised democracy in what was an unrealistically short time frame, the administration returned to the earlier policy of supporting anticommunist governments regardless of their authoritarian character. Looking for a more direct democratizing alternative, Congress then instructed USAID to encourage democratic evolution by working directly on political institutions and on promotion of "popular participation" in the development process. Projects for political development involved areas such as legal process and institutions, civic education, and legislative process. For various reasons, however, direct political development remained a marginal activity. In the 1970s, under the shift of American aid's focus from economic development to meeting "basic needs" of the poor, "participation" survived as a catchword for the policy of directing benefits to the disadvantaged and including the beneficiaries in the planning and implementation of the aided activities.[1]

It was not until the 1990s that the direct promotion of democracy emerged as a major subject for U.S. aid. As the end of the Cold War freed Western development assistance from the geopolitical exigencies of the previous four decades, many other bilateral donors also adopted democracy as a goal of their development assistance agencies. To maintain its apolitical credentials, the World Bank has confined its foray into political culture to encouragement of good "governance." (The standard list of attributes of good governance includes such things as accountability, transparency, efficiency, low corruption, and addressing market failures, all of which can be characteristics of an authoritarian regime.) In practice, democracy promotion has involved support for NGOs working on human rights; legislature development; strengthening of judicial systems; training of journalists; and technical and financial support for elections and for political party development. The end of the Cold War also saw a lessening in many developing countries of opposition to such donor country "interventionism" in governance and political process.

Thomas Carothers's recent book, *Aiding Democracy Abroad*, is the first comprehensive examination of the still brief record of direct assistance for the institutionalization of democratic process and political "culture." Recall our earlier discussion of the apparent long-term congruence among development, democracy, and nonviolent internal political process (and nonviolent interstate relations among democracies). If democracy aid could hasten the transition to, and solidification of, democracy—providing a quick, top-down fix—then the most direct route to conflict prevention would be aid for political engineering. Although it would appear inconsistent with former USAID Administrator J. Brian Atwood's conviction (cited in Chapter 1, pages 27–28) that state failure cannot be prevented by a top-down approach, democracy assistance was divided among "civil society," which included some bottom-up activities (NGOs, labor unions, civic education), and three top-down categories—rule of law, governance, and elections. According to Carothers, the mix of top and bottom activities reflected a bureaucratic compromise between the proponents of the two approaches. In any event, democracy became a major USAID objective in the 1990s. Funding for democracy programs rose from $165 million in 1991 to $637 million in 1999.

There is an important distinction implicit in the theorizing that rationalizes democracy aid as the antidote to conflict. Drawing on Atwood's explanation, the distinction is between management of social conflict and alleviation of the problems that produce such conflict—that is, between strengthening "indigenous capacity of people *to manage and resolve* conflict within their own societies" on the one hand, and providing technology to (*inter alia*) "increase food supplies, slow population growth and preserve natural resources" and to achieve "sustainable development" on the other. In effect, during a decade of stagnant or declining aid appropriations for development, funding to strengthen management of conflict rose at the expense of money to address underlying sources of conflict.

Was this transfer of funds and attention wise? Putting aside the presumed link between democracy and nonviolent conflict resolution, has this aid been an effective instrument for advancing its proximate objective, namely democracy? How can its effectiveness be evaluated? Needless to say, a mere decade in which this instrument has been going through its initial development is too short a period for reaching any definitive conclusion. For countries with governments, elites, and populations that are intent on democratic evolution and already well along in establishing democracy's basic institutions and processes, assistance for democracy may demonstrably advance its maturation. In countries in the early stages of transition from authoritarian rule, still saddled with leftover problems such as opportunistic leadership, subservient judiciaries, clientalist and hierarchical power structures, and a weak middle class, it is unlikely that external technical assistance and some incremental funding can bring off a rapid metamorphosis in which the society discards its inherited political culture and history.

Even where leadership is committed to democratic transition, there can be no assurance that the "Western" institutional forms and political processes the assistance is conveying will transplant successfully. The Western political parties generally have crosscutting economic and social agendas. Their agendas change over time in response to changes in voter preferences, and voter majorities often shift party allegiance from one election to another. In deeply divided societies, by contrast, parties tend to appeal to different ascriptively defined constituencies, and individuals vote for the party seen as identified with the interests of their own ethnic group, the party that interprets all issues in terms of effects on its own ethnic constituency. Adoption of Western party systems and processes (the American more than the European) is likely to require years of experimentation and socialization. Horowitz's insight about the fateful difference between the polarized party system of Sri Lanka and the coalition system in Malaysia stands as a warning for political engineers, especially as the less democratic Malaysian politics has maintained interethnic stability while the arguably more democratic system in Sri Lanka has led to civil war.

In Carothers's judgment (which he believes applies to all Western donors offering democracy assistance), the results to date have been decidedly "mixed." The U.S. effort has often been naive and simplistic, replete with mistakes. The democracy enthusiasts have learned some lessons, and their performance is improving, although the learning process has been a "constant struggle." The democracy promoters should be

> going beyond the simplistic use of U.S. models; moving from the reproduction of institutional forms to the nurturing of core political processes and values, such as representation, accountability, tolerance, and openness; coming to terms with the multiplicity of political trajectories that follow democratic openings; understanding the limits of electoralism; confronting the inadequate will to reform that hampers the reform of most state institutions; giving up the simple equation of advocacy NGOs with civil society; embracing more hands-on innovative methods of civic edu-

cation; not counting on the training of journalists as a solution to media reform. . . .[2]

Democracy programs too often rest on what is either a dreamy, or, seen in another light, a hollow view of politics. Democracy promoters frequently seem surprised by the most banal realities of politics—that power is only rarely given away cost-free, that principles trump interests only occasionally, that zero-sum instincts are as common as cooperative attitudes, that political violence erupts easily when power shifts are occurring, and that historical legacies, whether helpful or harmful to democratization, are extraordinarily persistent.[3]

In addition to the intellectual shortcomings of the practitioners, Carothers cites the inadequacy of the state of knowledge, the need for a "synthesis of economic and socioeconomic development work." He also criticizes the poor interaction between democracy promoters and development practitioners.

> Most democracy promoters believe that economic development and democracy reinforce each other. They have not, however, made many efforts to connect their work to other parts of the development assistance picture. . . . [They] have worked from a conception of democratization focused on political institutions and processes, which downplays socioeconomic forces and trends that affect democratization. In parallel fashion, even though many traditional developmentalists came around in the 1990s to the idea that democracy can be a positive factor in development, they have shown little interest in democracy assistance, whether out of skepticism about the possibility of shaping political development through aid or concern about "infecting" their social and economic programs with overtly political content.[4]

A project USAID conducted in Haiti between 1994 and 1996 was an interesting exception to this dichotomous practice. The project provided small grants for local economic improvement activities in a large number of communities throughout the country. The purpose was to help shore up the initial stages of the restoration of elected government after the ouster of the military regime. According to an evaluation, the Communal Governance Program (CGP), as a complement to the restoration by international diplomatic and military intervention,

> contributed to the democratization process by quickly moving into a new political space and providing badly needed material resources to enable local organizations to begin improving their communities . . . , a means for Haitians to express themselves freely both with one another and with their local representatives. This is resulting in local officials being more respon-

> sive to their constituents. . . . CGP has injected transparency and account-
> ability into programs and transactions. . . . CGP has started an important
> process to rebuild confidence in local government and lay the foundation
> for other democratization activities.[5]

The project was seen as a contribution to "facilitating the restoration of effective governance at all levels of Haitian society." The concept is interesting as a putative marrying of civil society, local officialdom, higher democracy, and economic reconstruction. Even if aid efforts subsequent to the brief CGP project have succeeded in sustaining what was certainly a novel set of relationships in Haitian society, there is little evidence that it has made any connection with, or contribution to, effective governance at higher levels. Haitian government at the top has been paralyzed since 1994.

Conflict-management at the national level can take different forms, of which some would be foreign to, or inconsistent with, constitutional principles underlying the political systems of some of the countries (mainly the United States) providing democracy assistance. Eric Nordlinger identified six political practices, one or more of which have been employed where nonviolent conflict management has succeeded for periods, if not permanently: (1) stable government coalitions between parties representing the antagonistic groups; (2) proportionality in allocating government positions or resources, rather than winner-take-all; (3) mutual veto (or concurrent majority), under which decisions in specified areas of public policy must be acceptable to all parties; (4) selected issue depoliticization, limiting involvement of government in divisive communal issues, devolving authorities to different jurisdictions, or avoiding public discussion of "conflict-laden communal issues"; (5) compromise on core issues, most feasible where there are several such issues giving scope for quid pro quo bargaining; and (6) unilateral concessions by the stronger among a set of antagonistic groups. Pure democratic majoritarianism may actually exacerbate conflicts in deeply divided societies.[6]

In sum, we should anticipate modest results from efforts of aid agencies to democratize the political culture and institutions of societies that are still retaining or newly emerging from authoritarian political cultures. Power accommodation through negotiation (in some cases achievable only after a civil war in which neither side prevails) may be a more realistic and more quickly attainable goal. As Malaysia illustrates again, power-sharing and its accompanying bargains can be the basis for long-term stability and for rapid economic growth and poverty reduction, even under a flawed, quasi-democratic political system that democracy promoters (and many Malaysians, of course) would judge needful of reform. The fundamental constraint on the effectiveness of efforts at direct aid-induced, or aid-assisted, reform of power relations and political process can be simply put. If a regime seeks assistance in good faith to adopt conflict-avoiding measures—such as power-sharing, decentralization, respect for minority rights, judicial independence, credible elections—the battle is already won. The really difficult problem is how to bring a government and a polity to that readiness.

An alternative, structural route to power-sharing may be through decentralization. We have seen how the *location* of power has been a central issue in countries like pre–civil war Pakistan, Sri Lanka, Yugoslavia, and Mozambique, where large ethnic groups are concentrated in specific areas or subnational jurisdictions. Division of powers between central and regional or local government is everywhere fundamental to politics and the structure of the state. Constitutional provisions establishing these distributions were important issues in the processes leading to post–World War II decolonization. The issue has been much studied by scholars and mediators concerned with countries (e.g., Nigeria) where the very integrity of the state is bound up with an unstable assignment of powers. Whether decentralization will exacerbate or ameliorate group tensions depends on such factors as the presence, or lack, of ethnic (or religious, racial, etc.) homogeneity in the subnational jurisdictions, the nature of the political and social agenda of the regional ethnic elites as compared with that of the national authorities, and the location and fiscal powers over resources. Despite the complexity of the issues surrounding state structure, there appears to be a presumption that decentralization is likely to be an effective solution in deeply divided societies.[7]

Thomas Carothers's work deserves close reading by aid policymakers and practitioners, and by anyone concerned with the dynamics of the post–Cold War world. Our sketchy use here of some of his conclusions is intended to fill out the context of international development agency work relevant to conflict prevention, and to convey the essential point that agencies' contributions to conflict prevention through their traditional main business—promoting economic development—cannot be short-circuited through a diversion into democratic engineering. It is all the more unfortunate, then, that the U.S. aid program has in recent years marginalized the resources and attention devoted to economic growth.

Development of Civil Society

The role of civil society has become an important area for the study of both economic development and the dynamics of collective action. Civil society, in the particular form of independent "advocacy" NGOs pursuing civil rights, women's rights, and democratic processes generally, has become an important subject for numbers of bilateral aid agencies. Encouragement of civil society for its economic development role, and for its potential enhancement of socioeconomic governance, has become an object of attention and financing for both bilateral and multilateral agencies. For many years, donors were drawn to supporting local NGOs for their self-help potentialities. For small groups of people who were poor, powerless, and ignored or unreachable by government services, these were vehicles to move from passive victimhood to initiators of collective action to improve their local agricultural, health, housing, or other circumstances.

In addition to spontaneous responses to environmental challenges or market obstacles, people also have formed collective-action organizations to defend immediate interests under threat. Albert O. Hirschman (1984) observed that the poor in Latin America "are used to their poverty, which they bear in silence and isolation, but the fact of being treated with *injustice* can bring out unsuspected capacities for indignation, resistance and common action." Hirschman's resistance examples had emerged in response to "aggression by society" (i.e., land swindles by powerful and unscrupulous persons) and destruction of slum housing and preemption of small agricultural holdings by "the state as aggressor." His grassroots examples were all being supported by national "intermediary" organizations (social activist NGOs set up to train and promote the grassroots entities) and/or by international aid donors. Hirschman captures the basic and classical NGO paradigm as follows:

> [T]here exists today an impressive, loosely integrated network of national and international organizations which, at the level of any single Latin American country, performs important functions of education, public health, housing improvement, agricultural extension, development promotion of handicraft and small business, etc. It is as though both the national and the international conscience about *basic economic rights* of Latin American citizens had outstripped what is provided by the state so that complex substitute or supplementary attempts at assuring these rights have come into being.[8]

When donors turn to NGOs as instruments of conflict avoidance, they are seeking a different paradigm. Instead of the classic self-help model, or the collective to act against economic injustice, they hope to empower NGOs that want to enhance a democratic political culture, act against group prejudice and victimization in any form, promote accommodation and understanding between groups in conflict, and in general undertake activities designed to prevent violent dispute resolution. To be meaningful for internal warfare prevention, such activities must have effects on large regional or national stages. This also suggests a need for an additional and different perspective and program objective, which we might term *distributional* rather than

functional—that is, a focus on creating and empowering civil society organizations internal to traditionally structured backward groups up to the level
of organization and capability of the more advanced rival groups.

Affirmative action policies (discussed below) are designed to favor individuals from a specified group(s). In effect, those individuals who are helped
to gain (favored) access are entering the mainstream structures and processes
of economic development where they and others of different ethnic origins
now will jointly participate. But affirmative action may also be seen as a
group rather than an individual-based program. Subordinate or disadvantaged groups are commonly perceived, even by themselves, as lacking critical behavioral attributes of the dominant or more advanced groups in their
society. Horowitz notes that the "collective" side of relative positioning is as
important as the individual side. "Backward groups very often believe advanced groups to be more cohesive, better organized, more given to mutual
cooperation and collective effort—including in-group favoritism—than backward groups are."[9] It is clear from his examples that these characterizations
(which Horowitz cites in a discussion of ethnic stereotyping) frequently mir-
ror reality. The Malay view of the Chinese minority as more highly organized was correct, although probably not any longer. Such collective
organizational thinness can be described as a near absence of modern institutions of civil society. Programs to eliminate this important basis for invidious group comparisons, and for real differentials in group strength—in effect,
a collective preference in civil society promotion—might make a significant
contribution toward conflict avoidance in a deeply divided society.

Conversely, although the narrowing of a civil-society gap might help reduce hegemonic imbalance, it would also deepen the structure of ethnic division. Divided countries that have ethnicity-based political parties tend to
have ethnically exclusive, parallel civil society organizations such as unions,
chambers of commerce, and social organizations.[10] The optimal objective
might be to encourage development of functional organizations that cross
ethnic lines and include significant multiethnic participation. In any case,
donors should not assume naively that all civil society organizations are inherently more pro-peace than are political parties.

As with many of the programmatic opportunities we are discussing, a
donor bias in favor of civil-society capacity-building among institutionally
weak and subordinated groups would generally not be feasible if opposed by
a recipient government. In fact, some governments have made known their
discomfort with the idea of a direct aid relationship between donors and civil
society (or the local private sector). As the World Bank noted: "The involvement of civil society and the private sector in the aid coordination process
remains controversial. Most donors strongly favor greater involvement, while

recipient governments express a variety of views, ranging from cautiously positive to skeptical, or even antagonistic."[11] Nevertheless, in a conflict-prone society, if donors judge that strengthening civil society would contribute to improved communication, and a better sense of minority capability for nonviolent representation and participation, an aid program along these lines would be a proper candidate for donors to pursue in their overall dialogue with government.

But what exactly is civil society, and what kinds of organizations are relevant for what particular objectives? Under its broadest definition, the concept refers to all associations, except private business and formal political organizations, which are "between state and family [and] which are separated from the state, enjoy autonomy in relation to the state and are formed voluntarily by members of society to protect or extend their interests or values."[12] The associational area between state and family in developing countries can be very large. It might include traditional kinship networks, patron–client networks, trade unions, professional associations, sports associations, cooperatives, farmer irrigation water-user groups, advocacy organizations, cultural organizations, welfare societies, and women's groups, not to mention criminal networks. In the many countries where an establishment religion has a close relationship with the state, only independent religious groups and hierarchies, and interfaith organizations, would fall into the area between state and family. Although donors have worked with such associations as water-user groups and village women's groups in the normal course of development projects, their interest in "civil society" has focused on organizations that aim to influence public policy, primarily to move government and society in the direction of greater democracy. Thus, the United States at least has tended to work with a narrow range of organizations and individuals, seeing civil society as a strategic instrument for advancing democracy.

> Given the breadth of the concept, efforts to support the development of civil society in transitional societies could in theory reach across quite a number of organizations, associations and collectivities. In practice, however, they have not. The U.S. civil society programs carried out under a democracy rubric have focused on a limited part of the broad fabric of civil society in most recipient countries: nongovernmental organizations dedicated to advocacy for what aid providers consider to be sociopolitical issues touching the public interest—including election monitoring, civic education, parliamentary transparency, human rights, anticorruption, the environment, women's rights, and indigenous peoples' rights. [Two] other areas of U.S. democracy assistance—media assistance, and aid to labor unions—also represent efforts for the development of civil society, though

when U.S. providers use the term "civil society assistance" they are usually referring specifically to their work with advocacy NGOs.[13]

In searching for the roles that civil society can play in conflict prevention, we can define four categories. First, *political engineering:* nongovernmental organizations (NGOs) dedicated to changing—in ways that promote inclusion, transparency, and accommodation—specific government policies, the political institutions and processes, and/or the "political culture," that is, the general orientation of the citizenry toward political behavior and the proper exercise of power. Second, *conflict management and resolution:* traditional or modern organizations specializing in good-office negotiation and mediation, and in related research. Third, *empowering representative institutions of an aggrieved group,* whose civil society is limited to traditional internally oriented networks. Fourth, *bridge-building between hostile groups* through promotion of common-interest organizations and activities that are (a) economic or professional, or (b) social, cultural, or charitable. A nuanced approach would try to distinguish among the types, functions, and membership of civil society organizations so as to focus on those most relevant to a program's objectives.

Building networks among professional and intellectual elites may be particularly strategic. Some of these elites may offer the best prospects for strengthening influential opinion that favors accommodation and nonviolent dispute management. They may also be more receptive to establishing (or reestablishing, postconflict) cross-ethnic associations. I surmise that such groups would include educators, medical and mental health providers, social workers, feminists, athletic organizations, and various academic faculties and "development" professions, including economics, anthropology, humanities, engineering, and political science.

Bottom-Up: Behavior Change and Civil Society

For those who adopt Kevin Avruch's "restricted" sense of conflict resolution (i.e., getting at root causes rather than relying on negotiated bargains between combatant leaderships), interventions aimed at psychological and perceptual change, at altering worldviews, deconstructing categorical prejudice, and socializing entire populations to tolerance are deemed essential for establishing an enduring basis for nonviolent group relations.[14]

As removed as this perspective may seem from *Realpolitik*, many bilateral government aid programs are carrying out small-scale, community-level, interpersonal projects, on the assumption that reeducation and improved interpersonal communication can make practical contributions to reconciliation and conflict avoidance. For such activities to have a hope of significance, they must be replicable and scaled up to include politically meaningful numbers of communities and ordinary citizens. Whether groundswells against aggression as public (or group) policy succeed or fail will depend on the circumstances. But strong nonelite support for accommodative politics may well be a necessary if not sufficient condition for the sustainability of peace accords.

There are several areas under this heading in which aid agencies have conducted development-oriented activities that merit reconsideration in the context of conflict prevention. Some investigators believe that formal education systems, starting from the earliest grades, can have a significant, possibly lifetime, effect on how people view and behave toward members of ascriptive groups other than their own. Programs of multicultural curriculum design, classroom integration, and integration in sports and other extracurricular activities have been widely adopted in the United States and elsewhere, based on the presumption that lifelong patterns of individual altruism or aggression grow at least partly out of early schooling experience. The potential contribution of such programs to subsequent adult propensities would, of course, be more limited in divided societies where different ethnicities reside in geographically separate regions. In contrast, on the other hand, amicable interethnic relations in leading urban areas, as in Brussels, for example, can contribute substantially to national conflict mitigation. Whereas programs to socialize children and adolescents to tolerance, to altruism, to the ideas of a shared humanity with people of different ethnicity or religion, and to democratic values are all undeniably important, the determinants of adult behavior in these respects, and the distinctions between individual psychology and the behavior of individuals in groups, are complex phenomena.

The experience of some local NGOs working to promote restoration of tolerance and pluralism in ethnically mixed Bosnian communities (with financial and technical support from USAID) illustrates some of the practical potentialities and difficulties of efforts to reshape attitudes and behavior. The NGOs had practical objectives: incremental steps to restore interethnic communication, participation in the same classes and community activities (e.g., neighborhood cleanup and restoration), and interethnic group counseling. Although reconciliation was a major objective, some of the NGO staff believed that the term "reconciliation" in Serbo–Croatian (as in English) implied a restoration of attachments that was infeasible so soon after such bitter conflict. However, those NGOs working with youth (eighteen and younger) found that reconciliation, not merely restored communication, was easily attained.[15]

One not atypical example is worth describing as an illustration of what ordinary common sense can accomplish even under inauspicious conditions. In the so-called divided city of Gornji Vakuf/Uskoplje, one voluntary organization located near the street separating the Muslim (or "Bosniac") inhabitants from the Croat began by offering computer and photography courses not available in the schools on either side of the line with their separate ethnic composition. At first the Croat and Muslim children came to the NGO facility on separate days. Cordial interethnic relations were restored, however, among the teachers at the facility. When summer came along in 1997, the NGO offered seaside vacations (financed by German aid) to groups of teenagers under teacher supervision. In this first round, the Muslim children went with Muslim teachers, the Croat with Croat teachers. In the following summer the children chose which other children and teachers they would prefer to join, readily crossing ethnic lines and erasing the previous ethnic structuring. After this second vacation, they began crossing the street to visit friends in their homes regardless of side. Although in 1999 the youth center was still the only facility in the city where Croat and Muslim teachers worked side by side, the programs were having "spread" effects, inducing teachers not connected with the center to move themselves toward restoration of prewar relationships. The number of children participating in center activities had risen to 2,500 and had drawn about 4,000 of the parents into involvement in the center's interethnic programs.

One would hope that in time activities of this sort would thrive, involving enough people to bring about fundamental change in interethnic relations at the community level, sufficient to force local politicians to base their electoral appeals on inclusion rather than on separated constituencies. Three years was apparently not enough to produce such signs of spread effect. No families had moved their residences across the line, no repatriated refugees of either ethnicity had returned to live in former homes located on the "other" side, and the city—formerly, as Gornji Vakuf, a single jurisdiction—remained politically divided, with separate administrations. In general, the NGOs under this project throughout Bosnia found that the return to preconflict civility and interethnic cordiality came most easily to youth, then to mothers, and most slowly to adult males. The NGOs themselves, it is important to note, were formed and staffed largely by women professionals (social workers, psychotherapists, etc.) working on a volunteer basis. Aside from their desire to respond to the needs of the war's victims for social services, they commonly expressed deep regret over how ethnonationalism had arisen and overwhelmed the multicultural society Bosnia had enjoyed before the conflict, indeed stretching back many generations.

The experience in Bosnia points to several considerations common to programs of support to bottom-up NGOs pursuing conflict amelioration and reconciliation. First, in many countries an effort to empower individuals who have the motivation and capabilities to undertake bottom-up activities will face the difficulty that the society has weak or no traditions of self-propelled NGOs. These individuals work, or previously worked, for government, or in private practice. Or they may be long on motivation and probity, but short on trained background. Almost universally, the NGOs remain small and cannot be sustained without technical assistance and external funding. External technical assistance can do its job in a very few years, especially if a local organization is established as a permanent technical support center. Donor financial support may have to continue for a much longer time before the local general public and/or private business community develop the financial capability and philanthropic habits that support NGOs in wealthier countries. Donor support, therefore, has been critical for the NGO segment of "civil society" development, a subject we return to below.

Second, the enthusiasm with which donors have seized upon the NGO sector does not mean these efforts have been without problems. An important one to mention here has been the problem of fit between donor preferences and the objectives and project preferences of the local NGO initiators. To remain eligible for financial support from a donor that has turned its attention to a new subject, NGOs may be forced to undertake the donor's newly favored activity in place of the activities they were originally motivated and competent to initiate. Thus, an NGO that starts out working on reconciliation may find that its donor has switched attention to microenterprise. To maintain its original focus and survive, an NGO may have to become adept at, and divert attention to, the art of international grantsmanship for finding replacement donors. The problem of financial sustainability has been widely recognized as critical for NGOs in developing countries. Success in securing several donors increases an NGO's reach and potential impact. It also forces the recipient to meet each donor's management and reporting requirements, and to bow to multiple programmatic preferences and restrictions.

Third, the Bosnia program illustrates a gender bias, of U.S. assistance at least, toward supporting NGOs dedicated to women's problems, interests, and empowerment. This makes sense when the objective is to address problems of war victims, refugees, and maternal and child health. As we have seen, NGOs run by women can also serve as entering wedges in an effort to rebuild interpersonal and communal relationships. However, such a gender focus overlooks the overwhelming importance of adult males in violent conflicts and the fact that the political actors and opinion leaders in most of the societies at issue are largely men. It is a commonplace that the females of our species are less bellicose than are the males. It is also commonly assumed that strengthening the role of women will help prevent conflict, even if such strengthening has no direct connection with the specific roots of a conflict. As the Carnegie Commission observed:

> There is great preventive value in initiatives that focus on children and women, not only because they are the main victims of conflict, but also because women in many vulnerable societies are an important source of community stability and vitality. . . . For women, this entails national programs that encourage education for girls, women-operated businesses, and other community-based activities.[16]

The gender point is debatable, of course, and rests on two assumptions. One, greater participation, organization, and training and funding support will lead to empowerment at different levels—from within the family, to the local community, to group and national political processes. Two, women are more likely than men to exercise power to resolve disputes in ways that avoid violent conflict. There is much evidence that NGOs at the local level can empower women by freeing them from total financial dependence, loosening social restrictions, and strengthening their collective voice in village deliberations. To my knowledge, however, no evaluation has been done to assess what impact such bottom-up empowerment may have had on local interethnic dispute resolution, or whether and how increased empowerment of women in developing countries has affected political processes where they have penetrated and risen in more than token numbers. Are the effects limited to "women's" issues, or has the presence of women legislators and politicians also had moderating and humanizing influence, especially where women have reached senior ranks in political parties, in their own social or ethnic groups, or in influential and decision-making national positions? Under what circumstances and at what levels in a polity has the increased presence of women had discernible impact? Thomas Carothers appears to share donors' enthusiasm for women's NGOs as instruments for promoting democratization, but he notes the open questions regarding this connection, the superficiality of some of the thinking behind it, and the limitations to which women's NGOs are not immune. (Although the apparently voluntary participation of women and girls in the genocide in Rwanda and in the cadre of the Khmer Rouge are exceptional cases, they serve as cautions to facile generalizations.)

> U.S. democracy aid does include a growing number of undertakings directly related to women, but there remains a tendency among numerous democracy promoters to view the subject as a narrow specialty rather than as a potentially powerful approach that can usefully synthesize many as-

pects of the democratic agenda. A focus on the political status and role of women obliges aid providers to go beyond the forms of democracy to grapple with the substance—how different sectors of a society are participating in political life and whether political systems are representing their interests. It also ties together the all too often separate components of the standard democracy aid template. It may entail simultaneously addressing issues relating to elections and political parties (such as preparing and encouraging women candidates), state institutions (increasing the presence of women in positions of state power and the extent to which state institutions are responsive to women's concerns), and civil society (heightening the degree of civic organization and participation among women). . . .

Programs to help increase the number of women in political office may meet their numerical goals but run up against the fact that merely having more women in office does not change much. Though women's NGOs are the most rapidly growing form of NGO in transitional countries, they still face the same problem as other donor-supported NGOs of elitism and disconnection from their intended base. Nonetheless . . . it is impossible not to be struck by the unusually intense interest and enthusiasm that democracy programs relating to women often generate. It is a domain with notably strong potential for further development.[17]

Fourth, we noted that youth were easily drawn into postconflict normalization and reconciliation activities. Conversely, most of the actual combatants in all violent conflicts are young males, even children. While the very young boys are commonly said to have been dragooned (as in Mozambique), they also commonly became socialized to violence. Restoring their mental health and resocializing them in the process of postconflict normalization is one of the unusual problems faced by these particular societies. The idea that youth in particular, as a conflict-avoidance measure, can and should be educated to insulate them against violence is attractive even if its efficacy is problematical.[18]

Fifth, if bottom-up programs are to have *significant* amelioration (or any other) effects, they need to be approached with the systematic conceptualization commonly applied to more standard subjects. For example, to have more than isolated impact, they need to be replicable. They also need to extend into a wide range of activities so that the bridge-building perspective becomes incorporated into different dimensions of interpersonal and community life and affects the different social classes within the society. Individual NGOs should not be encouraged to extend their clientele, locations, or program content prematurely, beyond their management reach and technical competence. Instead, replication and the development of complementary programs can be achieved through support of networks of NGOs selected for their interest in the relevant activities. Local concentrations of NGOs with similar bridge-building or disadvantage-minority focus—working with women, youth, or adult men, through activities involving skills training, sports, neighborhood improvement, performing arts, cultural exchange, and so forth—are more likely to affect communal relationships than if the same volume of activity is scattered and unintegrated over a large area. Achievement of critical mass along such lines is more likely if good coordination exists among all donors interested in promotion of civil society.

Finally, despite the enthusiasm with which donors have seized upon local social service and activitist NGOs, donors may (as was the case in Bosnia in the mid-1990s) view NGOs essentially as cheap service delivery vehicles.[19] Instead of sustaining their support as an effort at NGO institution-building in Bosnia, some donors and international NGOs lost interest in the local organizations, shifting their attention to other countries or subjects. Sustainability cannot be approached haphazardly. Donors should be prepared to support effective NGOs until sustainability has been achieved through income-generating activities, membership and local community or business contributions, and/or NGO mastery of international grantsmanship. In countries where none of the domestic sources will be significant options for years to come, donors should consider capitalizing an independent, local endowment foundation that can act as a reliable source of core funding for operating NGOs. Also, in addition to supporting individual NGOs working on the donors' chosen subjects, donors should examine the legal framework. Sustainability of the aided NGOs and of the entire nongovernmental organization sector may be at risk if the legal basis for NGO existence, and the regulatory environment, is undeveloped or hostile. Creation of an enhancing framework could be an important subject for technical assistance.

While bringing *large* numbers of people in opposing or hostile groups into harmonious relationships is critical if animosities are widespread, it would be a mistake to overlook the possible benefits from bottom-up activities that involve only relatively small numbers. Forms of NGO organization, potential leaders, and the effectiveness of alternative programs may have to be tested in small pilot projects before the feasibility of scaling up to large numbers of beneficiaries can be determined. Hirschman asked, "What does it all add up to?" in his essay on Latin American grassroots organizations. He cautions that doing good on any scale should not be denigrated by "comparing the resulting 'total' to some equally nebulous concept such as the General Economic Welfare or the Prospects for Democracy."

Still, the question remains, what effect can scattered microprojects have on the mass of untouched population? Hirschman suggests important social-change benefits. The projects were providing youth a new voice, an option other than guerrilla warfare: "the lives of Latin American middle-class youth have been enriched by the opening up of this vast new area of possible endeavors." He speculates that in the case of the anti-authoritarian reactions in Argentina and Chile in 1982 and 1983, "it is conceivable that the grassroots stirrings, together with the searchings of the social activitists, were an important underlying factor in preventing the social quiescence and introversion that are required for an authoritarian regime to take hold." Nevertheless, Hirschman still envisages major social change as a function of the scale of the change agents' movement. "A *dense network* of such movements, jointly with a large number of social activist organizations, is bound to change the traditional character of Latin American society in several ways, most of which are not yet well understood."[20]

The Sri Lankan irrigation experiences described earlier illustrate how development projects can either exacerbate local communal relations or ameliorate them depending on whether or not the inherent opportunities for bringing divided, even hostile, local communities into harmonious, economically meaningful relationships are taken. The farmer groups of the Gal Oya project have become celebrated examples of on-the-ground, integrative, and conflict-avoiding civil society. Comparable opportunities can be found in other types of projects: agricultural settlement schemes on land not previously occupied; farm-to-market road projects that traverse heterogeneous population areas and that are built, and possibly maintained, using labor-intensive methods; cooperative marketing systems that include producers from different ethnic groups; pastoral projects embracing different kinship groups; rural electrification systems that include consumer community representatives in their governance. The border zones of contiguous ethnic regions should be scrutinized for project opportunities that could bring the different groups together in common-interest relationships. As the Gal Oya project also shows, social engineering may have to be an essential component of such projects to ensure that the design and workings of the new relationships are conducive to a positive outcome despite the previous distance or hostility between the groups involved.

The creation of real common interests is likely to enhance the effectiveness of people-to-people programs that hope to change attitudes and behavior through sheer discussion. A large conflict-management/resolution network has developed in recent years. Organizations like the U.S. Institute of Peace bring small groups of people together in seminars and retreats designed to break down barriers and stereotypical thinking, and to facilitate negotiation and accommodation.

Conflict-avoidance facilitation through dialogue can operate at all levels, from local and youth groups up to national level decision makers. The

Carnegie Commission's "Project on Ethnic Relations" (PER), for example, is working in Russia and in Central and Eastern Europe, through "dialogue among government officials and ethnic leaders," support for local conflict-resolution institutions, and training of conflict management specialists. The PER "brokers" ethnic disputes. "Moderates on both sides were able to develop partnerships, begin to devise peaceful solutions and compromises, and create an atmosphere of mutual respect." To reduce the chances of conflict, PER adheres to certain methods—for example, create credible, neutral forums; redefine the parties' self-interests; work regionally; maintain communication with opinion leaders; encourage indigenous solutions.[21] The focus is on the process. Obviously, this is a large subject. It involves many institutions and field projects and has been much studied by scholars of conflict and diplomacy. Because this important dimension of international peace maintenance lies outside the scope of our own study, I mention it only in passing except to note that Churchill's precept—jaw-jaw is better than war-war—will be more persuasive, as the Carnegie Commission recognizes, if the jaw-jaw rests on a foundation of concrete grievance mitigation and interest harmonization.

In conclusion, it would be naive to assume that civil society is uniformly virtuous. Enthusiasts of civil society have tended to equate civil society with NGOs, especially advocacy NGOs, and to believe that civil society organizations naturally favor tolerance, accommodation, and democracy. Unfortunately, it has often been the case that civil society supports the agenda of aggressive national leaders, adding fuel to the flames. Donors need to be alert to the possibility, especially under nondemocratic systems, that apolitical NGOs they have nurtured only as programmatic instruments may be susceptible to being coopted for divisive purposes. Such coopting should not arise under government that is benign. Instead, donors need to be alert to the danger that excessive reliance on NGOs could deprive a development- and equity-oriented government of resources and technical assistance it would otherwise have received to help improve its performance. The Netherlands Institute of International Relations study found that donor funding and reliance on NGOs had been weakening governments in West Africa.[22] This is a striking observation that runs counter to the current vogue for civil society, and one that merits further exploration in other regions.

Notes

1. See Carothers, 2000, ch. 2, for a detailed account.
2. Ibid., p. 342.
3. Ibid., p. 343.
4. Ibid., p. 344.

5. Management Systems International, 1996, p. vii.

6. Nordlinger, 1972, pp. 20, 36.

7. A recent example in USAID is cited by Heather S. McHugh, in "USAID and Ethnic Conflict: An Epiphany?" in Esman and Herring, 2001, p. 74. McHugh refers to a USAID paper (authored by Harry Blair) as the basis for a study on governance: "The concept paper developed for this evaluation contains valuable indications on where future agency guidance may be directed and includes sections relevant to projects focused on ethnic conflict. For example, in the section on benefits of decentralization, the concept paper discusses two strategies: decentralization projects have the potential to indirectly empower marginal and ethnic groups who find little or no political voice at the national level; and decentralization can directly reduce ethnic conflict."

8. Hirschman, 1984, pp. 33, 92–93. Italics in original.

9. Horowitz, 1985, p. 169.

10. Ibid., 1985, p. 293.

11. World Bank, 1999, p. xi.

12. Gordon White, cited in Carothers, 2000, p. 209.

13. Ibid., pp. 209–210.

14. For one example, see Staub, 1989.

15. This account draws on Muscat, 1999.

16. Carnegie Commission, 1997, p. 84.

17. Carothers, 2000, pp. 345–346.

18. There is a "need to design projects aimed at youth and preparing them for involvement and progressive assumptions of responsibility in society." German Foundation for International Development, 1996.

19. The reference is to an evaluation by Ian Smillie, *Service Delivery or Civil Society? Non-Governmental Organizations in Bosnia & Herzegovina*. CARE/Canada, December 1996.

20. Hirschman, 1984, pp. 97, 98. Italics added.

21. Carnegie Commission, 1997, p. 53.

22. Netherlands Institute of International Relations, 1999, p. 90.

6. Economic and Sector Policies
Reforms, Preferences, and Harmonization of Interests

Across-the-Board Reform

The international development agencies have played an important role in the shaping and financing of the economic framework and development policies of most developing nations in the past half century. Both the scope and speed of the economic, social, and technological changes in this period have been historically unprecedented. It bears repeating that, over the long run, both economic development and modernization have been tides that raise most (but not all) boats. (Conversely, in countries suffering development failure, the economic ebb tide has left most boats stranded or lowered.) In the early stages of the development process, however, the distribution of the gains can be very uneven. At various times, different groups may be left behind to experience relative or even absolute deterioration in their material circumstances. The plight of the losers can be especially sharp and pregnant with conflict potentialities when their welfare deteriorates relatively quickly, particularly if the deterioration can be laid at the door of the government. Recall how the central government's slow and seemingly indifferent response to the typhoon in East Pakistan added to the Bengalis' sense of regional grievance before the breakaway. More commonly, grievances have arisen in response to perceived sins of commission rather than omission. When these sins are perceived as outcomes of economic policies, external agencies associated with the adoption of the policies may also be implicated.

As the policy front-runners among the international economic agencies, the World Bank and the IMF have been the principal targets for critics decrying the inequities and hardships attributed to policy change and reform programs. Sound economic management over time always requires policy adjustments to ensure that changing economic circumstances (often the consequence of external factors over which a country's policy managers have no control) do not destabilize an economy or derail its growth. Structural adjustment, the target of much criticism, differs from ordinary policy adjustment in its scope and timing. To restore economic balance and growth to the numbers of Third World economies that had become seriously destabilized, the structural adjustment programs of the 1980s and 1990s typically called for a multitude of policy changes. The change packages ranged from the relatively incremental to the drastic. Reform programs typically went beyond "stroke of the pen" changes, such as currency devaluation, to include "structural" changes—that is, changes in the economic rules of the game, in the role of government in the economy, and in the relative extent of government economic direction and public ownership versus private markets and private property.

The degree of change an economy and society had to undergo depended on how severe and unsustainable were the macroeconomic imbalances, and on how far (and for how long) previous governance had gone in the way of establishing nonmarket, centrally administered, politicized systems of resource allocation and economic management. Whereas the change processes in different countries frequently comprised similar policy packages, the most thoroughgoing end of the reform spectrum—the dismantling of the socialist systems in the former Soviet Union and Eastern Europe—has been differentiated under its own term of art, namely "economic transition." The economists' standard anodyne characterization of these processes as "policy reform" does not convey the depth of change entailed. As one investigator has observed, "Although each element of reform—price decontrol, privatization, stabilization, and so on—might seem familiar, the confluence of so many elements of such magnitude is unprecedented. The word 'reform' is surely a misnomer for what is occurring; 'revolution' is more fitting."[1] While this observation (written a few months prior to the collapse of the Soviet Union in late 1991) referred to Eastern Europe and the USSR, it is also apt for many of the IMF/World Bank structural adjustment programs in mixed-economy developing countries. In deeply divided societies, processes of such scope and systemic change, and which are planned for implementation over relatively short time periods, are not likely to be neutral in their effects on different ethnic or socioeconomic groups. They may well exacerbate social and political divisions, increasing the potentialities for violent conflict.

The substitution of competitive markets for the administrative determination of prices, resource allocation, and asset control, which was characteristic of socialist economies, has been at the core of the mainstream paradigm (the "Washington consensus") and of the wave of economic reform that has swept across the developing countries in the past two decades. It has been widely acknowledged that there will be losers during these transitions and that measures need to be incorporated to protect the most vulnerable. It is less well recognized that markets in deeply divided societies may not, over time, produce economic convergence between ascriptive groups. Whether owing to history, geographic resource endowment, discriminatory practices, or other reasons, competitive markets may, under some not-uncommon circumstances, widen group divergences. The literature on structural adjustment appears to have ignored this perspective.

For example, researchers into the politics of adjustment have focused on the question of implementation viability. Whose interests are hurt and how can governments (and aid agencies) limit that hurt and the resulting opposition to the program? The winners and losers are usually defined in traditional class terms as measured by income deciles, or by standard production factor groups—private enterprise, organized labor, public-sector enterprises, agriculture small-holders, and others.[2]

An examination of the conflict potential of a structural adjustment or market-transition program in a deeply divided society should consider the implications, in that context, of individual policy changes that would affect socioeconomic groups likely to be identified more by their communal or ascriptive character than by the standard crosscutting class and factor classifications. Examples would be policies that (a) reduce or remove economic rights long held by particular groups; (b) reduce or end subsidies or other transfers benefiting particular groups; (c) transfer land, manufacturing, infrastructure, or other assets from state to private ownership; (d) change government expenditure allocation by reforming the budget process to *(inter alia)* depoliticize expenditures by subjecting them to technocratic review and control; (e) centralize or decentralize aspects of the fiscal system (e.g., allocations of revenue and intergovernmental transfers between the center and regional/provincial jurisdictions; taxation and borrowing authorities), which would shift the previous balance of rights and controls; (f) reduce import tariffs and quantitative restrictions that have favored some groups at the expense of others (e.g., through urban bias impact on the urban/rural terms of trade); (g) devalue a currency, and/or unify a multiple-rate system, thereby affecting income distribution through the changes in implicit taxes on, and subsidies to, the producers or consumers of the affected goods; (h) reform labor markets in the "liberalizing" shape of eliminating hiring/firing restrictions (which would be conflict-ameliorating or enhancing if previous labor market policy included affirmative action, depending on whether such policy was designed to promote or to counter discrimination); or (i) introduce or strengthen safety-net provisions to offset deleterious effects that reforms (such as exchange rate liberalization or credit expansion ceilings) might have on defined groups.

The potentially conflict-exacerbating effects of these changes can be greatly intensified if many of them are introduced at once under a package of reforms. The political consequences can also be greatly magnified if the differentially affected groups are concentrated (the Yugoslav case) in separate jurisdictions (provinces, republics, etc.) under a decentralized federal sys-

tem, with the reform program in effect pitting some ethnogeographic jurisdictions against each other or against the central government.

Once the incidence and grievance potentials of the individual reforms
have been identified, the possible impact of the reform policy as a whole
should be considered. The study of the interrelationships among the different structural changes involved in these reform processes has produced a
large literature and much debate over the past decade. A great deal of attention has been devoted to issues of timing and sequencing. Many of the individual reforms turn out to be technically related in ways that make the viability
of some reforms dependent on the implementation of others. (For example,
to be effective, privatization may require changes in accounting and audit
standards and reforms in the banking system.)

Although the insights gained from research into these relationships have
been important for improving the design of reform programs, the really contentious debates have been over the politics of timing and sequencing, with
analysts divided over which approach is more likely to ensure the success
and permanence of the process. Advocates of a "'big bang"—implementing
and telescoping the full package as forcefully as possible—argue that speed
is essential to deny vested interests and other opponents the time required to
mount an effective blocking or undermining counterattack. The proponents
of more deliberate and gradual implementation argue the reverse: longer sequencing lowers the risk of a scuttling counterattack by reducing the startup
pain and giving different groups more time to adjust. Some reforms must be
introduced early and strongly on technical grounds, such as measures to sta-
bilize the economy and legal reform prerequisites for privatization, taxation,
banking system, or other components of the package. The timing of other
reforms may have greater leeway or be inherently more time-consuming.

> The most important strategic choices arise . . . out of the interplay between
> economics and politics. System-wide reform is an intensely political pro-
> cess: indeed, the main differences among reform strategies largely reflect
> differing views of what will be politically sustainable. The time needed to
> reform institutions, create skills, and value assets, argues for a measured
> pace of reform. But a slower pace has costs, including prolonged uncer-
> tainty and probably a longer period of poor economic performance, during
> which opposition can coalesce to block the reform process. A rapid ap-
> proach, in which markets are liberalized even before adequate preparatory
> steps, avoids the dangers of delay, but raises the potential for chaos.[3]

This summary of the core political economy issue (by a former chief economist of the World Bank and by a former chief of the World Bank's Socialist
Economies Unit) drew on the experience up to 1991 of socialist economy

transitions. It serves equally well as a caution for designers of reform processes in developing countries elsewhere.

As we observed earlier, the evidence does not show significant association between structural adjustment programs in general and subsequent conflict, except for the occasional "IMF riot" and the exceptional case of Yugoslavia. One might look for a relationship if a structural adjustment program fell heavily and suddenly on a portion of the population that was relatively poor and already politically mobilized over grievances against the state and/or a less affected, hegemonic "other." Many critics of structural adjustment have decried its alleged inequities (e.g., government budget cuts in the form of reductions in food subsidies for needy urban consumers or increases in unemployment caused by ceilings placed on bank credit expansion). Though some of these effects (e.g., increased unemployment) have been common, others have not. For example, many subsidy beneficiaries actually have been middle-class rather than the more needy poor; health service cutbacks have not affected the very poor in countries where the services never reached the poor to begin with. Some policy-change adjustments may benefit some groups of the poor while simultaneously hurting others. Thus, currency devaluation in African cases raised the (agricultural product export) earnings of rural poor but reduced the real incomes of those poor earning their living in the urban informal sector.

In Latin America, by contrast, devaluations were found to have hurt both the rural and urban poor.[4] A multiple-exchange-rate regime is like a system of trade taxes and subsidies, with differential price-raising or price-lowering effects on different import or export goods. A policy reform that moves to a uniform rate applied to all trade transactions will differentially affect producers and consumers of different goods, benefiting some and costing others. I cite these few examples only to demonstrate that a *general* argument against structural adjustment as being inherently antipoor is fallacious. Furthermore, where antipoor results did emerge, the IMF often had no alternative than to accept a government's decision not to pursue the relevant policies to their target levels and timing, while the World Bank responded by developing and funding "safety-net" programs.

Even where a structural adjustment program (or, more precisely, components of a program) is reducing the welfare of some of the relatively poor, such effects (even if not fully offset by safety-net programs) are intended to be of short duration. If structural adjustment overall achieves its stabilization and structural reform purposes, then growth should resume on a more sustainable path, gradually restoring employment and income levels. (There are caveats, of course: for other reasons, sources of growth like investment or exports may not recover despite the enhanced policy environment. Bolivia has been a case in point.) Economists who criticize structural adjustment have not argued that the reforms were not required; rather, they have asserted that the IMF (and the U.S. Treasury, but not the World Bank) erred in imposing "shock therapy," that is, requiring the implementation of the full package of reform policies within relatively short time frames, on the assumption that the political and economic viability of the reform would be threatened if the sick patient did not take the bad medicine all at once. Thus, a prominent critic, Joseph Stiglitz, accused the IMF and the U.S. Treasury of having deepened the 1997–1998 crisis in East Asia and worsened the economic transition process in Russia.[5]

Other critics argued that the really sick patients were the poor. To the extent that budget stringencies, job layoffs, or other elements of the process fell on those owning the fewest resources to tide themselves over before economic recovery, the adjustment programs at least should be redesigned to include social safety nets. An essential point was often ignored by critics of the earlier structural adjustment programs going back to the late 1970s, namely what would have happened had these programs not been undertaken?

The dilemma this oversight appears to place upon the IMF and World Bank is illustrated by the Netherlands Institute study cited earlier. Recall that the Netherlands Institute cited dissatisfaction over weak government capacity to deliver services as a factor contributing to the outbreak of conflict. The institute views the budget stringencies of World Bank/IMF-sponsored structural adjustment as further undermining these capacities, thereby in effect contributing to conflict.[6] Conversely, the study's examination of the Sri Lankan conflict is said to show that "economic decline and stagnation provide mobilizing incentives for extremist leadership."[7] If economic decline does hold such potentiality it must be reversed; but reversal is usually impossible without the initial stabilization reforms normally contained in structural adjustment programs, reforms that may unavoidably require reducing government expenditure in order to restore fiscal balance.

No criticism of any public policy that does not try to take account of the alternatives—doing nothing, or adopting a different policy—can be taken at face value. Where such efforts have been made, they indicate that

1. failure to undertake any significant policy change would have worsened the position of the poor, quite apart from the increasing general economic deterioration;
2. the successful cases illustrate how policies can be designed to avoid, or mitigate, adverse effects on the poor;
3. time does matter, that is, a faster return to sustainable growth is best for sustaining and enhancing the well-being of the poor; and

4. the particulars of each country situation have had major impact on the distributional consequences of policy alternatives within an adjustment program.

The last point is especially pertinent. It reinforces the importance of individual country assessments of conflict risk, quite apart from poverty impact analysis for its own sake. Whatever may be the elusive upshot of the debates concerning past structural adjustment and poverty, the apparent determination of the IMF and World Bank (responding to the charges of social insensibility) to give poverty impact and safety nets high priority should at least lessen inequitable, short-term distributional effects of stabilization and reform programs these institutions, and associated bilateral donors, support in the future.

In sum, within the overall consensus there has been much debate. Economists have differed on details, timing, the reasons for regional and country performance differences, the methodologies used in econometric examination, and the need for adjustments within the consensus—for example, concerning financial markets following the setbacks experienced by the East Asian "miracle" countries. The structural transitions undertaken by the majority of developing countries (including East European and ex-Soviet states) are a recent development, still in the early stages in most cases. Consequently, there has been relatively little empirical study of the relationships between transition and violent internal conflict.

I turn now to a closer look at some specific areas of economic policy reform and structural change. These are illustrations of policies with potentially significant distributional impact among competing groups. The examples are intended to look at policy reform in the context of conflict potential and obviously cannot be taken as full treatments of the policy changes in question.

Privatization: Transfer of State Assets to Private Ownership

The sale of government-owned enterprises to private ownership has been an important component of the transition process in most countries undertaking structural reform. *Privatization* is a standard element of the reform agenda promoted, if not demanded, by the World Bank and the IMF, and it has been supported by donor governments in principle and with technical assistance. The unloading of public enterprises has also been an important part of structural adjustment programs in countries that had long been market-based but that had traditionally reserved for government ownership certain sectors (e.g., power generation and distribution), or had adopted the principle of government manufacture of "commanding heights" products of heavy industries (e.g., steel).

Although there have been exceptions (such as some French state enterprises), the case against government ownership and management in developing countries rests on wide experience of inefficiency and economic drag.

> Managers in centrally planned economies faced distorted incentives that sooner or later led to poor enterprise performance. Transition requires changes that introduce financial discipline and increase entry of new firms, exit of unviable ones, and competition. . . . Once markets have been liberalized, governments cannot indefinitely control large parts of a dynamic, changing economy. [Privatizing] ownership is the best way to increase competition and improve performance.[8]

In addition to its salutary effects on enterprise efficiency, privatization can also contribute to economic reform and modernization by spurring the development of a country's capital market and ancillary legal, accounting, and other service sectors.

Despite the now extensive experience with privatization in a host of countries, and the availability of a library of case studies, much debate remains among economists and political scientists over issues of method and timing. The economic advisability of privatizing in principle is seldom questioned, even though the two most outstanding growth performers, Taiwan and South Korea, were clear laggards in this respect. These countries had unusual institutional characteristics that enabled them to avoid or minimize the management inefficiencies and corruption commonly found in the public enterprise sectors of developing countries. Different methods and sequences for privatization have been tried under different economic and political circumstances, with varying results. Enterprises have been sold (a) to domestic entrepreneurs, foreign ownership, or joint local/foreign ownership; (b) through management–employee buyouts; and (c) through voucher systems open to the general public. Under less orderly circumstances and weak regulatory systems, public enterprises have been privatized "spontaneously," that is, taken over by workers, or acquired at below-market value by political insiders. In countries with entrepreneurial classes inexperienced in management of large firms and/or having limited access to capital, privatization of large state enterprises may be possible only if the government is willing to sell ownership shares, often a controlling interest, to foreign investors.

Apart from the different efficiency outcomes of these various routes to privatization, the processes have drawn much attention to their political outcomes. The Russian experience has been paradigmatic for its lack of transparency and the acquisition of public-sector assets by tycoons who have then been perceived as wielding enormous backroom political influence, an outcome seen as undermining public support for the entire transition to a market-based economy and feeding public cynicism regarding the nature of the political transition to a democratic system. Crossing from the economic to the potential political effects of privatization, a World Bank review concluded that "Poorly managed privatization, even if it delivers short-term revenue or performance gains, may be seen as corrupt or highly inequitable, concentrating economic and political power in the hands of a domestic elite or foreign investors rather than expanding an independent and decentralized middle class."[9]

Two perspectives of this critique are interesting as illustrations of how a traditional, "technical" analysis overlooks potential outcomes in conflict-risk countries, outcomes arguably of much greater moment than the merely economic. First, the World Bank's perspective sees such political effects as suboptimal efficiency drags, unfortunate *results* from a process of institutional change that derives from, and is integral to, an economic reform program. These "crony capitalism" outcomes are technical distortions, opportunistic products that could be avoided were the process not "poorly managed." Some critics of the Russian experience have cited the plundering of state assets by a new class of oligarchs as a consequence of a fundamental error (attributable in part to the flawed advice of the IMF and the U.S. Treasury Department), that is, the disposition of the state enterprises before an adequate institutional infrastructure for a market economy had been put in place.[10] Second, the political economy lens through which this undesirable outcome is seen is traditional for economic analysis: the winners and losers are characterized by economic class (a socially undifferentiated domestic elite on the one hand, and everyone else, the nonelite, on the other) and by functional groups such as consumers, workers in the privatized firms, other enterprise stakeholders, and so forth.

The effects and desirability of privatization may look very different if the policy is introduced as an instrument for the extension of an elite's political dominance. A process of political spin-off to reward elite supporters is not likely to be structured to achieve efficiency results. Though technically devolved, the privatized enterprises may actually increase the extent of the political authorities' economic control compared with the previous situation under which the state-owned entities were controlled by diverse pieces of the bureaucracy. If the governing elite belongs to—and is using privatization to enhance the interests of—a dominant ethnicity, the process could widen ethnic power disparities and exacerbate perceptions of ethnic-group exclusion and exposure to fundamental political risk. Whereas several investigators have examined how politically driven privatization may produce perverse economic outcomes, one study of privatization under military regimes in sub-Saharan Africa found empirical support for the existence of political (rather than efficiency) derivation and ethnically skewed outcomes.

> To ensure complete power, privatization has often been used to control the country economically and politically. . . . Almost all of the African countries with military (as well as some civil) governments have adopted privatization on pure political grounds rather than efficiency. . . . Governments which undertake selective (political) privatization usually belong to a certain party or ethnic group. Their policies are, thus, more likely to be partisan than nationalistic.[11]

Acquisition may be additionally skewed through the allocation of politically influenced bank credits only to the favored buyers. Privatization then transfers state assets to the personal ownership of the same elites who controlled these enterprises when they were still state property, or to the ownership of their clientele. Several analysts have noted that the privatization that swept sub-Saharan Africa in the 1980s and 1990s produced exactly this unintended consequence. Even if a government had no intention to skew privatization for political purposes, the state assets might end up owned disproportionately by members of one ascriptive segment of a population because of "institutional" weaknesses (such as absence of open process, insider access, or below market or nonmarket valuation) that facilitate their capture by well-positioned groups. An ethnically skewed privatization might become a divisive issue, especially if the same group of beneficiaries appears to be gaining disproportionately from other aspects of public policy.

In the Mozambique case the aid technicians assisting the privatization process argued that, among the groups not acquiring state enterprises, there simply were no capable entrepreneurs. The experience in Kenya was very different. There it was widely recognized that public-sector enterprises were among the main sources for financing patronage and political support. In the first postcolonial period, under Jomo Kenyatta's presidency, the benefits of this system accrued largely to the Kikuyu. Under the succeeding Daniel arap Moi presidency, the ruling coalition of non-Kikuyu tribes has redirected in their favor the flow of resources and rents under government control or influence. When the privatization process began, the interests of those groups, and of the Moi administration, appeared threatened. The World Bank and the IMF were deeply involved and cognizant of the potential distributional consequences. Unlike in the Mozambique case, the external actors in Kenyan privatization made a sustained effort to depoliticize the process, which meant reducing to some degree the salience of tribal identity as a factor determining ownership outcomes.[12]

These potential outcomes on the relative positions of the elites of ascriptive groups have generally been ignored by the analytic studies of privatization. In one review of privatization experience, a World Bank study that was cited as an advance over "earlier partial studies" because it examined the effects of divestiture on "all important actors" apparently did not include ascriptive groups per se as "stakeholders" or "important actors" in the outcome. The review discussed methods of addressing the political problems that might arise when foreign owners acquire state enterprises, but did not consider how such devices might meet the special problems of domestic ownership, which is viewed as ascriptively "other" by a significant fraction of the society. As the investigators noted, the distributional effects of privatization need more thorough study.[13] A political economy perspective going beyond an oversimplified two-class model, of elite and nonelite actors, should be adopted for both comparative analytic studies and for individual country policy assessments.

Finally, it is worth reiterating an observation often made about a related reform consequence that may be necessitated by privatization. Where state enterprise profits have been a major source of revenue for government budgets, a government that is divesting must develop alternative revenues, usually through a mix of improved administration and collection and the introduction of new taxes, steps that in themselves may have important consequences for wealth distribution and for the relations between taxed groups and the state.

Labor Market Liberalization

Although seldom a central concern, labor market reforms may figure in structural adjustment. An important objective of adjustment programs has been to increase industrial competitiveness and flexibility. In addition to such measures as price liberalization and investment and production deregulation, industry may need access to a more efficient labor market as a complement to the other areas of liberalization. As explained in a World Bank review of adjustment programs during 1980 to 1992,

> Labor market regulations also served to impede the flow of resources to newly expanding subsectors in such countries as Cote d'Ivoire, Ghana, Indonesia, Mexico, and Senegal. In Cote d'Ivoire, for example, all firms are required to hire personnel from a single, government employment agency. Hiring and firing are tightly controlled by the agency, which also sets industrial wages. Undoubtedly, these regulations limited the private sector's ability to respond to the extensive liberalization of the export sector that took place under structural adjustment.[14]

The review concluded that regulatory reform, including reform of labor market controls, had been inadequate in many of the countries undergoing World

Bank–assisted structural adjustment, thereby limiting the gains that could have been realized through the price and other reforms that had been introduced. It recommended that the Bank needed to "refocus its attention on domestic market structure and performance."

Without gainsaying the importance of flexibility in the factor markets, proponents of freeing up labor markets need at least to be aware of the possibility that liberalization in ethnically divided societies may have perverse outcomes. Robert Klitgaard has warned against facile assumptions in this regard:

> [T]he creation of a national and competitive labor market does not necessarily lead to a reduction in ethnic inequalities. The colonial period in many countries marked the first establishment of a large-scale state apparatus, and it often led to an accentuation of both the perception and the fact of ethnic differences. The Brazilian example is interesting: "the creation, consolidation, and growth of the competitive social system did not help" the newly emancipated slaves overcome their economic handicaps. Contrary to the optimism of some economists, there is ample evidence that ethnic tensions and inequalities are frequently exacerbated rather than removed by the onset of competitive markets.[15]

Klitgaard makes the important observation that this outcome may derive from market imperfections even in the absence of deliberate discrimination.

> [I]f, for whatever reasons, groups differ objectively in performance and if information on individual performance is scarce and expensive, then we cannot count on free markets for labor or fair merit systems to drive out discrimination. . . . *If information is poor enough and it is difficult to vary wages according to performance, then the forces of competition may even reinforce ethnic inequalities. . . .*
>
> [A]n employer may have no intrinsic preference for one ethnic group over another, yet may rationally hire members of groups with higher expected productivity.[16]

Regardless of whether an ethnically segmented labor market derives from history, prejudice, or economic structure, one response may take the form of affirmative action, or preference systems, to which we now turn.

Changes in Group Economic Rights

Structural adjustment is only one of many policy-change processes that reshuffle economic rights. Loss of economic rights a group has already possessed can be a major source of grievance and conflict. The rights may be traditional, say from long occupation, or enshrined in law. The rights might be individual or pertain to a group's public property. The loss may be actual or only a credible threat. The loss might develop gradually over time or be imposed suddenly by edict or legal process. The changes in group economic rights may be unintended consequences of reforms undertaken only for economic purposes.

The recent conflict in the Moluccas was a violent response to an actual but gradual erosion of traditional individual economic rights, compounded by perception of a general threat of cultural and local power loss. In Nigeria, the Eastern Region's reductions in revenue allocations from oil production (of which the East was Nigeria's largest source) was a major grievance precipitating the Nigeria–Biafra civil war of 1967 to 1970. The breakup of Yugoslavia, as discussed earlier, has been attributed in part to the threat of loss of groups' public economic rights under structural adjustment. Most often, strategies for maintaining the viability of deeply divided multiethnic states center around devolution (rather than mere administrative decentralization) of powers. Devolution respecting subjects such as education, culture, judiciary, and some economic matters is common. The federal or central government commonly retains internal security, defense, foreign policy, and the core economic powers over monetary policy, foreign exchange, and public-sector external debt. Devolution in Yugoslavia had gone further than elsewhere, certainly further in economic policy management than would normally be considered prudent. The Yugoslav disintegration provides an example of the risks of moving in the opposite direction, of withdrawal of group economic rights previously devolved.

While the sense of grievance may be more acute when a group *loses* economic rights it has previously enjoyed, grievance over government *denial* of access to economic rights being newly created or distributed can be acute enough to fire up a movement for secession or conflict. As examples, such denial of economic rights could pertain to administrated allocation of foreign exchange earnings (the East Pakistan case), to land distribution (as in the Sri Lankan case), or (in Mozambique) to access to state enterprises up for privatization or to the bank credit that potential buyers will need to acquire those enterprises. As we have seen, donors may be involved in the policy deliberations respecting the creation and allocation of new economic rights, or the reallocation of existing rights, and in associated financing. The political economy of such processes should not be ignored.

Preference Policies

Preferential government policies, and/or preferential private-sector practices, have a long history. The granting of preference rights has represented a major structural change in the many countries where such preferences have been adopted, sometimes to widen, sometimes to narrow, economic differences. Many countries retain large group differentials in economic status and opportunity, either as legacies of now discredited past economic structures and policy regimes, or as the result of current policies and practices.

Negative preference (discrimination) and positive preference (affirmative action) regimes can take four general forms: (1) one group (or set of groups) dominates another group (or set) both politically and economically; preferences are discriminatory and exclusionary, with inequalities maintained by a policy regime that favors the already dominant; (2) one group(s) dominates (or, in democratic systems, preponderates over) a minority group(s) politically and economically, but the preference system aims to reduce inequalities, favoring the nondominant; (3) one group(s) dominates (or, in parliamentary systems, preponderates) politically, while another dominates (only) economically; the preference policy regime may be compensatory and inclusive, employed to reduce economic inequalities by favoring the politically dominant, or (4) confiscatory and exclusive, a zero-sum program at the expense of the politically subordinate.

In practice, the distinctions between groups and their relative advantages or deprivations may not be as clear as these categories imply. Rigorous cross-country comparison of preference programs and their outcomes would be difficult. Apart from data problems, the programs have differed in policy content, have ranged in scope, and have been carried out in very different contexts (e.g., India, the United States, and South Africa). Preference policies combined with large-scale resource transfers are likely to have more powerful effects for their beneficiaries (or on their victims) than preferences alone and would make the identification of preference effects alone even more difficult. By denying a country the potential growth contributions of the excluded group, programs of extreme exclusion may actually work to the disadvantage of the putative majority beneficiaries (as in South Africa, and in East Africa and Burma after the expulsions of South Asian commercial classes).

In logic, preferential policies designed to eliminate (or reduce to specified levels) differences in the social or economic opportunities or circumstances of different groups within a country should be temporary. Once the objectives are achieved (over a period that realistically may have to be measured in years, if not a generation), the policies would no longer be needed or justifiable. If progress along the way toward the objectives falls short of what was anticipated, the policies and objectives could be reevaluated, and adjusted or strengthened. After achievement (regardless of how much of the change can be attributed to the policies in question), continued application of the preferential policies may become perverse, putting the previously relatively advantaged group(s) at a disadvantage. The policies could then be seen as unjust and discriminatory by the groups not eligible for the preferential treatment. In the U.S. experience, a backlash against some affirmative action preferences, both in university access and in hiring practices, has developed long before the broad objectives of interethnic economic equality have been achieved.

Policies favoring one group over others may appear in a very different light depending on the economic context. Unequal distribution of *only the increments* of income and economic assets may be acceptable to, even if disliked by, the economically advantaged group if strong economic growth is yielding generous increments to all population segments. By contrast, discrimination that appropriates existing assets of one group or expels members of the nonfavored group from residence, occupations, or employment they already occupy is overtly negative-sum and unmistakenly punitive and expropriable. Preferential access to increments—if transparent, negotiated within a politically inclusive process, and framed with specific cutoff criteria—may be seen as morally justified and serve to avoid resentment sufficient to support ethnic radicalization.

As with so many programs of social engineering, the history of economic preferences shows mixed outcomes. Writing in 1990, Thomas Sowell came down against preferences based on his review of experience in several countries. He argued that the preferences once legislated usually remain in force despite their presumably temporary nature. Further, political pressures tend to expand preferential access to include ever increasing other "minorities" or "disadvantaged" groups, as has been the case, for example, in India. He also argues that the numbers show the policies are not very effective after all. After another decade, however, the record looks less negative.

In the United States a substantial black middle class has emerged along with a conservative reaction among some African-American intellectuals against further extension of affirmative action. There has been a substantial narrowing of the wage gaps between the "white" majority and the designated minorities. Black urban youth continue to pose complex problems of absorption into the mainstream, but the fact that the preferential policies have not been a complete answer to the difficulties facing the remaining disadvantaged does not gainsay their effectiveness in facilitating the inclusion of a significant portion of the population eligible for those preferences. For the purposes of this book, however, the Malaysian experience is more apposite and its outcome to date has been much more positive than in Sowell's earlier judgment.

The main economic objection to preferential policies has been that they distort and lower the efficiency of markets by interposing administrative requirements and by creating artificial incentives and disincentives. For example, for the rational employer who hires and retains workers based on skill and performance criteria, a government stipulation that he must hire (usually, some percentage of) workers of a specified ascriptive group, even if they are less qualified than other applicants, will lower productivity in the firm and raise costs. While the nonpreferred groups as a whole have presumably been enjoying disproportionate economic rewards (which is the rationale for introducing affirmative action preferences), nonpreferred individuals may have to bear private costs. Taxation to finance transfers to benefit a disadvantaged group may have the effect of reducing the incentives for the taxed to work at the now reduced net income level. An IMF handbook captures these dysfunctional outcomes: "[M]easures aimed at addressing distributional objectives have an efficiency cost. There is therefore a trade-off between equity and efficiency that implies a limit to the amount of redistribution which can be undertaken."[17] The micro costs may add up to a macro-efficiency drag.

The overarching benefit—social stability where reduced inequalities have helped reduce the risk of conflict—suffers in a comparison with the costs of market interventions because the reality of the benefit depends on a counterfactual argument: the preferences have helped prevent conflict that would have entailed heavy economic and humanitarian costs had it taken place. Obviously, no measurement is possible of a scenario the extent of which is only imagined, even though possibly ranging up to catastrophic levels. The what-if comparison looks very credible, however, in some cases. In Belgium, both the language issue and the accommodations it has required have "exacted costs in government efficiency and money and, in nontrivial ways for some, traditional individual and family prerogatives, *but not in lives or civil order*, when compared with other deeply divided societies."[18] In the case of Malaysia since the 1969 riots, the restoration and maintenance of social stability, squarely based on the extensive market-intervention preferences system, has avoided recurrence of ethnic conflict and enabled the country to record one of the highest growth outcomes among developing nations for nearly three decades before the interruption from the region-wide financial crisis of the late 1990s.

Preferences in the education system have been particularly important in countries employing affirmative action policies. Their importance flows from the plausible presumption that human capital disparities are at the heart of social and economic inequalities, and that educational equality is a necessary, if not sufficient, condition for eliminating other inequalities. Whether or not educational preferences (such as access quotas and differential scholarship allocation) ease or exacerbate group relations depends on the context and the political processes that lead to adoption and then modification and phasedown. In Sri Lanka, the university quota policy in favor of the underrepresented Sinhalese majority reinforced the Tamil perception of general exclusion caused by language and land policies. In Malaysia, the Malay university preferences caused ethnic Chinese resentment but were only one element of the general bargain and were put in place by the multiracial power-sharing coalition. In both Malaysia and Tanzania, as quota policies turned away many students who would otherwise have qualified for entrance on merit, parents responded by sending their children to schools in other countries and by creating a demand for local private schools, to which education entrepreneurs responded by creating a private school sector. The private costs of the minority-student families were arguably more than compensated for by their sharing in the public good of nonviolent interethnic relations. The stimulation of private-sector education was an unintended, but additionally beneficial, consequence in both cases.

In a critical vein, Horowitz pointed out some of the efficiency costs of quota systems that, perhaps unavoidably, lower entrance standards as preferenced places become filled with students who would not otherwise have been able to gain admission.[19] Because the relatively poor preparation (or rural, cultural, or other presumed causes) was part of the problem the educational preference was designed to help overcome, the lowering of admission standards should be seen as indicating a need for complementary strengthening of the primary and secondary systems, not as a weakness of the preference concept.

The preference system experiences in Sri Lanka and Malaysia show how powerful education admission problems can be as an ethnic issue. In Sri Lanka, "a new wave of Tamil separatist violence, including the assassination of policemen, rather clearly flowed" from the quota and entrance preferences for Sinhalese students. Horowitz cites a Sri Lankan writer who concluded that the system "convinced many Sri Lanka Tamils that it was futile to expect equality of treatment with the Sinhalese majority. It has immensely strengthened separatist forces with the Tamil United Front and contributed to the acceptance of a policy of campaigning for a separate state."[20] Conversely, educational preferences may contribute powerfully to ethnic harmony and conflict avoidance—again, depending on context, implementation flexibility, and private alternatives.

As the Malaysian case illustrates, preferences can make a substantial contribution to reducing historic inequalities of participation and economic power in private business. Education and business preferences can be mutually reinforcing. The increasing numbers of school graduates with technical and management skills and who belong to ethnic groups previously absent or underrepresented in business professions and trades enlarge the pool of those capable of taking advantage of the licensing, credit, ownership, and other business opportunities set aside for the preference eligibles. Although Horowitz correctly judged that 1981 (the year of a report he wrote for USAID on policies to deal with ethnic conflict) was too soon to draw strong conclusions from the Malaysian experience, his study remains useful for its discussion of some of the problems that may emerge in the early years of a business preference program. For example, access to licenses, contracts, or other opportunities supposedly set aside for a preferred ethnic group may continue to be captured by established nonpreferred firms that hire front men or give senior positions to token ownership. Corruption of the civil service may increase as members of nonpreferred groups pay bribes to obtain access they would otherwise lose. (Horowitz expressed concern that the increased costs of doing business to avoid the effects of business preferences could discourage investment in Malaysia or cause capital flight. While some ethnic Chinese entrepreneurs did emigrate to other countries—more likely to escape the totality of ethnic politics and the preference systems rather than merely the extra costs of doing business—the quantitative effect on investment and development in Malaysia was apparently negligible.) Governmental agencies set up to help Malay entrepreneurs were constrained politically from collecting on the loans they had extended.

Drawing on Indian and Malaysian experience, Horowitz cited several of the problems that arose in the programs these two countries (or individual Indian states) undertook to install ethnic preferences in employment. Here also, short-run costs were evident. For example, if a preferred group has had an educational deficit, the demand for qualified personnel from that group can quickly outrun the supply. "Unproductive employees may be added to the payroll to satisfy statistical requirements or, as in the case of representation in business, enforcement may be avoided through corruption."[21] Employment preferences for dominant ethnic groups in some Indian states led to movements among nonpreferred ethnic groups to secede in order to establish new states in which the nonfavored minority could become the dominant majority.

In Horowitz's view, judgments about the effects of preferential policies in business are difficult to make because short-term costs are "apparent" whereas long-term benefits are "difficult to estimate."[22] However, taking account of Robert Klitgaard's insights on the market-failure costs of ethnic discrimination in the labor market, there may be short-term benefits just as apparent as the short-term costs. A narrow economic comparison of costs and benefits of preferences should offset the short-term costs of affirmative action measures by the short-term gains derived from lowering the efficiency costs of prejudicial hiring practices. The short-term micro costs are generating (Klitgaard's unrecognized) short-term micro gains. The presumption that the net macro-efficiency effect of redistribution through preference systems is negative may be wrong.

Furthermore, a proper weighing of short- and long-term costs and benefits is a problem for many areas of public economic policy. The persuasiveness of long-term future economic benefits in day-by-day political calculation is normally low, and can be even further reduced if the normal financial concept of discounting future benefits to a present value is brought to bear. Such calculus could be affected substantially, however, where there is a credible risk that failure to address structural or prejudicial inequalities could trigger violent conflict.

Horowitz's general conclusions were, in my view, more negative than his own evidence suggested, especially given the importance he assigned to the Malaysian case. In addition, he cites employment outside the home ethnic region, which could be promoted deliberately through selected preferential hiring, as an important disincentive to Luo or Lozi secessionism, in Kenya and Zambia, respectively.[23] As in so many areas of public policy, the devil is in the details, and success lies in the implementation.

> The evidence is not complete yet on preferential policies and development. But it is clear enough that ethnic preferences pushed too far produce short-term economic and political costs—costs in efficiency, costs in unplanned expansion in education, costs in ethnic conflict. It may still be true, as it is assumed to be, that there will ultimately be less ethnic conflict if ethnic groups are proportionately represented in all sectors at all levels. One reason that the truth of this proposition remains elusive is that few, if any, societies approximate this description. If it is true, however, that does not mean that the end is worth any cost. In the developing countries, the short- and medium-run is very important. That preferential policies have not produced even more short-run costs is testimony more to the wisdom and political sensitivity of those who enforce such policies than it is to the policies themselves.[24]

We might also hypothesize that short-run costs may be minimized, and short-run conflict-risk most readily defused, if the initial effects of affirmative action are to narrow the economic and power gaps between *elites* of different groups. The first people to take advantage of many of the preferences in such programs are likely already to be members of their group's elite or, if not, will become so, thanks to the benefits they acquire. Of course, preferences are not promulgated as elite-promotion schemes, nor with the intent to increase vertical inequality within the preference group as a whole. Nevertheless, early inclusion of aggrieved elites may be highly effective for avoiding conflict in the short run, giving time for the preferences to reach wider and deeper into the eligible group.

Finally, it is worth repeating the two major lessons of the Malaysian experience. First, rapid economic growth that is also lifting the boats of the nonpreferred groups will moderate the political costs of a preference program and make it easier for a government to sustain and adjust. Second, government should implement preferences flexibly, allowing frequent exemptions. In a sluggish economy, or heightened atmosphere of ethnic tension, or where the number of potentially frustrated job seekers is large, preferences can be counterproductive. Thus, between growth and flexibility in enforcement, the employment preferences have caused much less resentment in Malaysia than in India.[25] The private efficiency costs of enforced hiring of less qualified workers can be offset by subsidizing on-the-job training periods. Preferences may be difficult to undo. Conversely, after preferences appear to have brought about a substantial lessening of employment disparities, the political cost of reducing the preferences may be eased if there is a reaction among some in the favored group against the continuation of schemes that imply its members have a permanent skill inferiority. Where disadvantaged groups are geographically concentrated, educational deficits can be narrowed by allocating sufficient resources to regionally equalize the quality of education, without imposing a preference system at the school level, or focusing the costs of the system on nonfavored individual students barred entry.

Whether through policy dialogue in connection with sectoral and project analysis and finance, or through their general advisory assistance on economic and development policies, donors should be alive to opportunities to consider adoption of affirmative action programs, where such might reduce group disparities, or the dismantling of preference systems that have achieved their original objectives or that were initially installed as instruments for exclusion. To be in a position to provide sound advice in this sensitive area, it would be helpful for donors to make a comprehensive review of experience, updating the work of Sowell, Horowitz, and others. For donors too strongly attached to government minimalism to contemplate support of preference policies, I would give the last word to Milton Esman. Noting that the advantaged economic position of particular groups had established at independence a nonlevel playing field in many former colonies, Esman asks, using the example of the Malays:

> When, under market processes, non-Malays gain control of most of the banks, manufacturing enterprises, construction companies, and commer-

cial firms in the private sector, should Malay elites meekly acquiesce in economic subordination? Or should they attempt to use the powers of government to rectify their disadvantaged status by revising the rules of access and of administrative intervention?[26]

Taxation

Tax policy reform and tax administration have long been subjects of donor interest, either through policy dialogue intended to advise or persuade governments to undertake reforms, or through technical assistance either to improve tax administration or the economic efficiency of the tax regime. Because questions of tax incidence (who pays and who benefits) have long been integral to economists' study of public finance, these issues of welfare effects have also been integral in donor involvement in this area. This has been so even when, as has often been the case, the activities have been carried out by academic and professional consultants or contractors in a technical rather than reform context.

Bad tax policies and administration are much more likely to exacerbate than to ameliorate economic conditions related to conflict. Besides their distorting impact on industrial efficiency and overall growth, tax policies can have differential regional and class distributional effects that can reinforce political, religious, or other sources of disaffection. Examples could be (1) commodity export levies that reduce farm-gate prices of crops cultivated largely by socioculturally distinct groups or in one ethnogeographic region; (2) controlled purchasing monopsonies of export commodity boards, tantamount to export taxation falling on similar groups; (3) sales taxes on products generally known for being bought only by a particular group; (4) taxation designed to fall only on economic activities or assets that are specific to a particular group; or (5) taxes that distort the industrial/agriculture terms of trade, usually to the disadvantage of agricultural regions.

Assessments of an existing taxation regime in a deeply divided society, or consideration of changes including imposition of new forms of taxation, should take into account (in addition to the usual criteria of incidence, efficiency, etc.) the actual or expected impact upon disadvantaged or aggrieved ascriptive groups. In such societies it would be prudent to adopt a working assumption that taxes are preferable that are at least neutral in impact among ascriptive groups, or (perhaps better) that fall relatively less or lighter on consumption or economic activities that are peculiar to disadvantaged ethnoregions or communities. Such group incidence criteria apply more appropriately to indirect than to direct taxes. Unequal application of individual income taxes based solely on ethnic group membership has little justification from either an equity or a political perspective. As noted below, corporate tax concessions offered as incentives for investment in lagging ethnic regions need to be moderate and time-bound. They should avoid creating a noncompetitive regional industrial sector that subsequently could become a source of contention, quite aside from the normal economic considerations that weigh against such structural distortions.

The effects of individual taxes or of the tax regime as a whole on intergroup relations depends both on the real incidence and (more importantly) on group perceptions of their absolute and relative after-tax positions. To have its desired fiscal and political effects, a tax regime designed (among other things) to advance equity among groups must be so understood by the groups in question. As economists often have difficulty determining existing tax incidence, let alone accurately projecting the incidence of a new tax, it is especially important in a divided society that perceptions be taken into account and that the process of establishing or altering taxation be transparent and well explained. Experience indicates that the greatest opportunities for substantial tax reform have come in the wake of major changes in political power.[27] In some of these shifts, especially in postconflict situations where completely new alignments and institutional arrangements may be put in place, the donors may have unusual windows of opportunity to help design a new tax regime, and other aspects of fiscal policy, that can contribute to preventing a resumption of hostilities.

The general advisability of any tax reform that will result in significant increases in government revenue cannot be determined without taking account of the expenditure purposes the revenue flow will support. These purposes depend heavily on the nature of the regime in power. If a regime is predatory, simply kleptocratic and devoted to self-perpetuation, assistance to increase tax efficiency (say, technical assistance to strengthen customs administration) would merely increase the flow of resources extracted from the economy, frequently to finance transfers to private external accounts. In a deeply divided society where a regime draws its support from one region or ethnic group, any revenue expansion would enhance the government's ability to feed its own patron–client networks, thereby exacerbating the enmity of the excluded groups. Whether in fact a regime prefers to extract transfers or to benefit from overall economic growth can make an essential difference in the conflict risk. The preference may depend on the relative size of the dominant group. Ruling elites from smaller dominant groups may be more likely to prefer systems of resource exaction compared with regimes that draw support from (and can expect future revenues from) a larger fraction of the population and a broader, growing taxable economic base.

The suggestions here on likely taxation strategies of ascriptive-group-based regimes are comparable to conclusions for economic growth that Robert H. Bates, Mancur Olson, and others have drawn from the policy performance of (mostly African) regimes that have been led by elites who frequently "sacrifice the general interest to extract rents and retain power." In the exaction/feeding interplay between regimes and taxed or supported groups, this literature defines the groups by their class and economic, rather than ascriptive, character.[28]

Internal Resource Allocation

Regional Preferences

Donors may affect the internal regional allocation of resources—and thus the relative costs and benefits experienced by different regionally concentrated groups—through (a) their influence on government expenditure patterns, (b) their influence on government economic and social policies, and (c) the distributive effects of the donors' own aid resources and projects.

It is often the case that the relatively poor economic circumstances of a restive disadvantaged group have resulted largely from a paucity of natural resources in the region they occupy. Poor resource endowment in a developing country commonly means some combination of agricultural deficits, such as soil that is saline or has low natural fertility or poor water-retaining characteristics; limited possibilities for irrigation; irregular or insufficient rainfall; excessive flooding. With or without such deficits, an economically backward region may have disadvantages of remoteness from urban markets or poor access to ports for shipping potential export commodities. Between remoteness and economic backwardness, and the political weakness that commonly results, such regions have often suffered also from neglect in the provision of education and health services and in the amount of agricultural research devoted to raising productivity. In sum, such regions tend to be disadvantaged in natural resources, physical infrastructure investment, human capital, and technological attention. As in some of our case studies, donors face the problem that investing scarce aid resources to the development of such regions reduces the resources available for investment in other areas where higher returns will make a greater contribution to a country's overall economic growth.

There are no simple answers to the backward-region problem. An extended treatment here would take us far beyond our subject, but a few observations drawn in part from the case studies point to conflict-relevant perspectives that donors should take into account. In the interest of strengthening the viability of the local economy and the traditional attachments to a region that underlie a disadvantaged population's culture and sense of identity, investments in agriculture should not be rejected automatically because they fall below the expected profitability criteria applied to projects in areas with more favorable agronomic endowments. Further, even poorly endowed regions often have pockets with better soil or with minor irrigation potential. A recent review by the International Food Policy Research Institute (IFPRI) pointed out that agricultural investment in the long favored areas has been facing diminishing returns.

Because such investment has lagged, the modest research advances that have accumulated open up opportunities that may now have higher returns on the margin than do further investments in the favored areas.[29] Investment in regional survey and planning may uncover local potential that has been previously overlooked and unsuspected. Contract farming and niche production of high-value produce for export have enabled some disadvantaged areas to join in mainstream development. Reducing isolation and lowering transport costs through highway and farm-to-market road projects is essential for realizing whatever prospects a regional agricultural economy may have for sustained income growth. Investment in marketing infrastructure may also be needed to help develop active and competitive produce and input markets where none existed before.

Although some concessions, such as purchasing and/or price guarantees, may also be needed to enhance a region's (or a regional project's) initial momentum, they should be held to modest levels to avoid encouragement of production that has weak long-term competitive prospects. To avoid saddling a national economy with permanently uncompetitive regional industries, it is generally best to eschew the substantial tax and other incentives that would be necessary to lure manufacturing into areas where such location would not be competitive otherwise.

Investment in human capital is likely to offer the highest long-run returns, both private and social. Education and health services should be brought up to national standards. Regional university(ies) could be created to increase tertiary education opportunity and to undertake research on local socioeconomic problems less likely to be explored by faculties at national, urban institutions. Social integration can be enhanced through the interregional migration of elites whose higher education affords them national competitiveness in the markets for advanced skills. Efficient interregional labor markets and associated low-cost transportation are important so as to facilitate seasonal migration; backward agricultural regions typically have annual alternating seasons between months of heavy labor demand and months of labor surplus. Investment in regional tourism and institutions of cultural preservation and promotion can be especially effective for reducing isolation and preserving regional identity.

The location and resource disadvantages of some backward regions may be so great that regional development programs alone are unable to bring income levels close to the levels of the more advanced areas. Per capita income convergence may be possible only through permanent migration to more dynamic areas, creating in effect an internal diaspora that supplements the incomes of those who remain behind (often the elderly, the children, and the more traditional minded) through a permanent flow of remittances. Taken altogether, however, backward-region development and cultural enhancement can go far toward overcoming grievances over neglect, relative deprivation, and cultural condescension. The IFPRI's arguments for anticipating satisfactory returns to investment in backward regions, and for reversing past neglect, are especially cogent where such possibilities are located in areas that are ethnically distinct and at risk for seeking radical redress.

Two other locational perspectives can be drawn from Esman's suggestion (noted earlier) that donors in ethnically divided societies allocate resources to projects that create interethnic common interests, and to projects that create intercommunal interdependence (i.e., divisions of labor that reward cooperative rather than competitive behavior). Where ethnic groups dwell in contiguous but separate homogeneous regions, the border areas may offer possibilities, not otherwise feasible for the populations located farther apart, for projects that involve groups from either side. An active search for such possibilities may turn up interdependence options that might otherwise be overlooked. Options for common-interest projects should be more readily apparent in ethnically heterogeneous areas. Within some heterogeneous areas, as in the Gal Oya project in Sri Lanka, the different ethnic groups may be locally concentrated in nearby, separate homogeneous communities but can be drawn into the unifying framework of a common project. Esman cites a carpet-producing project in Tadjikistan designed to create common interdependence between two hostile ethnic communities; one was provided the machinery for making the carpets, the other for producing the wool.[30] Needless to say, projects that introduce entirely new economic structures embracing hostile communities may end up creating either new cooperative relationships or new bases for conflict (especially if they prove unprofitable), depending on how astutely the projects have been designed and handled. Alternatively, heterogeneous groups may share the same villages or neighborhoods, where opportunities for involvement in common-interest activities and enterprises may be created more easily and naturally.

Choosing Among Alternative Projects

Knowledge about differentials in group income should be used to inform policy and project planning. For many years, development agencies have taken income disparities into account in the appraisal of proposed development projects. In calculating the potential benefits of a new project, it was acceptable to give greater weight to benefits expected to accrue to the poor compared with the valuation of benefits to accrue to members of higher-income classes. In practice, weighting might be merely implicit in a decision to scratch around for any investments that might yield something for the relatively poor.

Before income weighting was formally sanctioned in project analysis methodology, a project could be made to meet a minimum expected rate of return by fudging the assumptions and expected output figures. Although elaborate project-appraisal methodologies that, *inter alia*, use weights and shadow-prices to value benefits to the poor appear to have dropped out of fashion, a similar concept could apply to the valuation of benefits expected to accrue to a relatively depressed or backward *group*, compared with benefits expected to accrue to a dominant group more advanced economically and socially. Benefits expected for members of the same income class across groups could be given a higher valuation if they accrue to members of an ascriptive group that is generally backward, especially if such a group suffers from political and prestige discrimination and bears a general sense of exclusion or subordination. Such weighting would tend to skew the allocation of projects and their content to help reduce group asymmetries. One can imagine different magnitudes of weighting depending on the depth of the society's social divisions and antagonisms. The larger the specific asymmetries being addressed, the greater the weight that would be applied to the benefits to accrue to a disadvantaged or excluded group. Greater weight might be applied if the asymmetries had already entered the consciousness, rhetoric, or mobilization agenda of the disadvantaged group. The greatest weight could be employed if the grievances over these asymmetries were reinforced by dissatisfactions over wider issues of subordination. Establishment of such a practice in a given situation would have greater impact if the bias were accepted by the host country as a decision tool for its own policies and projects.

Formal Education

Programs to assist the development or reform of education systems typically run the gamut of schooling requirements: system planning; school construction; educational equipment; teacher and management training; curriculum, books, and teaching materials. The aid effort may be underpinned by a sector study that examines and projects the country's educational resource needs, the weaknesses that need to be overcome, policy issues (e.g., school financing and fees), and the part each donor can play. Implicit in the mere expansion of the primary and secondary levels to nationwide coverage (essential for modern economic development) is the long-term effect that universal education can have on national unity through exposure of the entire next generation to a common learning and socializing experience. Many newly independent developing countries have made the inculcation of common national symbols, values, and histories an explicit objective of their education systems. The donors may bear some responsibility for the software and socialization processes, especially if project assistance includes textbooks.

Donors should satisfy themselves that the physical expansion plans do not exclude or accord lower priority to minority areas, or jurisdictions where opposition parties have dominant support or have won local government elections. Ethnic group exclusion or discrimination in education is likely to have much more pernicious effects on social stability than neglect or discrimination applied to female schooling, an education problem donors have pursued vigorously in recent years. Donors working on education development should not be passive in the face of the divisive effects of segregated schooling, even of the "separate but equal" variety.

The health of the education system, and the impact the system has on the society as a whole, may depend on finding the right balance in teaching materials among "nation-building" commonality, multicultural knowledge and respect, the teaching of particular histories and traditions in schools in predominantly local or distinct cultures, and on policies respecting languages of instruction and the recruitment and placement of teachers of different ethnicities. These questions may take different forms and call for different responses in school systems in ethnically heterogeneous areas compared with areas where the student body is ethnically homogeneous. Also, donors involved in curriculum development or teacher training should not overlook possibilities for inculcating students with values of respect and tolerance through programs in the performing arts or through after-school nonformal education.

Although overtly hostile discriminatory policies, which include language among other forms of rights violation, raise issues for the basic relationship of donors to recipient governments, language alone may serve as a tool of more subtle discrimination that might be relevant to donor activities on a project level. For example, university development may be assisted by projects focusing on individual faculties or on the upgrading of physical plant; if the university is discriminating in its admission procedures (as in Pakistan against certain language groups[31]), the donor might not be aware if admission practices fall outside the boundary of the project and its normal prefinancing appraisal studies.

Donors may or may not have useful things to suggest or do regarding such issues. Donor involvement may not be welcomed in some sensitive areas, or may be acceptable only from an international agency like the United Nations Educational, Scientific, and Cultural Organization (UNESCO). The minimum requirement in education, as in other aid subjects, is to develop an awareness of divisive or ameliorative potentialities, and to avoid exacerbation, even if such conflictive effects would be unintended consequences of aid activities assumed to be "technically neutral." More proactive donor involvement in the distributive aspects of a country's education system may be appropriate where aid is being given in the form of education budget support. The apparent recent increase in arrangements calling for release of such support in tranches (partial disbursements), tied to performance of a government's education policy commitments, could provide an effective basis for expressing donors' distributive interest.[32]

Moreover, the relative ease with which teachers in the Bosnian NGO project (described earlier) were able to induce rapid interethnic reconciliation among Bosnian youth serves as an example of the potentialities for socializing the young to values of tolerance and civility. The idea that school systems can so shape the worldview and behavior of youth (with lasting effect over their adult lives, it is hoped) has led to some aid-funded intercommunal pilot projects and to general calls for education systems to play a greater role in conflict prevention and postconflict reconciliation. However, the past century saw many examples of the obverse: formal secular and religious education systems that taught targeted hostility to domestic minorities or external "enemies." In the recent flood of analyses of the roots of Middle East–based terrorism, various investigators have pointed out that virulent anti-Western, anti-Israeli, and/or anti-Christian inculcation has become embedded in some school curricula in the region, probably enhancing the ability of extremists to recruit youth for violent organizations. Wherever a curriculum has such inculcating content, donors should attempt to effect its removal, or, failing that, should withdraw from the education sector.

In a positive context, schooling should be able to educate and socialize youth to mores of nonviolent conflict resolution. Despite all good intentions on the part of local project staff and on part of donors providing financial support, however, pilot education projects that demonstrate reconciliation feasibility among the few students involved, or among their few parents, are unlikely to have wide impact if the government is not committed to replication throughout the system. A successful example of replication of a primary education model with general grassroots reconciliation impact appears to be evolving in El Salvador. Through a locally managed system that tapped the shared desire for better education for each community's young children, the widely known EDUCO project (Educacion con Participacion de la

Communidad) has won support from all the country's political parties. What began as a rural pilot project had grown (with World Bank and Inter-American Development Bank support) to cover 20 percent of the nation's enrollment through grade six in 1996. The good educational results aside, the program stands as a striking demonstration of formal education's reconciliation potentialities in a society (postconflict in this case) where the desire for child education is strong on all sides and where the political environment is reconciliation-enhancing.

> [T]he EDUCO experience has played a significant role in bringing elements of civil society and the political spectrum in El Salvador together in their assessment of an initiative of vital importance for the future development of the country. This finding of "common ground" constitutes a contribution to the sustainability of the continuing peace process. This is no mean achievement.[33]

Language Policy

We have seen how divisive language policy can be and how language questions can arise in various contexts. I have not come across any occasions where a donor agency was involved in the internal politics surrounding establishment of an official indigeneous language(s) to the exclusion of other languages spoken in a country. Among ex-colonial donors, France has probably been the most forceful in its pressing of Francophone countries to maintain French as the main second language. Although French policy on this score has caused problems among the donors in some cases (in the case of Cambodia, resentment among local officials who preferred to shift toward English, but could not risk the loss of the French aid program), the important point is the advantage that knowledge of any international language brings to the speakers and whether that knowledge is confined to dominant groups.

Even without any awareness of their language implications, donors may have some impact through various kinds of projects. For example, in what language are the road signs written along routes built or reconstructed with donor funds? Are public relations materials on donor programs, including announcements of forthcoming procurement and of employment and training opportunities, issued in the translations needed to ensure widest access? Does any one ethnic group have an inherent advantage in access to training opportunities tied to a specific foreign language?

Most importantly, in a society where language differences are salient markers of deep ascriptive divisions, donors should not support or passively tolerate the establishment or implementation of a language policy introduced for hegemonic ends or that is opposed by significant numbers of speakers of excluded or disfavored languages. At a minimum, donors in such situations should insist (or make their own arrangements) that government documents concerning subjects or processes in which donor technical, advisory, or other assistance is involved be issued in major languages other than the official language. Even apparently benign language discrimination can be a major obstacle to economic mobility.[34] If language discrimination is accompanied by other prejudicial programs to impose cultural assimilation (as in Bulgaria in 1984 when the government tried to prohibit its Turkish minority from using the Turkish language, wearing traditional dress, or performing circumcision, among other things), such violation of human rights should trigger strong donor response.

Agriculture

Struggles over agricultural resources reach back into ancient history in many parts of the world. In modern times these struggles, essentially over land ownership or use rights and over access to irrigation water, have often been central issues among the root causes of group conflict. (Although local and scattered conflicts over encroachments on the traditional lands of "indigenous" peoples have broken out in many countries—attracting severe criticism when development agency projects have been involved, and the attention of international human rights and environmental groups—these hostilities often involve relatively small populations that are politically marginal and do not scale up to generalized warfare.) Land policies can also be instruments for reducing rural economic inequalities and demonstrating inclusion. In the case of Sri Lanka, we have seen both how exclusionary policies governing access to new land settlement exacerbated interethnic relations, contributing to Tamil loss of trust in the state, and how at least local trust and amicable communal relations could be restored through jointly administered water-sharing systems. In Malaysia, government-financed settlement schemes gave small or landless Malay farmers land holdings (and credit and technical assistance) that substantially improved their economic prospects.

Donor projects may affect the communal outcomes of such programs and policies. Specific issues with collective distribution implications that might involve donors, or merit their attention, include

1. illegal intercommunal land seizure;
2. land seizure sanctioned by government legalization;
3. access to new land opened up by irrigation, and the associated rules for selection of beneficiaries;

4. irrigation system design (location of canals and water distribution, between alternative settled areas);
5. selection of beneficiaries for access to unoccupied arable land;
6. resettlement or internal migration programs (or voluntary, private migrations) that bring previously separate groups into close proximity, especially if the settlement area is already populated by people of a different ascriptive group;
7. development of the legal frameworks for land markets and for establishing clear property rights, especially in countries making a transition from socialist ownership systems;
8. rural credit access;
9. communal dimensions of beneficiary participation in project planning and project governance;
10. policy reforms that free up domestic markets for agricultural commodities that might have differential income effects on different regional or ethnic groups;
11. liberalizing imports of foodstuffs grown by previously protected domestic producers;
12. location of investment in rural roads;
13. location of research stations and selection of crops for research attention;
14. regional allocation and effectiveness of agriculture extension systems; and
15. location of agricultural universities.

All of these may impinge upon assistance programs, or be the subject of technical or economic aid. Depending on local circumstances, they may be frought with implications for domestic stability.

In land-settlement programs the economic assets being provided should be sufficient for sustained income growth. Otherwise the disadvantaged group being helped to narrow the intergroup income gap may be disadvantaged again if its holdings are too limited in size or productive potential to sustain more than a short-term increase in output. An insufficient short-term measure would first facilitate a rise in productivity, then act as a ceiling on further income growth, as was the case in early rubber and oil palm settlement schemes for Malay small landholders.

Civil Service Reform and Modernization

This is an old subject in development assistance, known earlier under the rubric of "public administration." A common objective of civil service reform is to move to a system of recruitment and advancement based on merit, on a Weberian concept of technocratic bureaucracy, matching people with job descriptions, giving them rank and pay depending on their entry credentials and their subsequent performance and in-service training. Many regimes in developing countries have used civil service appointment to build patron–client networks or to entrench the ethnic group of the governing elite. Many also inherited colonial bureaucracies that had been staffed under a combination of merit and ethnic affiliation.

Civil service reform programs, typically necessitated by administrative inefficiency and budget stringency, often call for retrenchment and the introduction of personnel systems based on competitive recruitment and merit-based promotion. Although some civil servants may be "shadow" employees—on the books and drawing pay but never showing up at the office—thereby easier to dismiss, reductions in actual employees may result in, or offer an opportunity for, changing the ethnic composition of the bureaucracy. If ethnic composition has been seriously disproportionate, or reflects an ethnic or ethnoregional dominance of government that could be an interethnic issue, any donor providing technical assistance (or, in some instances, finance to help those dismissed make a smooth transition to private employment) needs to be cognizant of the possibility of such problems. If ethnic composition is found to be an issue, the donor should determine whether the assistance being provided is having some relevant impact. If the donor adopts a posture of technical neutrality (i.e., formally oblivious), the reductions the donor is pressing and possibly financing might fall disproportionately on the already underrepresented ethnic group(s). If reform projects can contribute to an easing of such problems, so much the better. At a minimum, it is important to be aware of any impact, and to avoid contributing to a worsening of the situation or overlooking an opportunity for amelioration.

Some standard guidelines for effective public administration are especially important in deeply divided societies. For example, Arnold C. Harberger advised developing countries to "avoid the all too common trap of endowing regulators, administrators, and other government officials with wide discretionary powers. Such powers are dangerous even in economies well supplied with trained talent, and with an informed and vigilant public. They can be utterly noxious in countries with fragile bureaucracy of relatively low administrative competence and a public that does not and probably cannot subject public decisions to careful scrutiny."[35] The recommendation is particularly apt where the service is staffed largely by people drawn from a dominant ethnic group. Harberger's observations about government rule-making are also sound guidelines for limiting the scope of arbitrary and biased administration. "Perhaps the first thing that occurs to outside observers when they contemplate all the tasks confronting so small a group [i.e., the tiny cadres of educated civil service technicians and professionals] is the urgency of keeping the processes of government—the laws, the regulations, and the procedures and indeed the very scope of the public sector—as simple as possible. Taxes should be simple and easy to collect. Budget processes should be straightforward and clear. Legislation should be drawn so that exceptions and special cases are very rare."[36]

Conclusion

Most of the actions I am suggesting would aim to protect or benefit economically disadvantaged or repressed ethnic groups. In effect, the development agencies would be undertaking programs and promoting policies that, if effective, would contribute to empowerment of the groups so assisted. Even if an assessment concluded that such a bias was not required, or that circumstances limited the scope the agencies might have to shape their programs in such a manner, the agencies should hold to a Hippocratic rule of doing no between-group harm. They should not reinforce any conditions that have led to existing political or socioeconomic inequalities. They should ensure that information about their programs—project locations, access procedures, training opportunities, procurement and contracting opportunities—be widely available, and that program implementation does not reinforce inequalities.

Not all of the measures we have suggested are relevant in every divided country, or in any one country at one period of time. Just as a conflict-avoiding agreement or program will usually involve a whole set of policies, incentives, and trade-offs, so international assistance could include a selection of components to support such a program, or to help it materialize if a conflict-prone society has not yet gotten to the point of general bargaining. One of the things an assessment should do is consider whether the country would be better served by an attempt to develop an ambitious package to help bring the opposing groups to a general bargain, or whether it would be better, perhaps more feasible, to develop incremental accommodations on issues easier to sell. Further, a successful broad "bargain," as in the Malaysian case, will require a mix of political and socioeconomic, perhaps even symbolic, components. The development agencies are not likely to be lead advisors to local parties ready to design comprehensive constitutional arrangements. But they—most likely the World Bank—can provide negotiators with objective information and analysis of the relevant economic dimensions, propose policy and program options, comment on the economic implications of political structuring proposals on the table, and offer financial support if the parties follow the agreement in good faith.

If an advance for one group under some particular program is feasible only at some cost to another group, an acceptable package should include positive incentives for the latter. As noted above, the inclusion of such compensation for population displacements (if not simply avoiding projects with displacement effects) has become established policy for the World Bank. As complex as the problems of appropriate and acceptable compensation for (the typically small) groups involved have turned out to be in practice, they are conceptually and politically easier to manage than the balancing of costs and benefits among large and sharply defined population segments.

An intervention of primary importance for group relations in one country may be of slight importance in another. This may seem too elementary to merit saying, but it serves as a reminder that general conflict theorizing cannot substitute for individual country assessment. Cross-country analysis may dismiss a factor that is statistically insignificant compared with many other variables in a large number of countries, but that *is* important in a particular country one is concerned about. Furthermore, in the same country, a set of policies that effectively promotes accommodation and political stability for even a long period of time (as was the case in Lebanon where the highest-level positions in the political structure were reserved for specified allocation to leaders of the different religious communities) may become counterproductive when the underlying conditions change (as in Lebanon when the changing communal demographics undermined the rationale for the reserved allocations) or when the country is destabilized by outside forces. It is important to retain flexibility and to keep a door open to recurrent assessments and dialogue with objective outside institutions.

Postscript: Demobilization

Demobilization is an important component of conflict settlements. The primary expected benefit is prevention. Cutting the size of the opposing armed forces, often with the intent to integrate the residual military into a single national force, can serve as a confidence-building measure while reducing the ability of either side to resume combat. In addition, the consequent reduction in military expenditure is commonly seen as a "peace dividend" that can increase the resources available for reconstruction. In a successful demobilization, the new integrated national military structure should be placed under civilian control, removed from politics, professionalized, and retrained. Peace settlements may also call for development of a professional, nonpolitical police force to complete the separation of the military from domestic functions.

International involvement in conflict resolution typically includes important roles in the negotiation and implementation of demobilization. Where the development agencies have been involved, their role has included planning, retraining, and financing of the return of military personnel to civilian life. In a departure from its traditional areas of competence, the World Bank has done some pioneering work on the design of demobilization and the planning for reabsorption of soldiers into the civilian economy.[37] The political aspects of demobilization—integration of the armed forces, redefinition of military functions and command structure, identification of units to be dissolved, and selection of individuals to be mustered out—are the responsibility of the political/ diplomatic negotiators and of the international (mainly U.N.) political and military authorities involved in helping to implement peace accords.

The demobilization record is mixed, at best. Whereas some efforts (e.g., in El Salvador and Mozambique) have been qualified successes, others (e.g., in Angola and Cambodia) were deeply flawed or outright failures. The military provisions of the Bosnia accords have not yet been implemented. Troops were trained in civilian occupations before being demobilized in Haiti, but the process had no provision for securing them employment; as a result, many kept their weapons and turned to banditry when they found that the depressed economy offered few jobs. Postconflict crime was also a serious problem in El Salvador and Mozambique. In many cases the creation of new efficient and uncorrupt police forces has fallen well short of expectations. A recent review of postconflict security programs found a troublesome "demobilization dilemma":

> In a postconflict environment, the rates of violent crime, especially assault with automatic weapons, are apt to be soaring. Government security forces are typically demobilized or restricted to cantonments, creating a void in public order after years of harsh and repressive rule. As public alarm mounts, the retention of elite units and leadership cadre who have had the benefit of extensive training and years of experience becomes very appealing. The dilemma arises because these same individuals and elite units are often guilty of grave human rights abuses and rampant corruption.[38]

Even where a successful demobilization program has taken place without an upsurge in criminal violence, a further dilemma may present itself. If the officer corps has been dominated by one ethnic group in a deeply divided society (a common destabilizing element in Africa, examined at length by Horowitz),[39] a demobilization program could fall selectively on officers and ranks of other ethnicities, leaving the same ethnic group with a monopoly of military power, even though reduced in size. Although development agencies helping to finance and implement portions of a demobilization program are not likely to be involved in the design of the military aspects of a stand-down, they should have responsibility for its economic aspects and should try to ensure that adequate account is taken of its potential sociopolitical effects. Demobilized troops (and their families) will comprise only a small fraction of the population needing postconflict resettlement, reabsorption, and employment. However, because the demobilized are the most readily remilitarized element of the society, their normalization programs (civilian occupation training, job search, small enterprise credits, mustering-out grants, etc.) merit high priority for international agencies involved.

Notes

1. Peter Murrell, "Symposium on Economic Transition in the Soviet Union and Eastern Europe," in *Journal of Economic Perspectives* (Fall 1991): 3–4.

2. See, for example, Joan M. Nelson et al., *Fragile Coalitions: The Politics of Economic Adjustment*. Washington, DC: Overseas Development Council, 1989.

3. Stanley Fischer and Alan Gelb, "The Process of Socialist Economic Transformation," in *Journal of Economic Perspectives* 3, no. 4 (Fall 1991): 104.

4. Lyn Squire, "Introduction: Poverty and Adjustment in the 1980s," in *World Bank Economic Review* 5, no. 2 (May 1991): 183.

5. Joseph Stiglitz, "What I Learned at the World Economic Crisis," *The New Republic*, April 17, 2000.

6. Netherlands Institute of International Relations 1999, p. iv.

7. Ibid., p. vi.

8. World Bank, *From Plan to Market: World Development Report 1996*. Washington, DC: Author, 1996, p. 44.

9. Ibid., p. 53.

10. See Joseph Stiglitz, "What I Saw at the Devaluation: Why the IMF can't be trusted to run the world economy," *New Republic*, April 17, 2000, pp. 56–60.

11. Suliman and Ghebreysus, 1998, pp. 6–7.

12. Cohen, 1995, pp. 38–43.

13. Sunita Kikeri, John Nellis, and Mary Shirley, "Privatization: Lessons from Market Economies," in *World Bank Research Observer* 9, no. 2 (July 1994): 241–272.

14. Carl Jayarajah and William Bronson, *Structural and Sectoral Adjustment: World Bank Experience, 1980–92*. Washington, DC: The World Bank, 1995, p. 198.

15. Klitgaard, 1991, p. 209.

16. Ibid., p. 209. Italics in original.

17. Ke-young Chu and Richard Hemming, *Public Expenditure Handbook: A Guide to Public Expenditure Policy in Developing Countries*. Washington, DC: IMF, 1991, p. 23.

18. Martin O. Heisler, "Hyphenating Belgium: Changing State and Regime to Cope with Cultural Division," in Joseph V. Montville, ed., *Conflict and Peacemaking in Multiethnic Societies*. Lexington, MA: Lexington Books, 1991, p. 179.

19. Horowitz, n.d., p. 77.

20. Ibid., p. 77. The citation is from C.R. de Silva, "Weightage in University Admissions: Standardization and District Quotas in Sri Lanka," in *Modern Ceylon Studies* 5, no. 2 (July 1974): 166.

21. Horowitz, n.d., p. 84.

22. Ibid., p. 79.

23. "Why is it that the Luo in Kenya, whose home is in the west and who resent the domination of the Kikuyu, have never 'seriously contemplated a Biafra-type (secession)'? Clearly, it is because they hold influential positions in major Kenyan towns outside their region, especially Nairobi and Mombasa. Like the Lozi in Zambia, but unlike the Ibo, ethnic conflict has not forced them to return home. Secession is less attractive if it is likely to mean a forfeiture of abundant opportunities outside the home region." Horowitz, n.d., p. 31.

24. Horowitz, n.d., p. 93.

25. Horowitz, 1985, p. 676.

26. Esman, 1994, p. 232.

27. Reviewing the case histories for a conference volume on tax reform, Robert Bates observed that "the cases suggest that reforms clearly were facilitated by the comprehensive restructuring of power brought on by military occupation (Japan in the 1940s); coups (Liberia, Brazil, Indonesia, Chile, and Venezuela, among others); and massive electoral victories (Sri Lanka, Jamaica, and Peru). Decisive shifts in power help to define which interests are in and which out. By structuring power relations, such large-scale political changes constrain the range of blocking coalitions. And they therefore make possible stable solutions to a political game which contains significant possibilities for redistribution." See "A Political Scientist Looks at Tax Reform," in Malcom Gillis, ed., *Tax Reform in Developing Countries*. Durham, NC: Duke University Press, 1989, p. 486.

28. For a recent example, see Benno J. Ndulu and Stephen A. O'Connell, "Governance and Growth in Sub-Saharan Africa," in *Journal of Economic Perspectives* (Summer 1999): 41–66.

29. John Pender and Peter Hall, eds., *Promoting Development in Less-Favored Areas*. Washington, DC: International Food Policy Research Institute, 2020 Focus brief, November 2000.

30. Esman and Herring, 2001, p. 247.

31. Klitgaard, 1993b, p. 8.

32. I am indebted to John Eriksson for bringing this point to my attention in a personal communication, July 2001.

33. World Bank, 1998, Vol. III, pp. 37–38.

34. "If Spanish is the official language but Quechua is not, one group is obviously disadvantaged in entering public life. Peru has made Quechua an official language, but Spanish is still exclusively used in government documents and business." Klitgaard, 1991, p. 217.

35. Arnold C. Harberger, "Policymaking and Economic Policy in Small Developing Countries," in Rudiger Dornbusch and F. Leslie C.H. Helmers, eds., *The Open Economy: Tools for policymakers in developing countries*. Washington, DC: The World Bank, 1988, p. 251.

36. Ibid., pp. 250–251.

37. See, for example, Nat J. Colletta, Markus Kostner, and Ingo Wiederhofer, *War-to-Peace Transition in Sub-Saharan Africa: Lessons from the Horn, the Heart, and the Cape*. Washington, DC: World Bank, n.d.

38. Oakley et al., 1998, pp. 521–522.

39. Horowitz, 1985, several chapters.

7. Persuasion, Leverage, and Sanctions

The Role of Ideas: Against Utopianism, Triumphalism, and Ignorance

Utopianism has been at the heart of much misery and conflict throughout human history. An idea is utopian if it purports to point the way to perfection in the social or political order. Movements spouting utopian ideals have often attacked or swept away an old and allegedly flawed social order—one based on purportedly outmoded and unjust religious or social conventions—in the name of a perfected society that the righteous survivors would build over the ruins of the past. The utopian ideologies of our time have typically been cynically exploited by their propounders, often accepted by masses of people who have all been fooled for some of the time, and implemented with extraordinary brutality. Their adherents long see (or claim to see) no contradiction between the barbarism of the means employed and the higher civilization these means are supposed to bring to birth. Based on a crude distortion of social Darwinism, the European utopianisms of fascism were frankly exclusive; the allegedly superior civilizations of fascist Italy, Nazi Germany, and Falangist Spain were to rest on the degradation or murder of those not participating, whether domestic groups who disagreed, or, more widely, foreign peoples whose cultural and ethnic inferiority was sufficient grounds for imperial control or worse. Communist utopianism was inclusive and multinational; its benefits, and the new egalitarian society to be created, were to be extended to all except the nonegalitarian and exploitative classes, who by definition lacked a moral claim for further survival and dominance. Communist utopianism in power exacted a heavy price from the purportedly transitional generation, and it became a blind for old-fashioned nationalism. In Asia, inspired by the Chinese Cultural Revolution, the Khmer Rouge designed the most extreme utopian distortion, combining a national gulag-collectivism with utter extermination of their own inherited culture and of all Cambodian citizens deemed tainted with foreign association or learning.

The means by which the leadership of these totalitarian states mobilized sufficient domestic support for their policies have been studied in great depth, as have the differences in the programs and behavior, including the harshness, of ideologically similar authoritarian regimes in different countries.

The striking differences between the fascist programs of Germany and Italy, and the very different responses of their populations to the drumbeat propaganda extolling hatred of alleged internal enemies, reflect (among other things, of course) fundamental differences in culture. Kevin Avruch has an important insight in this respect. He observes that those who cite and manipulate a specific "culture," in order to mobilize the support and acquiescence of the large mass of a population who see themselves as sharing this "culture," are able to do so because people have basic misconceptions about the presumed homogeneity, generality, and historical continuity of their culture and its particulars. He describes misconceptions, of which the following are especially pertinent to our concern:

1. that any specific culture is free of contradictions and inconsistencies (which enables one to characterize all the members of a culture with sweeping prejudicial denigrations, or to mobilize a culture's members with undifferentiated "instructions"), and as a result,
2. that a culture can be reified, leading to easy dismissal of the reality of intracultural diversity;
3. that the members of any one culture can be lumped together because they think and behave uniformly;
4. that every individual possesses only a single culture, devoid of differentiation or cross-cultural aspects of identity (an idea deriving from anthropological description of village level, and relatively remote microcultures); and
5. that cultures are timeless and changeless (he cites the idea that the "Arab mind" has descended unchanging from Mohammed's Mecca).

According to Avruch, these baseless notions are employed

> when culture is objectified by actors and used in politically charged—usually nationalistic, racialistic, or ethnic—discourses. Many of these discourses go way beyond the injuries inflicted by [Matthew] Arnold's snobbery or even the class system of nineteenth century England. As Rwanda, Burundi, Bosnia, and before them Nazi Germany all demonstrate, they are capable of provoking genocide. In fact, we have now identified one way in which the culture concept, used as an ideological resource by contestants, is itself a source—or accelerant—of social conflict.[1]

Avruch then draws out a suggestion for conflict prevention:

> One strategy for conflict prevention immediately presents itself: the proactive destruction, in the sense of debunking and unmasking, of those inadequate ideas. At least, this strategy logically falls out of seeing culture's

role in the conflict. The enactment of such a strategy in places like Rwanda, Burundi, or Bosnia is, of course, another matter entirely.[2]

It is easy to share Avruch's skepticism about his own suggestion. Against the fear and ferocity experienced in such places, a campaign of historical revisionism, of convincing violent actors that neither they nor their enemies are what they have thought they are, seems to be without hope of practical effect. Nevertheless, it should not be dismissed altogether as lacking any potentially beneficial impact *before* antagonisms have been mobilized and divisions hardened, long *before* the Rwandas are ready to explode. One might speculate, in retrospect, if the emerging hegemonic conceptual framework of the Sinhalese (long before independence) might have been modified or rendered less militant had the mythic distortions of history by the leading Sinhala intellectual of the late nineteenth and early twentieth century, Anagarika Dharmapala, been discredited or at least challenged by other thinkers.[3]

> The upshot of Buddhist revivalism, as represented by Anagarika Dharmapala, was to provide a warrant for intolerance, for viewing as inferiors and discriminating against "peoples perceived as obstacles to what rightfully belongs to the Sinhala." There are precedents for such intolerance with the chronicle tradition. But the particular character and intensity of Dharmapala's intolerance depended on special religious, cultural, and political conditions and influences in the nineteenth and early twentieth centuries. To that extent, Dharmapala's intolerance was "invented" or "new."[4]

In recent decades, there has been much scholarship showing how cherished traditions (historical myths, clothing conventions, national celebratory rituals and pageantry, triumphalist distortions of military history, etc.) rest on dubious factual bases and are often recent inventions, deliberately crafted to create historically unjustified beliefs of shared tradition.[5] In the United States, the triumphalist tradition with respect to the American Indians has been totally repudiated. I cite this not as a conflict-reducing advance, but as an indication of how scholarship and media attention can alter an entire nation's idea of the content of its traditions. Although this U.S. experience was not the product of a deliberate, government-inspired effort, it suggests that initiatives along such lines might be fruitful as instruments for reducing stereotypical and prejudicial thinking and for weakening appeals to ethnonationalist exclusion and chauvinism. Such cultural "intervention" might be feasible under international auspices such as that of UNESCO, or by private foundation support of local institutions capable of independent scholarship and dedicated to conflict prevention in their own societies. Cross-cultural education to reduce stereotypical thinking and prejudice, as a part of the regular school curriculum, is already under way in some countries, with international technical assistance. In countries where the state stands for rule of law and human rights, and where it serves as arbiter rather than partisan, programs along the lines of Avruch's suggestion might be feasible.

Correction of triumphal and denigrating fictions could serve several useful purposes. It could strengthen the basis for apologies and help make restitution politically feasible. It could help reduce threat perceptions. It could help undermine the plausibility of chauvinism and the credibility of hegemonic claims. And it could clear the ground for resurrecting facts of past amicable and integrated relationships.

Ordinary Development Research: Illuminating Frictions and Fictions

The development agencies conduct a great deal of individual country information-gathering and research as a part of regular business—project reconnaissance missions, project feasibility studies, market analyses, project monitoring and evaluation, recurrent studies of general economic conditions, sector studies, and so on. These professional missions and studies may provide objective, empirical information and analyses regarding conditions and problems that are currently sources of ethnic grievance and contention or that contain the seeds of potential social conflict, even if the studies are not being drawn upon for systematic conflict assessment as suggested earlier.

Take, for example, allegations that one ethnic group is exploiting another. Members of ethnic majorities frequently believe they are being exploited by a minority merchant class given to sharp commercial practices, sometimes individually and sometimes in marketing conspiracies. Such views are common where a minority, especially of immigrant descent, serves as produce buyers and small credit suppliers for "indigenous" farmers. In some countries emerging from colonialism, such beliefs were the rationale for large-scale expulsions. In others, the beliefs were used to justify discriminatory policies. Objective market research may be able to establish whether or not monopsonist or monopolist conditions actually exist. If the allegations are shown to be groundless, the research will have provided the means for fact-based refutation. If the allegations are correct, the research will have established a basis for informed policy, such as measures to promote competition or adopt Malaysia-style preferences.

Another example might be drawn from the Mozambican privatization experience described above. If early monitoring of the privatization process had established (as subsequently alleged) that the domestic entrepreneurs acquiring the state enterprises derived largely from a single ethnic group (which was associated with the ruling political party), aid-sponsored research could have put the issues on the table and explored the purported factual explanations (a paucity of entrepreneurs of other ethnic origin) and allegations of favoritism (political/ethnic bias in the associated credit extension and enterprise awards). If paucity rather than favoritism had been demonstrated to be the problem, measures could have been devised to bring about a more ethnically diverse outcome (such as extending the time frame, marking a group of enterprises as set-asides, and locating among the underrepresented groups suitable entrepreneurs or talent who could become capable with technical and financial assistance).

Persuasion and Leverage

Effective influence on policies is often a combination of persuasion and leverage. As a term of art in the aid context, leverage goes beyond persuasion, referring to steps that donors might employ to elicit decisions or actions a government would not take otherwise. The balance that donors may seek between persuasion and leverage will vary from case to case, depending on factors such as the importance of donor interests at stake, the extent of democratic legitimacy of the government involved, the particular policies at issue, and, of course, the (usually problematical) extent to which donors have real leverage to exercise. The international acceptability or respectability of the concept of leverage has risen and fallen over time. Circumlocutions have become common as the term "leverage" has taken on an invidious character. International agencies for many years have used the term "policy dialogue" to refer to sensitive interlocution (which may or may not cross the fine line between persuasion and leverage) with recipient governments.

Governments seriously intent on economic development normally are receptive, even eager, to adopt changes proposed or designed by aid-financed expertise in agriculture, transportation, and other areas and disciplines. Economic policy changes were long a more difficult sell. Economists and donor agencies who urged developing country governments to adopt policies of private ownership and the operation of competitive factor markets had to compete with the command-economy, public-ownership model, which was viewed as a viable alternative until the collapse of the socialist economies. Even in the "mixed" economies that comprised the developing country mainstream, partial or single-policy reforms (such as rationalizing import protection systems, correcting foreign exchange rate distortions, or introducing water-use charges in irrigation projects) have often been difficult to sell. Our case studies showed examples of successes and failures in such attempts, where the policies in question were relevant to deep societal divisions. There is a considerable literature on the subject of aid influence. Because aid agency work on governance institutions, political development, and human rights is of relatively recent origin compared with work on "technical" economic and sectoral policies, interest in the question of aid influence and how such influence might be effectively exercised long focused on tactics related to reforms of macroeconomic management policies. The kinds of changes we are considering here are arguably more sensitive, more difficult to bring about, because they relate to fundamental issues of distribution, hegemony, and identity. Nevertheless, some of the lessons learned from donor experience with economic policy dialogue may apply when donors attempt to exercise aid influence for conflict prevention.

In their efforts to engage governments on economic problems and policies, donors have given great weight to professional expertise and analysis. Well-founded research results can be persuasive enough in themselves. They may bring public attention to issues that have been neglected or suppressed. If there has been divided opinion among serious bureaucratic professionals, analysis and advice from outsiders with respected credentials can tip the scales. Donor support can strengthen the hand of technocrats unable to move power-holders away from discredited or dysfunctional policies. Naturally, the politics of donor involvement in internal decision processes can be tricky. Donor support of groups espousing policy changes viewed by other groups as detrimental to their interests carries a risk. Donors can be accused of intervention; officials they support can be accused of suspect loyalty. Conversely, the attachment of policy conditions to aid loans is accepted practice and is often fully justifiable on grounds of technical viability or policy credibility. The degree of sensitivity and the scope for charges of improper intervention may also differ, depending on a government's relations with individual donors or agencies. For historical reasons, individual countries may have more trust in one donor government than another, or more receptivity to policy recommendations from a multilateral institution than from an individual donor government.

The use of leverage, as opposed to persuasion and good offices, raises different questions. Leverage can be exercised in more or less forceful ways. The disbursal of loans in tranches released only after a borrowing government has met the policy commitments it made when negotiating with the lender(s) is common practice. Leverage that takes more forceful forms, such as withholding a loan tranche, or threatening to withdraw aid from specific programs, or threatening to suspend or cancel the aid relationship, relies on credibility to be effective. That is, representations that a donor judges government (potential or actual) policies or actions to be unacceptable to the point of undermining the aid relationship will lose credibility if, in the event, the donor shrinks from carrying out the forewarned or stipulated suspensions or cancellations. A donor's seriousness respecting such intentions is likely to be strengthened if the donor has actually carried through in such a scenario at some time with some recipient government. In practice, drastic leverage scenarios are more credible and easier to carry out, the more misguided or objectionable the policies and actions at issue, and the more united the donors involved. Conditions or pressures attached to aid programs may or may not be associated with diplomatic pressures, trade sanctions, or other forms of strong advocacy or compulsion, depending on the extent of international disapproval of a government's actions.

It is generally preferable for policy commitments to be unambiguous and to be defined explicitly when quantifiable actions or target dates are involved. One USAID study's conclusion about the benefits of clarity in the undertakings of both parties to an aid-related agreement respecting macroeconomic policy reforms—"the program must be definable in terms specific and explicit enough to permit a reasonable unequivocal judgment about the adequacy of performance later on"—should certainly apply to programs touching distribution, inclusion, nondiscriminatory governance, or other aspects of deep social division.[6] The sheer number of policy alterations or new program initiatives that donors wish to bring about should be commensurate with the resources the donors are willing to provide and the implementation capacities of the responsible government units. Although advice and discreet alliances with like-minded political or professional interlocutors may cover a wide range of policy areas, especially where government is not a promoter of division or a hegemonic partisan, the application of pressures or leverage is best focused on a limited number of the most critical issues. Where feasible, an incentive structure is best that links aid to positive performance, rather than in the negative form of penalties and withdrawals.

Perhaps most important was the USAID's finding that external assistance needs to be sustained over time when the changes that the donors are urging and supporting are structural, such as tax and trade regime reforms, compared with stroke-of-the-pen reforms (e.g., shifts to nondistorting interest and foreign exchange rates). This point applies very forcefully to changes in distribution and governance intended to promote inclusion and harmony over division and hostility.

Resource Allocation Among Countries: From Support to Withdrawal

The first allocation question any donor faces is whether or not to provide any financial and development assistance resources to a country in the first place, in any form whatsoever. There have always been wide differences in the amount of aid provided to different recipient countries, and these differences have been more marked among bilateral donors than among the multilateral organizations. Former colonial powers have tended to focus on their former colonies in order to sustain historical and cultural ties or promote trade and investment. Japanese aid has favored Asian recipients. Some donors favor recipients that follow strongly egalitarian policies. Aid during the Cold War was heavily skewed, by donors on both sides, to countries being wooed or rewarded. Large fractions of American aid have long been allocated to a handful of countries with highest priority in U.S. foreign policy. Both U.N. and multilateral bank allocations have been more evenhanded, more affected by technical and performance criteria, although not immune from a small-country effect (i.e., recipients with small populations tend to receive substantially more aid per capita than do large-population nations).

World Bank and IMF country allocations have also been affected by political considerations when major donor shareholders on their governing boards have strongly opposed extending loans, at one time or another, to particular recipients. The U.N. Development Programme allocates its core funds through an apolitical arithmetic method based on factors like per capita income and population, a system that appears to leave little room for discretionary country-by-country adjustments. Over the years the World Bank has moved toward increasingly transparent allocation systems based on population, per capita income, and objective criteria of performance and need. When developing nations reach some (undefined) range of per capita income, their receipts of concessional development aid begin to phase down toward total "graduation." Aid eligibility policies may be transparent and formal, as with the per capita income ceiling of the World Bank's "soft" window, the International Development Association, or, more commonly among bilateral donors, graduation may be an informal process not made explicit in any policy statements or practiced with any uniformity.

Some allocation or eligibility criteria are technical or legal. For example, the World Bank will not extend new loans to a country that surpasses a certain threshold of debt default, or a country that is not in good standing with the IMF. A special problem is posed when a country emerges from an extended conflict during which unserviced debts owed to the World Bank and IMF have mounted from accumulating arrears. The outstanding debt to the IMF in particular must be repaid (in the Cambodian case, for example, the outstanding arrears to the Fund were paid by France) before the World Bank can resolve its own debt problem with the country and before the decks can be cleared for new reconstruction financing. Commonly, an important criterion concerns a country's short-term economic management policies. Persistent pursuit of policies causing serious economic instability or structural distortions is likely to bring about a rupture in a government's relationship with the IMF. A formal breakdown in the relationship with the IMF may in turn affect the flow of resources from the World Bank, the regional development banks, and bilateral donors. Some legal criteria are political in nature, like the provision in U.S. legislation that mandates a suspension of American aid to a country if its democratically elected government is overthrown by a military coup.

Donor responses to conflict situations have affected aid allocation in ways that depart substantially from the business-as-usual standards above. The options have ranged from large-scale aid levels far exceeding what a country would have been eligible for otherwise, to total cancellation. Where donors are funding a "normal" aid program and face a government carrying out inequitable, injurious, or unacceptable policies that may or may not eventuate in violent conflict, they can try to exercise leverage on those policies by threatening, or acting, to lower or suspend their aid. Drastic lowering or cancellation of development aid may be part of a general punitive policy of economic and diplomatic sanctions or isolation. Or, if humanitarian needs are strong, donors may continue or increase their funding of programs conducted by (truly independent) nongovernmental organizations, while reducing or suspending allocations to the government and public sector agencies. Because the multilateral development banks do not conduct humanitarian programs, the ultimate performance sanction on their disbursements would be suspension.

The largest outpourings of aid, huge in absolute volume and very high in annual per capita terms, have been allocated to postconflict reconstruction. Donors commonly reward countries that have reached peace agreements by providing a few years of massive funding for reconstruction before allocations are returned to "normal" aid levels. The reasons for these extraordinary allocations have been part humanitarian and part hard-nosed self-interest; the donors hope that successful reconstruction—including repatriation, reconciliation, and new political institutions shaped to facilitate nonviolent dispute resolution, buttressed by palpable improvement in economic conditions— will prevent a recurrence of the conflict and contribute to regional stability.

A similar calculus should apply to prevention programs that help to avoid violent conflict in the first place. Suppose a deeply divided developing country settles on a mutually agreed program of accommodation that holds out a credible prospect of long-term stability. By the same logic that has been applied to preventing recurrence in a postconflict situation, the international community should be willing, in a preconflict situation, to raise aid levels substantially if the settlement requires large up-front funding (e.g., for land reform, or an ambitious regional development program). A preventive aid surge, preconflict so to speak, is likely to be substantially smaller than a surge postconflict, when destroyed physical capital must be restored merely to bring the economy back to its prewar condition.[7]

It has long been common for donor disapproval of a country's economic policies to be signaled through provision of less assistance than the country requests, or than it needs, based on standard resource flow analyses. Disapproval can also be indicated by reducing the level of aid committed in one year, compared with previous years. Commitments are normally easier to use in this manner, compared with disbursements. The multilateral development banks normally are in position to reduce or halt disbursements under an ongoing loan only if the borrower has failed to meet the precise conditions that have been specified in the loan agreement. Once a loan agreement has been signed, with the borrower perhaps paying up-front commitment fees, the banks regard the loan as "belonging" to the borrower. As a practical matter, projects requiring the presence of foreign technical advisers can also be interrupted if local security conditions become a threat to their safety.

In the recent past, as part of the process of increasing international willingness to apply pressure or intervene if a sovereign government endorses or carries out gross violations of the human rights of its own citizens, donors have threatened to suspend, or have actually suspended, aid flows. The threat of a freeze on planned IMF funding and on major bilateral aid programs was apparently an important factor in the Indonesian government's decision to accept the results of the East Timorese vote for independence.[8] For countries with significant dependence on aid flows, suspension is the most powerful and substantive "intervention" available to the international community, short of economic sanctions on trade or investment or of military action. It represents a level of pressure that most donors would consider applying only under crisis circumstances as an eleventh-hour tool.

But what is a "crisis"? Should the aid relationship in its entirety be reconsidered when circumstances might be judged to be heading toward a crisis? Should the ultimate aid sanction be employed, at least as a tool of persuasion, when a government's economic and social policies are clearly aimed at promoting the hegemony of the ethnicity controlling the state and at excluding or discriminating against subordinate groups? In the eyes of a subordinate minority, a significant policy change designed to weaken their status or reduce their rights (e.g., promulgation of a discriminatory language policy) could be perceived as a crisis. For the international community, the crisis calling for a powerful response might not emerge until several years later, after the deprived minority had mobilized the determination and capability for launching violent conflict.

Though statements of regret over inaction before the crisis of violence erupted have become common in recent years, regret is seldom expressed for failures to respond to the preceding policy measures and events that were the precursors or, more precisely, the beginnings of what should be seen as an extended crisis in which the violent conflict was an inherent culmination.

There is now a strong body of opinion that it would have been legitimate for the international community, working through the United Nations, to intervene in Rwanda to prevent the bloodbath. The focus of the expressions of regret over the failure to do so has been on the hours or weeks at most when the specific intentions of the extremists became unmistakable. The intervention principle here is based on credible evidence of murderous intent and capability, and it should be applicable even if the evidence is discerned months before, or earlier. The more difficult question is how the international community should respond at the crisis precursor stage, when events are being set into motion that, if not deflected, could well result in violent conflict, but in a future that can always be painted in different scenarios.

A large fraction of international financial assistance flows directly to and through governments. World Bank, regional development banks, and IMF loans are extended directly to a borrowing government or its public agencies. Although these resources generally are not intended (especially since the end of the Cold War) to support particular regimes, the funds do strengthen the incumbent government and its senior power-holders. This is especially the case when donors provide straight money (i.e., balance-of-payments support and funding for the government budget). But it is also the case, even if indirect and "politically neutral," where donors provide technical assistance to build the institutional capabilities of segments of the government bureaucracy, capabilities that strengthen the capacity of any regime to do what it chooses. As described earlier, Rwanda was a particularly noxious example.

The international development banks generally lend directly to central governments. If the banks extend loans to local jurisdictions or other domestic entities, the loans must be guaranteed by the central government. Thus, it would be unusual for the World Bank or a regional development bank to be able to finance a project its borrower, the central government, did not want. On the other hand, the banks are not without influence. Often, when their funds are large in relation to the resources at the disposal of the government, the banks are able to persuade the borrower to make changes in its allocation priorities. Bilateral donors may have more flexibility in many countries, especially because in recent years the bilaterals have been allocating increasing shares of their grant resources directly to local jurisdictions and NGOs. With rare exceptions, the bilaterals cannot finance activities the central governments are dead set against. (One such exception is Cambodia where bilateral donors finance civil rights NGOs, and the local U.N. human rights monitoring office, which have been tolerated by the government only because it cannot afford to jeopardize the flow of external aid.)

Despite the rising interest in, and importance of, NGOs as aid recipients and implementing agencies, we should not overlook the fact that central governments have been the principal aid recipients and policy interlocutors over the five decades of post–World War II development assistance. The postcolonial independent states (India was an important exception) generally inherited highly centralized governmental systems. The donors viewed centralization (even if moderated through some implementation decentralization) as an asset for helping to transform administrative bureaucracies into development instruments. Between the essentially government-to-government, and multilateral agency-to-government, character of the international aid system, and the view that government in newly independent developing countries was a critical designer and generator of economic growth, the aid process deliberately financed and strengthened the state. In a deeply divided society where the state has been captured as the instrument of one group rather than serving as impartial mediator and rights guarantor, external aid filtered through the state can have the perverse effect of contributing to the likelihood of violent conflict.

In sum, donors should presume that development aid normally strengthens the state. If donors intend to circumvent a regime, or fill in for its distributional deficiencies, they should deliberately assess the effects of aid in this context and consider the kinds of measures suggested in this chapter.

When Nothing Else Works: Sanctions

Most of the interventions we have considered address the situation where violent conflict is still only incipient, and where the hostility emanates from weaker groups that are relatively backward, disadvantaged, or excluded by the group (usually a majority, but sometimes a minority itself, as in Iraq and Burundi) that controls the state. Where a dominant ethnicity has gone to some length to use the power of the state to repress, the bottom-up or other options discussed here are not likely to be effective or even feasible. A repressive government is not likely to allow an external agency to shape development activities so as to strengthen the very groups the government views as internal enemies, especially if such groups begin to show potentiality for achieving the very empowerment the government is determined to avoid.

In general, aid agencies should take a strong stance where individual rights are violated under government policies of selected group discrimination. Because such policies have frequently led to political instability or violent conflict, the development process can be seriously compromised, whereas outright warfare causes destruction of physical capital, some of which has been financed with aid money. Moral considerations aside, development financiers have a prudentiary interest in the prevention of such growth loss and physical destruction. Parliaments and taxpayers in the case of bilaterally financed programs, and capital markets in the case of borrowing institutions like the World Bank, need to have confidence in the long-term sustainability of the development process in the recipient clients. Surely the avoidance of the marginalization of significant population groups and of civil instability or warfare is at least as critical for a viable development process as is the adoption of the sound macro- and sector policies that often have been central to the relationships and frictions among the IMF, World Bank, and some bilateral agencies on the one hand, and developing countries on the other.

The implication here is that the bilateral donors, or the governing bodies of development agencies, should consider the use of aid sanctions where recipient states are violating international rights conventions or otherwise pursuing policies of group exclusion or repression. Quite apart from, even prior to, U.N. resolutions or decisions that might cite a government for violating international rights conventions, or call for sanctions of one kind or another, donors may have practical and fiduciary grounds for applying sanctions independently. A range of options of increasing severity would be available for negotiating for, or pressing for, policy changes. They run from formal conditionalities written into (relevant) individual project and loan agreements prior to signing; prior conditionality applied to the entire aid package, more forceful if done by a group of donors in concert; freezing of new projects and loans in the pipeline; withholding of disbursements for ongoing projects; cancellation of ongoing projects; to suspension of further aid eligibility. Donor countries can also use their voting weight on the governing boards of the multilateral agencies to press for parallel multilateral sanctions.

There are times when the position of those in power is neither black nor white. The government is not pursuing a policy of empowering minority ethnic groups or reducing discrimination or economic inequalities, but is also not violating human rights of minorities or pursuing policies deliberately harmful to the economic, cultural, or other interests of the minorities. Or a change in the majority's leadership may bring on an effort to accommodate and heal relations, perhaps despite the call of extremists for policies of exclusion and hegemony. Aid conditionality might then assist governments in the middle—that is, governments willing to move toward inclusion and reduction of inequalities. Such governments might be able to strengthen their position with their own ethnic group by pointing to the international support and resources an accommodating policy would garner. Conditionality should be made as acceptable as possible by linking it with technical assistance in the design of a reformist agenda, and with sufficient financial support to bring benefits to both sides.

In some situations, of course, aid conditionality on sensitive political questions can be counterproductive. A government accepting aid under unpopular conditions may risk attack from rivals within its own ethnic group on the grounds of selling out to foreign pressures. If a government is divided between hard-liners and reformers, donor pressures may strengthen or weaken the position of the reformers. Much depends on the issues that the conditions address and on the effectiveness with which the requisite policies are explained to the public. Conditionality may be more effective and acceptable if it is used to nudge a willing, albeit reluctant or hesitant, government to adopt incremental policy changes, rather than being used to attempt to move an exclusionary government to make a complete about-face. In the case of highly repressive regimes, stronger incentives or disincentives would be needed if, indeed, any external influence is possible at all.

The term "political conditionality" is commonly applied to the use of aid—the threat of withdrawal, or actual cutoff—to induce a government to desist from policies, normally of political and rights repression, that the donors find highly objectionable and unacceptable. When the ultimate aid sanction has been employed, donor governments have generally linked its use with other strong diplomatic and economic pressures. Because our concern in this book has been on measures the development agencies can pursue to address root causes, well before conditions approach the crisis stage at which ultimate sanctions arise for consideration, we will not attempt to add any further to the literature on political conditionality. As Michael Lund showed in his (1997) review of that literature, there appear to have been few successes among the numerous attempts to elicit changed political behavior from the kinds of "obdurate" regimes that have driven donor governments to resort to (among other instruments) the ultimate aid sanction. Aid cutoffs, or threats, have elicited the liberalization or other political changes the donors insisted upon, only where a long list of conditions (not likely to be found in most cases) has occurred. Lund's conclusions regarding lessons learned echo the point we have made repeatedly on the hazards of cookbook generalizing. Comparing three main types of donor influence (aid with conditions, aid support without conditions, and persuasion), the literature shows that "No two applications, even of the same mode of influence, will have the same results. . . . These variations reflect the complexities of each specific development and conflict situation and the nature of the donor involvement in it, which defy one to predict consistent, universal patterns that follow when any course of action or policy is applied."[9]

Donor Coordination: Practical Obstacles

Despite the proliferation of conflict-prevention meetings, publications, research and Web sites among the donors, one cannot naively assume that their apparent determination to develop effective prevention roles will translate readily into cooperative programs. Donor coordination for all other worthy developmental purposes has had a long and checkered history. For many years, the major donors have recognized the need to maintain and improve coordination among themselves, and with recipient governments, through the Development Assistance Committee of the Organization for Economic Cooperation and Development, headquartered in Paris, and through formal coordination mechanisms. As more countries have become donors over the years, the number of official donors in individual recipient nations can range up to fifty or more. The number of NGOs working in developing countries has shot up in recent years. In some individual nations, the number of international and local NGOs working on the same problems as the official international development agencies has risen to over a thousand.[10] Of course, the coordination that matters for conflict prevention—for aggregating sufficient influence, resources, or pressures, to make a critical difference—will involve a relative handful of key donors. Even so, the record shows that the aid community may not automatically rise to the occasion when joint action might be fruitful.

A recent World Bank paper on aid coordination identifies three levels of donor cooperation: information sharing and consultation; strategic coordination—consensus on policies, objectives, and procedures; and operational coordination—programs or projects carried out and financed jointly. The literature indicates that "aid coordination becomes more difficult for participants as they try to move from one level to the next. Instances of strategic and operational coordination appear to have been most common during periods of crisis brought about by severe economic deterioration, food shortage, war, and prolonged violent conflict, rather than in 'normal' times."[11] In our perspective this implies, ironically, that donors will see no extraordinary need for coordination during years of preconflict "normality" when there is time and scope to make a difference, and will be increasingly ready to coordinate their efforts (in this case, toward conflict mitigation) as impending or actual crisis is reducing the likelihood that their actions can be consequential.

There is also a kind of ideological difficulty with the notion that external donors should present a common front to a government, especially against aspects of a government's domestic development and socioeconomic policies. The difficulty stems from the growing conviction that it is politically incorrect, and less efficient, for the donors to run the aid process. Starting from the coordination arrangements (formally initiated in 1958 when the World Bank chaired the first donor meeting on India) characterized for many years by a sharp distinction between donor officials who lectured and recipient officials who requested, the idea developed that the relationship should rightly be construed as a partnership. The ideal aid process would put the recipient in the chair and shift the coordination role from donors to the recipient government. The World Bank recently formalized this preference in a Comprehensive Development Framework for donor–recipient relations that makes partnership a major objective. In mid-1999 the aid ministers of Germany, the Netherlands, Norway, and the United Kingdom issued a call for better coordination and for putting the recipient countries in the aid "driver's seat."[12] Earlier donor guidelines in the 1980s had already called for coordination to be primarily the recipient government's responsibility.[13] Earlier still, in the mid-1970s, a senior Indian government official gave me over lunch his extreme minimalist view of how the donor–recipient relationship should operate. Through a door at one end of an empty room, the donor enters and places his money on the table. After the donor has left, the recipient enters from the other end, takes the funds, and leaves. There is no conversation. The donor has discharged his moral obligation and the recipient uses his own judgment as to the best use of the funds.

There is an obvious problem with these sentiments, especially those of my Indian colleague. They assume implicitly that the recipient government is working for the betterment of the population as a whole and has not been captured by one segment (or by a kleptocratic or vicious leadership) that is using the state to establish hegemonic and exclusionary policies. As some of the country experiences have shown, it has not been uncommon for the donors to be providing development assistance, in purportedly "normal" times, to countries ruled by governments that were pursuing policies inconsistent with donor political values, even policies leading to violent internal conflict. Placing coordination of aid policies with a recipient government under such circumstances would be irresponsible and would risk making the donors a party to the policies of that government and to their consequences.

If there is any aspect of the aid relationship where there should be zero tolerance for poor donor coordination, it is in conflict prevention. There have been encouraging examples of improved coordination in the urgent atmosphere of some *post*conflict countries.[14] Without the development of a comparable *pre*conflict sense of urgency, one cannot be optimistic that business as usual will not prevail. There is a parallel here between international response to crises of violent conflict on the one hand, and crises of economic destabilization on the other. Many economists drawn to the practical business of policy change see crises as the periods of greatest opportunity. One of the leading practitioners of economic policy reform, Arnold C. Harberger, believed that

> [T]aking advantage of crises . . . is one of the true secrets of great finance ministers, . . . great statesmen. The idea of taking advantage of crises is closely related to the old debate concerning a big push versus gradualism. . . . Most of the time a true big push will emerge in the wake of a major crisis. The important message is that governments have to be ready to take advantage of the crisis when it happens. In doing so they should recognize in advance that, precisely because of the crisis atmosphere, their actions will be limited in number and will have to be taken quickly. In a crisis atmosphere it is possible to do more than normally, but there are still limits. The true lesson is to be able to move with deliberate speed. That is to say, try to do the best all the time—when there is a crisis and when there is no crisis.[15]

The bulk of the work on reforms to prevent violent conflict has also taken place in the wake of, rather than prior to, crises. Unfortunately, it is often the case that the apparent wide scope, the big window of opportunity, for systemic political and economic change is actually constrained by the urgency the international community has felt to cobble together the minimally acceptable set of new arrangements and policy frameworks that will translate a cease-fire into a peace accord.

Conclusion

I have written this book in the optimistic conviction that many conflicts in developing countries can at least be mitigated if not prevented. I have tried to show that the development process may be shaped to prevent interest differences from degenerating into violent conflict, and that the international development agencies are perforce significant actors in that process. At a minimum, they should adopt the Hippocratic oath: Do no harm. Agencies should avoid supporting policies or projects that can deepen conflict in an already deeply divided society. Deliberate attention on their part to their past and potential effects on conflict can help them to realize contributions to mitigation that may have been only latent thus far. Even where antagonisms are exacerbated by symbolic, ethical, or cultural issues (e.g., religious exclusivity, fundamentalism, or proselytizing; historical legacies; language differences) that appear to be fall outside the scope and mandates of the development agencies, they may still be in position to undertake mitigating interventions.

Economic development also creates complexity; economic, occupational, educational, professional and other sources of personal identity and self-interest can cut across and dilute historically sharp differentiations (of race, religion, and ethnicity) that have led to deeply divided societies. Many of the components of the development process that contribute to this complexity can affect the roots of conflict, exacerbating or mitigating enmities, whatever their character. I have suggested how country policies and projects that are the bread and butter of the development agencies' involvement in this process—concerning areas such as structural adjustment, education, agriculture, and the rules of the marketplace—should be assessed for their conflict implications and designed accordingly.

In many developing nations, the perspective of conflict risk should be at least, if not more, important than the more standard criteria for aid allocation and usage. There is always a danger that these agencies and their practitioners will view a call to raise the priority of one set of objectives compared with others as yet another in a long line of successive enthusiasms pressed upon them by new management, new political masters, or outside critics or supporters. Too often the requirement to take a new subject into account in formal "assessments" in connection with appraisal of new project proposals (e.g., environment, gender, social impact, poverty, etc.) becomes an additional time-consuming and routine paper exercise that serves to ward off or pacify yet another interest group. In the case of conflict prevention, this would be an unfortunate outcome. Violent conflict undoes much of the economic, educational, or health progress that has been achieved for the women, children, poor, or other groups under "targeted" aid programs; its worst impact, of course, is to kill large numbers of these "beneficiaries." And these conflicts cause general economic decline, if not disaster, bringing severe deprivation to entire populations, including especially the previously most disadvantaged. Thus, in terms of loss avoidance and the enabling of regular continuing development, the benefits from a dollar spent (successfully) in a deliberate conflict-prevention mode are likely to exceed greatly the benefits of a dollar spent on any other purpose, especially if an avoidable conflict is virtually certain to undo or frustrate these other purposes entirely.

Finally, September 11, 2001, and its aftermath should reinvigorate public debate over the aid, trade, and other policies through which the rich nations affect the well-being and destinies of the poor. The reach and destabilizing potential of international terrorism have made plain how today's impoverished and geopolitically remote country can become tomorrow's source of a far-reaching crisis. With a modicum of foresight, and sufficient aid resources, the international development community can make a more substantial contribution to the spread of nonviolent conflict resolution.

Notes

1. Avruch, 1998, p. 16.
2. Ibid.
3. See Little, 1994, pp. 21–36, for an account of Dharmapala's career and influence.
4. Ibid., pp. 33–34.
5. See, for example, Eric Hobsbawm and Terence Ranger, eds., *The Invention of Tradition*, Cambridge, UK: Cambridge University Press, 1984, which is a study of purportedly ancient British, Indian and African colonial, and European traditions, of recent invented origin.
6. Agency for International Development, *The Use of Program Loans to Influence Policy*. Washington, DC: 1970, p. 30.
7. The readiness of donors to provide large-scale restoration funding to a country whose antagonists have agreed to stop warring presents a potential, perhaps only theoretical, problem of "moral hazard." That is, if a regime initiates violent suppression that leads to open conflict, presumably with the expectation that it will win, it can credibly expect that the donors, relieved when the conflict is ended, will substantially restore the losses of physical capital resulting from the regime's aggression. Such an outcome would depend, of course, on the nature of the peace accord and the ability of the regime leadership to avoid being charged with prosecutable crimes of war and against humanity. Thus, the record of postconflict reconstruction aid creates a basis for a future aggressive regime to discount capital destruction as a possible cost to itself, which might otherwise weigh against a decision to incur that risk.
8. *Far East Economic Review*, September 23, 1999, p. 9.
9. Lund, 1997, Section IV.B.
10. World Bank, 1999, p. 2.
11. Ibid., p. 3.
12. Ibid., p. 1.
13. Ibid., p. 5.
14. World Bank, 1998.
15. Arnold C. Harberger, in Vittorio Corbo et al., eds., *Adjustment Lending Revisited: Policies to Restore Growth*. Washington, DC: The World Bank, 1992, p. 92.

Selected Bibliography

Abrahamsson, Hans, and Anders Nilsson. 1996. *The Washington Consensus and Mozambique: The Need to Question the Westernised Development Paradigm in Africa*. Gothenburg, Sweden: Gothenburg University.

Addison, Tony. 1998. *Rebuilding Post-Conflict Africa: Reconstruction and Reform*. Helsinki: UNU/WIDER.

Anderson, Mary B. 1999. *Do No Harm: How Aid Can Support Peace—or War*. Boulder, CO: Lynne Reinner.

Avruch, Kevin. 1998. *Culture and Conflict Resolution*. Washington, DC: U.S. Institute of Peace.

Azam, Jean-Paul, and Christian Morisson, with Sophie Chauvin and Sandrine Rospabe. 1999. *Conflict and Growth in Africa*. Vol. 1: *The Sahel*. Paris: OECD Development Centre.

Ball, Nicole. 1992. *Pressing for Peace: Can Aid Induce Reform?* Washington, DC: Overseas Development Council.

————, with Tammy Halevy. 1996. *Making Peace Work: The Role of the International Development Community*. Washington, DC: Overseas Development Council.

Barro, Robert J. 1991. "Economic Growth in a Cross-Section of Countries." *Quarterly Journal of Economics* 106: 407–444.

Bennett, Andrew. 1999. "Case Studies and Typological Theories on Political Violence and Instability." Paper read at the Conference on Alternative Approaches to Assessing and Anticipating Political Instability, Vienna, VA, March 23–24.

Blair, Harry. 1998. *Spreading Power to the Periphery: An Assessment of Democratic Local Governance*. Washington, DC: USAID.

Boyce, James K., and Manuel Pastor, Jr. 1998. "Aid for Peace: Can International Financial Institutions Help Prevent Conflict?" *World Policy Journal* 15:2 (Summer).

Brass, Paul R. 1997. *Theft of an Idol: Text and Context in the Representation of Collective Violence*. Princeton, NJ: Princeton University Press.

Brautigam, Deborah. 1997. "Institutions, Economic Reform, and Democratic Consolidation in Mauritius." *Comparative Politics* 30 (October): 45–62.

Brogan, Patrick. 1998. *World Conflicts*. London: Bloomsbury.

Brown, Michael E., and Sumit Ganguly, eds. 1996. *Government Policies and Ethnic Relations in Asia and the Pacific*. Cambridge, MA: MIT Press.

Callahan, David. 1997. *Unwinnable Wars: American Power and Ethnic Conflict*. New York: Hill and Wang.

Carnegie Commission on Preventing Deadly Conflict. 1997. *Preventing Deadly Conflict*. Washington, DC: Carnegie Corporation of New York.

Carothers, Thomas. 2000. *Aiding Democracy Abroad*. Washington, DC: Carnegie Endowment for International Peace.

Cassen, Robert, et al. 1986. *Does Aid Work?* New York: Oxford University Press.

Cekic, Smail. 1995. *The Aggression on Bosnia and Genocide Against Bosniacs.* Sarajevo: Institute for the Research of Crimes Against Humanity and International Law.

Cohen, John M. 1995. *Foreign Aid and Tribal Issues in Kenya.* Cambridge, MA: Harvard Institute of International Development (draft).

Cohen, Marc J., and Torsten Feldbruegge. (n.d.). *Acute Nutrition Crises and Violent Conflict.* Washington, DC: International Food Policy and Research Institute (draft).

Collier, Paul. 2000. *Economic Causes of Civil Conflict and Their Implications for Policy.* Washington, DC: World Bank.

———, and Anka Hoeffler. 2000a. *Greed and Grievance in Civil War.* Washington, DC: World Bank (draft).

———. 2000b. *On the Incidence of Civil War in Africa.* Washington, DC: World Bank.

———. 2000c. *Aid, Policy, and Peace.* Washington, DC: World Bank.

Cortright, David, ed. 1997. *The Price of Peace: Incentives and International Conflict Prevention.* New York: Rowman and Littlefield.

Creative Associates International. 1997. *Preventing and Mitigating Violent Conflicts: A Guide for Practitioners.* Washington, DC: Creative Associates International.

Davies, John L., and Ted Robert Gurr, eds. 1998. *Preventive Measures: Building Risk Assessment and Crisis Early Warning Systems.* Lanham, MD: Rowman and Littlefield.

Deng, Francis M., et al. 1996. *Sovereignty as Responsibility: Conflict Management in Africa.* Washington, DC: Brookings Institution.

———, and I. William Zartman. 1991. *Conflict Resolution in Africa.* Washington, DC: Brookings Institution.

Dwyer, Denis, and David Drakakis-Smith. 1996. *Ethnicity and Development: Geographical Perspectives.* Chichester, UK: Wiley.

Eriksson, John. 1996. *The International Response to Conflict and Genocide: Lessons from the Rwanda Experience.* Synthesis Report. Copenhagen: Steering Committee for Joint Evaluation of Emergency Assistance to Rwanda.

Esman, Milton J. 1992. "The State and Language Policy." *International Political Science Review* 13, no. 4: 381–396.

———. 1994. *Ethnic Politics.* Ithaca, NY: Cornell University Press.

———, and Shibley Telhami, eds. 1995. *International Organizations and Ethnic Conflict.* Ithaca, NY: Cornell University Press.

———. 1997. *Can Foreign Aid Moderate Ethnic Conflict?* Washington, DC: U.S. Institute of Peace.

———, and Ronald J. Herring, eds. 2001. *Carrots, Sticks, and Ethnic Conflict: Rethinking Development Assistance.* Ann Arbor: University of Michigan Press.

European Platform for Conflict Prevention and Transformation. 1998. *Prevention and Management of Violent Conflicts: An International Directory.* Utrecht, The Netherlands: European Platform for Conflict Prevention and Transformation.

Feil, Scott R. 1998. *Preventing Genocide: How the Early Use of Force Might Have Succeeded in Rwanda.* New York: Carnegie Commission on Preventing Deadly Conflict, Carnegie Corporation of New York.

German Foundation for International Development. 1996. *Development Cooperation as Preventive Peace Policy.* Report of an international roundtable, April, Berlin.

Goudie, Andrew, and Bilin Neyapti. 1999. *Conflict and Growth in Africa.* Vol. 3: *Southern Africa.* Paris: OECD Development Centre.

Gurr, Ted Robert. 1998. *Minorities at Risk*. Washington, DC: United States Institute of Peace Press.

Hirschman, Albert O. 1984. *Getting Ahead Collectively: Grassroots Experiences in Latin America*. New York: Pergamon Press.

Horowitz, Donald L. 1985. *Ethnic Groups in Conflict*. Berkeley: University of California Press.

———. (n.d.). *Ethnicity and Development: Policies to Deal with Ethnic Conflict in Developing Countries*. Washington, DC: Agency for International Development.

International Crisis Group. 1999. *Is Dayton Failing? Bosnia Four Years After the Peace Agreement*. Brussels.

———. 2000. *Indonesia: Overcoming Murder and Chaos in Maluku*. Brussels.

International Federation of Red Cross and Red Crescent Societies. 1998. *World Disasters Report*. New York: Oxford University Press.

Jayarajah, Carl, and William Bronson. 1995. *Structural and Sectoral Adjustment: World Bank Experience, 1980–1992*. Washington, DC: The World Bank.

Jentleson, Bruce W., ed. 2000a. *Opportunities Missed, Opportunities Seized: Preventive Diplomacy in the Post–Cold War World*. New York: Carnegie Commission on Preventing Deadly Conflict.

———. 2000b. *Coercive Prevention: Normative, Political and Policy Dilemmas*. Washington, DC: United States Institute of Peace.

Kapur, Devesh; John P. Lewis; and Richard Webb. 1997. *The World Bank: Its First Half-Century*. Washington, DC: Brookings Institution.

Keyes, Charles F. 1987. *Thailand: Buddhist Kingdom as Modern Nation-State*. Boulder, CO: Westview Press.

Klitgaard, Robert. 1991. *Adjusting to Reality*. San Francisco: ICS Press.

———. 1993a. *Better States, Better Markets*. Paper presented at the South African Economics Society Biennial Conference, Pretoria, October.

———. 1993b. *Bribes, Tribes, and Markets That Fail: Rethinking the Economics of Underdevelopment*. Inaugural lecture, University of Natal, South Africa, October.

Klugman, Jeni. 1999. *Social and Economic Policies to Prevent Complex Humanitarian Emergencies: Lessons from Experience*. Helsinki: United Nations University World Institute for Development Economics Research.

———, Bilin Neyapti, and Frances Stewart. 1999. *Conflict and Growth in Africa*. Vol. 2: *Kenya, Tanzania and Uganda*. Paris: OECD Development Centre.

Kumar, Krishna, ed. 1997. *Rebuilding Societies After Civil War: Critical Roles for International Assistance*. Boulder, CO: Lynne Reinner.

Landell-Mills, Joslin. 1992. *Helping the Poor: The IMF's New Facilities for Structural Adjustment*. Washington, DC: International Monetary Fund.

Little, David. 1994. *Sri Lanka: The Invention of Enmity*. Washington, DC: U.S. Institute of Peace.

Lund, Michael S. 1997. *Impact of Donor Incentives and Disincentives in Reducing Violent Conflicts: A Survey of Extant Literature*. Prepared for the OECD/DAC Task Force on Peace, Conflict and Development (draft).

Management Systems International. 1996. *Evaluation of the Haiti Communal Governance Program; Funded by the USAID Office of Transition Initiatives and Implemented by the International Organization for Migration*. Washington, DC.

Mason, Edward S., and Robert E. Asher. 1973. *The World Bank Since Bretton Woods*. Washington, DC: Brookings Institution.

McCoubrey, Hilaire, and Nigel D. White. 1995. *International Organization and Civil Wars.* Brookfield, VT: Dartmouth Press.

Messer, Ellen; Marc J. Cohen; and Jashinta D'Costa. 1998. *Food from Peace: Breaking the Links Between Confict and Hunger.* Washington, DC: International Food Policy and Research Institute.

Montville, Joseph V., ed. 1991. *Conflict and Peacemaking in Multiethnic Societies.* Lexington, MA: Lexington Books.

Moynihan, Daniel Patrick. 1994. *Pandaemonium: Ethnicity in International Politics.* New York: Oxford University Press.

Muscat, Robert J. 1990. *Thailand and the United States: Development, Security and Foreign Aid.* New York: Columbia University Press.

———. 1994. *The Fifth Tiger: A Study of Thai Development Policy.* Armonk, NY: M.E. Sharpe, Inc.

———. 1999. *Umbrella Grant for Trauma and Reunification in Croatia and Bosnia-Herzegovina: Final Evaluation.* Bethesda, MD: Development Alternatives.

Nafziger, E. Wayne, and Juha Auvinen. 1997. *War, Hunger and Flight: The Political Economy of Humanitarian Emergencies.* Helsinki: U.N. University/World Institute for Development Economics Research.

Nash, Manning. 1989. *The Cauldron of Ethnicity in the Modern World.* Chicago: University of Chicago Press.

National Intelligence Council. 1999. *Global Humanitarian Emergencies: Trends and Projections,* 1999–2000.

Netherlands Institute of International Relations, Clingendael. 1999. *Causes of Conflict in the Third World: Synthesis Report.* The Hague, Netherlands.

Nordlinger, Eric A. 1972. *Conflict Regulation in Divided Societies.* Cambridge, MA: Harvard University Center for International Affairs.

Oakley, Robert B.; Michael J. Dziedzic; and Eliot M. Goldberg. 1998. *Policing the New World Disorder: Peace Operations and Public Security.* Washington, DC: National Defense University Press.

Oberschall, Tony. 1999. *Political Instability: The View from Collective Action Theory* (draft).

Organization for Economic Cooperation and Development, Development Assistance Committee. 1998. *Conflict, Peace and Development Co-operation on the Threshold of the 21st Century.* Paris.

Predergast, John, and David Smock. 1999. *Putting Humpty Dumpty Together: Reconstructing Peace on the Congo.* Washington, DC: U.S. Institute of Peace.

Robinson, Thomas W. 1991. *Democracy and Development in East Asia: Taiwan, South Korea, and the Philippines.* Washington, DC: AEI Press.

Rothchild, Donald. 1997. *Managing Ethnic Conflict in Africa.* Washington, DC: Brookings Institution.

Rupesinghe, Kumar, ed. 1989. *Conflict Resolution in Uganda.* Oslo: International Peace Research Institute.

Sellstrom, Tor, and Lennart Wohlgemuth. 1996. *Study 1, Historical Perspective.* Copenhagen: Steering Committee of the Joint Evaluation of Emergency Assistance to Rwanda.

Sirageldin, Ismail. 1994. *Population Dynamics, Environment and Conflict.* Working Paper 9413. Cairo: Economic Research Forum.

———, and June Taboroff, eds. 1992. *Culture and Development in Africa: Proceedings of an International Conference Held at the World Bank.*

Snodgrass, Donald. n.d. "Managing Economic Growth and Ethnic Diversity," unpublished manuscript.

Sowell, Thomas. 1990. *Preferential Policies*. Stanford, CA: Hoover Institution.

Staub, Ervin. 1989. *The Roots of Evil: The Origins of Genocide and Other Group Violence*. Cambridge, UK: Cambridge University Press.

Stevenson, Jonathan. 2000. *Preventing Conflict: The Role of the Bretton Woods Institutions*. New York: Oxford University Press.

Stremlau, John J., and Francisco R. Sagasti. 1998. *Preventing Deadly Conflict: Does the World Bank Have a Role?* A Report to the Carnegie Commission on Preventing Deadly Conflict. Washington, DC: Carnegie Commission on Preventing Deadly Conflict.

Suliman, Osman, and Ghirmay Ghebreysus. 1998. *Privatization and X-inefficiency in Selected Sub-Saharan African Countries: Is Privatization Politically Induced?* Cairo: Economic Research Forum for the Arab Countries, Iran, and Turkey.

Swedish Ministry for Foreign Affairs. 1999. *Preventing Violent Conflict—A Swedish Action Plan*. Stockholm.

Tellis, Ashley J., et al. 1997. *Anticipating Ethnic Conflict*. Santa Monica, CA: Rand.

Touval, Saadia, and I. William Zartman, eds. 1985. *International Mediation in Theory and Practice*. Boulder, CO: Westview Press.

Tulane University/USAID. 2000. *Conflict Vulnerability Analysis: Issues, Tools and Responses* (draft).

United States Agency for International Development (USAID) and the Woodrow Wilson International Center for Scholars. 2001. *The Role of Foreign Assistance in Conflict Prevention: Conference Report*. Vienna, VA: Evidence Based Research.

Uphoff, Norman. 1992. *Learning from Gal Oya*. Ithaca, NY: Cornell University Press.

Uvin, Peter. 1998. *Aiding Violence: The Development Enterprise in Rwanda*. West Hartford, CT: Kumarian.

Van de Goor, Luc, et al., eds. 1996. *Between Development and Destruction: An Inquiry into the Causes of Conflict in Post-Colonial States*. The Hague: Netherlands Institute of International Relations, Clingendael.

Verstegen, Susan. 1999. *Conflict Prognostication: Toward a Tentative Framework for Conflict Assessment*. The Hague: Netherlands Institute of International Relations.

Weissman, Stephen R. 1998. *Preventing Genocide in Burundi: Lessons from International Diplomacy*. Washington, DC: U.S. Institute of Peace.

Woodward, Susan L. 1995. *Balkan Tragedy: Chaos and Dissolution After the Cold War*. Washington, DC: Brookings Institution.

World Bank. 1994. *Governance: The World Bank's Experience*. Washington, DC.

———. 1998. *The World Bank's Experience with Post-Conflict Reconstruction, Synthesis*. Vol. I, and four case-study volumes: Vol. II: *Bosnia and Herzegovina*; Vol. III: *El Salvador*; Vol. IV: *Uganda*; Vol. V: *Cambodia, Eritrea, Haiti, Lebanon, Rwanda, and Sri Lanka*. Washington, DC.

———. 1999. *The Drive to Partnership: Aid Coordination and the World Bank*. Operations Evaluation Department, Washington, DC.

———. *World Development Report*, various years.

Zartman, I. William, ed. 1995. *Collapsed States: The Disintegration and Restoration of Legitimate Authority*. Boulder, CO: Lynne Reinner.

Index

About the Author

Robert J. Muscat is a development economist with experience as a practitioner and scholar. He has worked for the U.S. Agency for International Development in Thailand, Brazil, and Kenya. As the agency's chief economist, he was economic adviser to the Thai development planning agency and the Malaysian Ministry of Finance and was planning director for the U.N. Development Programme. He has consulted for U.N. agencies and the World Bank. Among his publications are books and monographs on reconstruction, technical assistance, food aid, nutrition and development, population, and other subjects. He has been a visiting scholar at Columbia's East Asian Institute and at the Institute for Conflict Analysis and Resolution at George Mason University.